THE YEAR OF YES

THE YEAR OF YES

a memoir

Maria Dahvana Headley

NEW YORK

LIBRARY OF CONGRESS CATALOGING-IN-PUBLICATION DATA

Headley, Maria Dahvana.
The year of yes : a memoir / Maria Dahvana Headley.
p. cm
ISBN 1-4013-0230-0
1. Headley, Maria Dahvana, 1977—Relations with men.
2. Single women—New York (State)—New York—Biography.
3. Dating (Social customs)—New York (State)—New York.
I. Title.
HQ800.2.H43 2006
306.81'53'092—dc22   2005052525

Hyperion books are available for special promotions and
premiums. For details contact Michael Rentas, Assistant
Director, Inventory Operations, Hyperion,
77 West 66th Street, 11th floor, New York, New York 10023,
or call 212-456-0133.

Book design by Richard Oriolo

FIRST EDITION

3   5   7   9   10   8   6   4

For Robert Schenkkan,

whom I adore beyond all reckoning.

How did I ever get so lucky?

AUTHOR'S NOTE

THIS IS A TRUE STORY. That means that within these pages are plenty of people who actually exist. Some of these people are completely out of my life, and have been for years. Others, I still know and adore. In neither case do I want to break up any marriages, pry open any barricaded closet doors, or otherwise ruin any lives. Therefore, names have been changed to protect the indignant, the infantile, and, of course, the innocent (all three of you). Pretty much the only names I didn't change are my own (because I have no problem with muddying my own character), and Big White Cat's, because he is housebound and doesn't care if I tell the world his secrets.

One more thing. This book has been reconstructed from memory. *My* memory. Subject to vagaries, hangovers, emotional meltdowns, and the occasional unrequited vendetta. Some of the people in this book are gonna be happy about this, and some of you aren't. I've tried to be kind where I could be, and if I couldn't be entirely kind while still telling the truth, at least I've edited out some of your bad dialogue and made you wittier than you were.

THE YEAR OF YES

A DAY IN THE LIFE
OF A NAYSAYER

IN WHICH
OUR HEROINE
DECIDES TO
START SAYING
YES . . .

That woman speaks eighteen languages,
and can't say "no" in any of them.
—DOROTHY PARKER

IMAGINE FOR A MOMENT THAT YOU ARE YOUNG, FEMALE, AND APPALLINGLY, POSSIBLY UNATTRACTIVELY, WELL READ. You grew up in a small town in Idaho, but now you live in New York City, the most exciting and romantic place in the country, and feasibly in the world. According to the literature you're choosing to apply to your current situation (you've carefully forgotten that you ever read *Last Exit to Brooklyn*), you are supposed to be wearing sequins to breakfast and getting your hand kissed by a heterosexual version of Cole Porter. Incandescently intelligent men are supposed to be toasting you with Dom Perignon. Instead, you're sharing a cockroach-ridden outer-borough apartment with two roommates and one dysfunctional cat. You're spending your evenings sitting on your kitchen floor, drinking poisonous red jug wine, and quoting Sartre. Hell is not only other people, it is you, too. You're not getting laid, because even if you were meeting something other than substandard men, you don't have a bedroom to call your own. And instead of the smoldering, soul-baring, Abelard-to-Heloise-sans-castration solicitations you rightfully deserve, you're getting stupefying lines like: "I'm listening to NPR. Do you want to come over and make out?"

That would be a direct quote.

Let me back up. Seven A.M. on February 14th, and I was lying on my lumpy mattress, alone again. The noises of NYC had ceased to metamorphose into the hopeful bird trills and tender love songs I'd imagined when I'd first arrived, a year before, and instead sounded like what they were: garbage trucks, honking horns, and the occasional cockroach scuttle. Granted, my last doomed relationship had been significantly more crow than canary, and more Nirvana than Sinatra. Still, it was Valentine's Day, and I was considering a backslide. It didn't matter that ceasing communication with my most recent disaster, Martyrman, an actor twice my age and half my maturity, had unquestionably been the right decision. It didn't matter how many times I told myself that I was the brainwashed victim of propaganda created by sugar lobbyists in order to engender mass consumption of chocolate. Waking up on February 14th without someone to love was depressing.

I was becoming convinced that I was going to be lonely for the rest of my life. It wasn't that I wasn't meeting men. I was. It was just that they all drove me crazy. I was not a member of a modern-day Algonquin Round Table, populated with the pretty, witty, and wise, as I'd moved to New York envisioning I'd be. Instead, I was a denizen of something more along the lines of the Holiday Inn Card Table, populated with the zitty, twitty, and morally compromised. I wasn't yet to the point of Dorothy Parker's infamous quote—"Ducking for apples. Change one letter and it's the story of my life."—but that was only because I didn't have time to approach my own bed, let alone anyone else's. The main problem of living in the city that never slept was that neither did I.

When I got home from my usual exhausting day of racing uptown and downtown between classes at NYU and my various temp jobs, all I did was crumple up on my mattress, muttering to myself and reading books that made my problems worse. The night before, for example, when the front neighbor's lullaby of sternum-thumping bass had made it clear to me that I wouldn't be sleeping, I'd picked up *Prometheus Bound*. Reading Aeschylus had thrown me into a waking nightmare of being stretched on a rock, my liver plucked at by rapacious turtledoves.

Somewhere nearby, someone was practicing an aria from *The Ring Cycle*. Whoever was singing Brunhilde was flat. Worse than that, someone small, soprano, and canine was singing harmony, sharp. My downstairs neighbor, Pierre LaValle, had started his daily apartment sanitization process. For someone with linoleum floors, the man had an unhealthy relationship with his vacuum. Add to this the revival tent set up at the end of the adjacent block, the house party two buildings down, and the fact that the back neighbor's illegal psycho rooster couldn't tell headlights from sunlight, and the night was pretty much a wash.

The opera singer switched to "What's Love Got to Do With It?" The canine backup started in on a rousing counterpoint of "Girls Just Wanna Have Fun." I let fury course through my veins. My sleep deprivation was partially my own fault, admittedly, but since I hadn't had a good time the night before, I was blaming it on everyone else.

I'd arrived home at 3:00 A.M., having spent the evening with a fellow New York University student. We'd eaten Korean barbeque, discussed Kierkegaard, and split the check in half, despite the fact that he'd eaten four times more than I. He'd then tried, and failed, to wheedle the traditionally clad waitress's phone number from her "perfectly symmetrical lips." At the subway, he'd given me a rubbery smooch on the cheek and told me he thought we'd really had a meeting of the minds.

I levered the window open and stuck my hungover head outside. Everything looked bleak. I felt disturbingly Steinbeckian, as though, at any moment, I might find myself begging my roommates to "tell me about the rabbits." My life was a great big fat NO. It wasn't like I didn't want to be happy. It just seemed that happiness was eluding me.

My landlady, Gamma, was standing outside in our Astroturfed courtyard, feeding a pack of feral cats a platter of shriveled hot dogs. Gamma's six-year-old granddaughters, the twins, were sharing a ketchup-covered hot dog with a notch-eared tabby. One bite to each child, one to the tomcat. Gamma was not known for her vigilance.

"Probably rain," Gamma announced.

"Probably flood," I said. Never mind the clear skies. I was embracing pessimism.

"World's ending sometime next week," Gamma informed me. Gamma liked to talk about only two things: the Apocalypse and the Weather Channel. One of the twins gave a war whoop, and pitched the rest of the hot dog at my window. It landed inches from my face and slid down the building. The twins shrieked with mirth.

"What do you think you're laughing about?" demanded Gamma, and herded them indoors. It was clear from the rear view that one of the twins had wet her pants in the excitement. This was my home. These were my neighbors, the urban equivalents of the hicks I'd been desperate to leave behind in my home state of Idaho. Give Gamma and company a little more space, and they'd have had a few rusted-out cars, some scrabbly hounds, and a stockpile of *The Book of Mormon*. I'd thought things would be different here. No.

"NO," I SAID, TO THE WORLD AT LARGE. "No. No. No." I thought that maybe if I chanted it enough times, all the aggravating things in my life would stumble away into oblivion. Then I'd be free to have the existence I wanted, something much more glamorous and gratifying.

The "no" was nothing new. It had, after all, been the first word I'd ever spoken. There were photos of me, posing prissily as an infant, my arms crossed over my chest, and a look of pointed fury on my face. By the time I was two, the initial no had become a string of nyets, neins, and the occasional sarcastic ha! I'd swiftly learned to read, and books had been the end of any social aptitude I might have possessed. I'd retreated from whatever unsatisfactory experience was coming my way, be it hamburgers (I was, from birth, vegetarian) or PE class (steadfast refusal to play for anyone but myself caused issues with team sports), a volume of something clenched firmly in my hand. My mother maintains that I wasn't rude, but I think about the kind of child I must have been, interspersing meows (my cats were my only real friends, and I'd developed an unfortunate nervous tic that caused me to meow in stressful situations) with the vocabulary of a seventeenth-century noblewoman, and I do not know how I survived my childhood. Time was spent in both Special Education and Gifted and Talented programs.

From a second grade report card: "Maria has a good sense of humor, but doesn't tend toward social interaction and instead just laughs to herself. She could also use some supervision when it comes to her school clothes."

I'd learned to use a sewing machine at the age of seven. Sometimes I came to school dressed in quilt fragments and safety-pinned togas.

In high school, I got in massive trouble during an assembly, because I'd laughed at soon-to-be-elected Congresswoman Helen Chenoweth, who'd pleaded ignorance of her own policies. I was not the only person in opposition (Chenoweth turned out to be embarrassing even to the Republicans—in 1996, when her GOP primary opponent stripped nearly naked during a televised interview, and spent the month prior to the election in a psych ward, he still got 32 percent of the vote), but I was the only one dumb enough to think that everyone else would laugh, too. Moreover, I was, alas, sitting in the front row, wearing a ruffled orange frock and purple combat boots. When Chenoweth started crying, her cohort, Senator Larry Craig, shook his finger in my face and told me that I was a "very, *very* bad girl." It was a familiar theme. The only thing that kept me from being expelled was my friend Ira petitioning the principal with the suggestion that I was "a little bit retarded." My mode of existence obviously didn't work for everyone, and half the time it didn't work for me, either, but I was resigned. It was how I was made. I was a protestor. I was such a protestor that I regularly protested things that might have been good for me.

When I'd moved to New York, after high school, I'd begun to suddenly, miraculously, sort of fit in. Unfortunately, I'd said no to so many things that I wasn't sure how to say yes anymore. This was problematic, considering that what I'd thought I'd wanted had turned out to be a shifting target, and that every day, the city gave me new things to say yes to, things I'd resoundingly denied in the past. My nos had begun to tremble, particularly in the dating category. I'd tentatively started saying yes, but it had turned out that my judgment of who to bestow my yeses upon was deeply flawed. After a year in New York City, I'd dated plenty of people, but none that had even come close to whatever I thought my ideal was. That was the other problem. I was looking for something different, but I didn't know what it was.

Certainly nothing that was outside my window. Across the way, I could see my neighbors wandering around half-naked. It seemed that everyone in my neighborhood was always in a state of unappealing undress. Not only that, they were always screaming at each other, even at 7:00 in the morning.

"Please be quiet," I whispered, not just to the neighbors, but to the whole damned city. "Please, just let me sleep." And for a moment, peace. I closed my eyes. I tucked myself back into bed.

Rrrrrrrrrringgggggggggggggggggggggggggggggggggggg!

I'd never been a person who could just let a telephone ring. I always thought that the person on the other end might be someone

I'd been dying to talk to for my entire life. Say, William Shakespeare calling from beyond the grave. Never mind that this had never happened. Lately, it had been the Sears collection department, searching for another Maria Headley, who owed them $15,000. She'd apparently binged on appliances, and was even now hidden in some dank cave full of stand mixers. Even though I wasn't the right Maria, I always ended up talking to Sears for at least half an hour. I'd grown up on one of the last party lines in the known universe, and phone privileges still seemed precious to me.

"Good morning!" I trilled. It wouldn't do to have Will Shakespeare thinking I was cranky. Particularly on Valentine's Day. What if he thought I preferred Kit Marlowe? I suspected that the last good man on the planet had died 413 years before I was born, but some part of me was still waiting for Mr. Shakespeare to whisper some sweet iambic pentameter into my ear.

Alas, no. Instead, I heard the husky voice of the Director, an acquaintance from a writing workshop I'd attended the year before. The Director was in his mid-forties and divorced. He was an intelligent person, with extensive knowledge of two thousand years of theater history. There was just one problem. Sweater vests. I couldn't date a man who wore sweater vests, any more than I could date a man who was a mime. Everybody had phobias. Sweater vests threw me back, not to my charming grandpa, as they would some people, but to my skeezy high school geometry teacher, who had recently gone on trial for attempting to calculate the surface area of his female students' breasts. (My phobia of mimes was simpler: I was a playwright, and words were my business. I took miming as a personal insult, but more on that later . . .)

The Director, with his sweater vests, with his husky voice, was not my first choice for someone I wanted to speak to at 7:30 in the morning. I liked him, but I didn't like him like that. We were supposed to see a play that night, and he was suggesting we meet up earlier. I said sure, but that I was still in my pajamas. He said he was really looking forward to seeing me, I said great and tried to say good-bye, and then, something went very wrong.

"I'm listening to NPR," he suddenly stammered. "Do you want to come over and make out?"

Well. I was finally going nuts. It was about time. Other people in my family were nuts. Why had I thought I'd been skipped?

"I didn't quite hear you," I said, just to make sure I was really losing it.

"I'm listening to NPR," the Director repeated. "Do you want to come over and make out?"

It wasn't a delusion. He'd offered me a radio rendezvous. Making out to *Morning Edition*. I had one question.

WHOSE LIFE WAS THIS?

"Is it for me?" yelled my roommate Victoria, but I didn't respond. I was itemizing the things I'd said to the Director that might have caused him to think that National Public Radio turned me on. I could think of nothing. I liked public radio, of course. Who didn't? But my attraction was strictly platonic.

A TINY LITTLE EXISTENTIAL CRISIS BEGAN TO NIBBLE AT THE BACK OF MY LEFT EYEBALL. Maybe it had been there for a while, and I just hadn't noticed it. My life left little time for reflection, given that my typical day involved rising at 5:30 A.M. to write a paper I'd inevitably forgotten, flying to the subway in order to get to NYU in time to attend an 8:00 A.M. lecture, where I'd usually fall asleep, flinging myself onto the train again for five or six hours of midtown temping, then a mad dash downtown for a few more hours of classes. I'd get home, write half a play, then go out again for a rehearsal until midnight, at which point I'd return home, write some more, and fall into bed for my usual three hours of sleep. I was fried. Most of my energy was spent on surviving, and I filled in the gaps in my nights with a series of unsuccessful love affairs.

At some point, my dissatisfaction had hit critical mass, and things had started to overflow. The Director didn't really deserve my contempt. He was probably just trying to woo me in some new and intellectually stimulating way, but the result of his comment was an extreme allergic reaction. NPR? What had I done to make the Director think he could get into my pants with NPR? I knew some kinky people, but I didn't know anyone who'd spread her legs for *Car Talk*.

I needed coffee, I needed sleep, and I needed better judgment when it came to men. In the scant year I'd lived in New York City, I'd accumulated a sheaf of romantic failures roughly comparable in length to *Remembrance of Things Past*. There were entire genres of food I now had to avoid as a result of Proust's madeleine effect; memories of bad dates that I didn't want to conjure up with an errant bite of ramen noodle. Because many of my worst debacles had occurred in dives misleadingly named Emerald Garden and the Cottage, I was having to avoid cheap Chinese food, normally a collegiate staple, altogether. Not to mention art house movie theaters, the NYU library, and basically all of Bleecker Street.

"Is it Brittany?" asked my other roommate, Zak, trying to grab the receiver. Brittany was his girlfriend that week, and I was lobbying heavily against her. Zak usually dated what I called Perilously-Close-to-Underage Nymphets, and what he called "Oh God! So Hot!!"

I shook my head at Zak, and pressed the heel of my hand into my eye socket. The existential crisis had grown into something the size and shape of a hamster. I moaned.

"That sounds pretty good," said the Director.

"I have a headache," I protested, weakly.

"I can fix that," said the Director. There was a growl in his voice, the kind of anticipatory rasp usually heard in commercials for sex hotlines.

"Mrrrooooow," said Big White Cat, our demonic angora adoptee, introducing his claws to my pajama pants. On Big White Cat's list of favored things to annihilate, silk was second only to expensive leather jackets belonging to visitors. He'd been an inadvertent acquisition, a friend-of-a-friend cat-sitting episode made permanent when his actor-owner went on tour and abandoned him. Big White had a Dickensian past: The actor had abducted him from a front lawn in Alabama, during a production of *The Diary of*

Anne Frank, and named him Mr. Dissel, after his character in the play. I liked my cats dark, sleek, and self-sufficient. Big White (we couldn't bring ourselves to call him Mr. Dissel) was needy and bitchy, not to mention fluffy. It was yet another example of how my life had gone awry.

"NO," I yelled, prying Big White Cat's talons out of my thigh, and forgetting to cover the receiver.

"But, *Morning Edition* is on," said the Director, trying to somehow excuse himself.

"You're kidding," I informed him, attempting to keep my crisis contained. Surely, he didn't think that NPR was my open sesame. We hadn't even kissed!

"I'm not, actually," he said, sounding a little hurt.

"No? Come on!" I laughed uproariously, hoping to lead him to confess that he'd been joking. Even if he had to lie. Ha! Ha! Ha! Ha! Ha! Ha! Ha! Ha! Ha! Ha! Ha! Ha! Ha!

"So, you're not coming?" His voice seemed to be trembling.

I stopped laughing, chagrined.

"You know, I guess I'm not," I said, trying to modulate my tone into that of a Compassionate Rejecter.

"Right. Good-bye, then." Dial tone.

Damn it. Now he'd go out into the world, telling all our mutual acquaintances that I'd brutally laughed at his heartfelt declaration. And I really wasn't a bad person! I tried to be kind! Unfortunately, for every pleasant date I had, there were equally as many messes. I got asked out frequently. It wasn't that I was gorgeous; I wasn't. In my opinion, and in the opinions of plenty of people in my past, I was distinctly odd looking. It was location. The Hallowed Halls of Academe were known for their tendency toward echoing loneliness, unnatural partnerships, and flat-out desperation. As a result, a significant percentage of my recent life had been spent dashing through campus buildings, my collar pulled up to hide my face from the scattered tribe of the Miserably Enamored—NYU men who'd spend hours comparing me to Lady Chatterley, who'd try to pass off Philip Glass compositions as their own, who'd diagram their desire for me in interpretive dance cycles pilfered from Martha Graham. This might have been fine for some girls, but it wasn't turning me on. At all. Maybe it was ego run amok, but I thought I deserved better.

The existential crisis was now the size of a rabbit. It beat its back feet against my sinuses and gnawed a piece of my brain. The crisis grew into a rat terrier, then a mule, then an elephant. It trumpeted. It stomped and shook my foundations, and then unfurled a banner, which informed me that I would never be happy. No one would ever, ever love me. Furthermore, I would never love anyone, because, in fact, I was incapable of love. My life was going to be a ninety-year no.

I frantically opened my address book and searched it for someone, anyone, who'd moved me, who'd been good in both bed and brain. No. A slew of the so-so. A list of the losers and the irrevocably lost. And, oh yes, my mom. I shut the book, nauseated.

The existential crisis had evolved into a dinosaur. It opened its toothy maw, raised its shrunken front legs, and gave me a mean pair of jazz hands.

"You're screwed, baby, seriously screwed," it sang, in the voice of Tom Waits.

Senior year of high school, I'd written a play, the title of which, *Tyrannosaurus Sex,* had been censored to *Tyrannosaurus ...* At the time, I'd been bitter, but now it occurred to me that I much preferred the ellipses to the actuality. The whole world of sex and love had turned out to be far too much like living in the Land of the Lost. I'd wander across lava-spattered plains for a while, miserably lonely, and then run into some Lizard King, who would seem nice, until he bared his teeth and went in for a big bite of my heart. Even more depressingly, there'd been times when the lizard had behaved perfectly pleasantly, but I'd somehow found myself spitting and roasting him anyway. True Love combined with Great Sex was the goal, but I had a feeling I was going to end up fossilized before I found anything close. I held my head in my hands and whimpered.

Zak approached, cautiously. He shook two Tylenol into his hand and offered them to me, patting my shoulder. He'd had significant personal experience with existential crises, usually related to the same topic as mine: love, and lack thereof. I swallowed.

I FELT LIKE I'D DATED AND THEN HATED EVERY MAN IN MANHAT-TAN. This was, I reminded myself, not strictly true. In fact, I'd gone out with a lot of writers and actors, a lot of academics—the kind of men who maintained hundred-thousand-dollar debts as a result of graduate school, the kind who possessed PhDs in Tragedy. In order to attend NYU's Tisch School of the Arts Dramatic Writing Program, I'd moved sight unseen from Idaho to New York, dragging all my worldly belongings in a bedraggled caravan of psychedelic pink Samsonite suitcases from the Salvation Army. I'd had my fortune of four hundred scraped-together dollars hidden in my bra, because my mom had told me I'd probably get mugged immediately upon leaving the airplane.

Taylor, a brilliant actor I'd met the summer before, had speedily taken the role of my only friend in the city and met me at JFK.

"You have to learn to take the subway sometime," he'd announced.

I was fully ignorant of mass transit, and had to be led onto the train. Upon disembarking into the flattening heat and humidity of August, we'd discovered that we were roughly five thousand miles from my dormitory. Taylor had manfully carried most of my luggage, as I'd begun to have a total nervous breakdown and was unfit to be responsible for anything but my backpack. The elevators in my building were, of course, broken, so Taylor had lugged the endless bags up eleven flights of stairs. Then he'd taken me to a burrito joint, bought me a beer, and told me it would be okay.

Taylor'd been right. I'd fallen in love with New York City anyway. In the cripplingly Caucasian Potato State, my olive skin and brown hair ("ethnic") had rendered me dateless. Revise. I'd been asked out, yes, but I'd never any intention of accepting the offers. Only creepy people liked me. Gray-ponytailed hippies often stalked me at all-ages poetry slams, reciting lascivious odes that referred to me as "a luminous, nubile woman-child." They'd get my mom's number from information, and then call incessantly, inviting me to accompany them to the beatnik mecca of Denny's for "coffee and cigarettes." No thanks. I'd been delighted to discover that the men of New York City were not only ponytail free, they had no reservations about my skin tone.

I'd met the first of my failures only hours after hitting the city. He was a dweeby Cinema Studies major from Cincinnati, who did not, in all the time I knew him, ever manage to zip his fly. It had only gone downhill from there, but still, I'd been dazzled by the dating options available to me: Men with Books! Men with Biceps! Men with Encyclopedic Knowledge of French Farce! I'd felt like I'd been wandering in a cultural desert for my entire life, and had miraculously stumbled upon a shimmering city of intellectual splendor, every man bearing a bejeweled braincase. It was a mirage, of course, but that hadn't kept me from repeatedly immersing myself in its sand dunes.

I'd wasted the year flinging myself into abortive relationships with a bunch of brilliant losers. I'd been forced to imagine myself as a thesis committee, so that my dates could practice defending dissertations on such varied topics as Misery and Maiming in the Russian Literary Canon; Masturbation Metaphor in Shakespeare—A Design for Contemporary Life; and Images of Insects in the Films of David Lynch. I'd spent a month or two in Drama with Donatello, an NYU graduate film student who preyed on freshmen. He was Haitian, via rich parents in Florida, and in possession of a rickety skateboard on which he could perpetually be seen flying half-drunk from the marble banisters of historic campus buildings. He'd been so peerlessly self-confident that he'd managed to convince me he was necessary to my emotional development, and thus had enjoyed the privilege of torturing me with a recurrent alleged joke: "You're so racist. I can't believe you don't see it."

"If I'm racist, why am I hanging out with you?" I'd point out. But his argument involved subtleties, like me being inherently against ethnic mingling even as I was kissing him. He'd taken me on a date to a screening of the unfortunate 1952 Orson Welles black-face *Othello*. During the Desdemona murder scene, he'd stage-whispered, so loudly that every cinephile in the theater could hear him, "Are you worried?"

I felt that I somehow might have deserved this. It was a given that I was underexposed to any kind of racial diversity. Maybe I *was* racist, and just didn't know it. I was white, after all, even though in Idaho I'd been frequently assumed to be Mexican. Anytime I'd fool-ishly admitted my home state (which had been, for many wretched years, the homebase of the Aryan Nation's skinhead compound), people would say things like, "Huh. So you're a neo-Nazi?" Don-atello had been ingeniously confrontational with everyone. One day, walking on Broadway with him, me hoping that we were finally hav-ing romance, he'd pounced for an hour on a Hare Krishna, "just be-cause."

We'd finally imploded one morning in my dorm room, as he'd meticulously directed the application of my makeup, forming his hands into the universal symbol for "I Am Now Framing a Shot." Ini-tially, I'd been flattered, but then he'd started using the close-up to point out zits. When I'd thrown him out, he'd earnestly declared that he'd expected to be my boyfriend for "seven years, but now you've fucked it up, so it's your loss." Then, he'd called for weeks, aggrieved that I was no longer speaking to him. I'd picked up the phone once.

"No," I'd said.

"No, what?"

"Just. No."

It wasn't that I had anything against intellectual men. I liked them. Indeed, I sought them. The problems happened later. We'd be on the verge of kissing, and they'd suddenly lurch away, whispering irrelevant lines clearly memorized in high school. Keats's "Ode on a Grecian Urn" was a favorite recitation among college-age males. "Thou still unravish'd bride of quietness," indeed. I was unravish'd far too often for my taste. "Never, never canst thou kiss" seemed to be a life philosophy for some of my paramours. One guy, engaged in the study of possibly pedophilic Victorian authors, had given me a scrap of "Jabberwocky" ("And, as in uffish thought he stood/The Jab- berwock, with eyes of flame/Came whiffling through the tulgey wood/And burbled as it came!") before attempting to do something that I speedily decided was anatomically inadvisable. Other guys tried quoting the drunken renegade poet Charles Bukowski's "love is a dog from hell." Frankly, I was weary of hearing about dogs as an ex- cuse for not being able to deal with pussy. The poem was about nei- ther dogs nor love. The title was the best thing about it. This was often the case with men, as well as poems. When I'd called my mom to tell her I was going out with a PhD in English Literature, it had sounded terrific. But what it'd really meant was that I was planning to subject myself to endless discussions of *Middlemarch,* capped off with the theoretically kinky suggestion that I pull a George Eliot and crossdress. An evening with a sensitive Virginia Woolf expert had ended with him gently closing his apartment door, and suggesting that perhaps "you just need a room of your own."

I did not want a room of my own! I just wanted to find a guy I wouldn't mind sharing a room with. It didn't seem too much to ask. New York City was theoretically populated with the most attractive and intelligent men in the world. I could think of no explanation for my failure. Except that, as Shakespeare would no doubt have in- formed me, the fault was not in my stars, but in myself. Or rather, in my no policy. I'd always believed that I knew exactly what was good for me, but clearly this wasn't true. I was no longer a trustworthy guardian of my heart. I was twenty years old, and I hated everything.

I was sick of the intelligentsia. I was sick of poetry. I was sick of theses and screenings of student films. I was sick of sweltering the- aters, populated with unintelligible actors in Kabuki makeup and vinyl loincloths. I was sick of expensively disheveled tweed jackets and designer spectacles.

I was sick of the species of man I was meeting.

I was from Idaho, goddamn it! The Wild West! I wanted to meet a real man! Well. Maybe not a cowboy. I'd had significant in- teraction with cowboys, and it had been less than positive. At some point, in high school, I'd seen one engaged in intimate dealings with a bovine. I was a vegetarian. Anything that enjoyed meat, in that way, had no business coming near me. And, since I was being specific, maybe I didn't want a banker. And maybe not a trucker. And maybe not a lawyer, a construction worker, a fireman, a goth, a taxi driver, a mime, a Republican, anyone with blond eyelashes, anyone in tight jeans, anyone I knew . . .

And maybe I was a bit too judgmental.

"Zak?" I called to the kitchen. "Am I too critical?"

"Is that a question?"

"Vic?"

"Obviously," said Vic. "That's why we get along." Victoria and I had met as assigned roommates in the NYU dorms, and become friends largely because we hated everyone else.

Fine. I could change. I could switch my acid-green tinted glasses for a rose-colored pair.

IT WAS TIME FOR A NEW POLICY. I decided, in that moment, to do with men as I'd done with books. Read them all.

In seventh grade, I'd started in the A section of the library, and by the end of high school, I'd made it to N, checking out twenty books at a time. If only life were like the library! My mother had no idea the kind of guys I'd met between the stacks. F. Scott Fitzgerald. Allen Ginsberg. John Irving. Franz Kafka. D. H. Lawrence. Some hadn't even been guys. Marguerite Duras. Anaïs Nin. Toni Morrison. Between A and N, there was not only a lot of great writing, there was a lot of hot literary sex. Granted, I'd allowed myself, by F, the luxury of judging books solely by their covers, and I'd been doing it ever since, probably to my love life's detriment. At J, I'd been at once daunted by, and desirous of, James Joyce. My gaze had wandered to the Rs. *The Satanic Verses* seemed an easy read in comparison with *Finnegans Wake*. What could be more enticing to a rebellious teenage girl than a fatwa? Once I was in the Rs anyway, I'd taken a foray into the smutty paradise of Tom Robbins, with whom I'd fallen rather speedily out of love. He had far too many sex scenes involving things that did not sound pleasurable to me. Goat horns. Engage-ment rings lost in cavernous vaginas. I'd fled Robbins for *Ulysses,* where the proclivities of Molly Bloom had scared me even more.

Regardless of the overall quality, I had, with my reading policy, found plenty of things I'd liked. I'd found authors I would never have given a second glance, predisposed as I'd initially been toward pretty covers and Piers Anthony. Surely, I reasoned, it'd be the same with guys. If I just went out with all of them, there'd have to be some in there that I'd want to read again. See again. Either.

AND SO, I DECIDED THAT I WOULD SAY YES TO EVERY MAN WHO ASKED ME OUT ON A DATE. I'd go out with all of them, at least once. I'd stop pretending to be deaf when my taxi drivers tried to tell me I was cute. I'd stop pretending to be crazy when strange guys walked too close to me on the street. I'd turn toward them, and smile. And if they wanted to go out with me, I'd say, "Sure."

No more nos.

Well. A couple of exceptions. No one who was obviously vio-lent, or too drunk or drugged out to walk. No one who introduced himself by grabbing me. And the dates could be flexible. "Date" was an almost obsolete term at that point, anyway. Mostly, you'd end up "hanging out," possibly going to a bar, possibly going to dinner, pos-sibly getting naked. Most of the women I knew yearned, at least a lit-tle bit, for the days before the sexual revolution, when men were forced to commit to the Official Date, arrive in a sport coat (yes, it was dweeby, but at least it signified a certain intention), and take the girl out for surf, turf, and Lovers' Lane. Now, it was hard to know whether or not you were actually dating someone. He might call you up and blurt a string of frenetic phrases involving anything from *Star Wars* to Egon Schiele before he finally got to, "So . . . you wanna, like, hang out?"

You might "like, hang out" for six months, and still have com-pletely different ideas of whether or not you were a couple. At least if I went out with guys who asked me out on the street, they'd be asking me out based on some kind of established attraction, as opposed to the guy who (for example) happened upon my number while making spitballs.

> **LOSER:** I was, like, *so intensely bored,* and I called a couple of other people, but no answer, but then I saw your number, and wondered if you wanted to, you know, hang out.
>
> **MARIA** *(trying in vain to sleep)*: I'm busy.
>
> **LOSER:** But, like, I wanted to, you know, *get* busy.
>
> *(He emits a maniacal stoned giggle. A water bong burbles into the receiver.)*
>
> **MARIA:** Wait. Who *are* you? Do I know you?
>
> **LOSER:** Devin's roommate.
>
> **MARIA:** I don't know a Devin.
>
> **LOSER:** Devin got your number from Kevin.
>
> **MARIA:** Kevin?
>
> **LOSER:** Kevin is, like, in your Modern Drama class.
>
> **MARIA:** I didn't give Kevin my number.
>
> **LOSER:** Classroom directory. He made a list of cute girls. Wanna hang out or what?
>
> **MARIA:** Not at all.
>
> **LOSER:** Your loss, man. Whatever. Yeah, crossing you off the list. Finito.
>
> *(Maria throws the phone and addresses the audience.)*
>
> **MARIA:** You get the picture. At least guys I met on the street would be asking me out due to something other than boredom. No matter how pitiful this sounds, it was better than the current situation.

HOW TO PUT MY NEW POLICY INTO ACTION? It wouldn't be hard. I was in New York City, after all. There were around four million men in the five boroughs, and one thing that could be said of the men of the Big Apple was that they invariably had Big Balls. If you were female in New York, you'd been hit on by a stranger. It was built into the way the city functioned. Pedestrians. Subways. Contact with strangers, 24/7. In my travels around the city, about ten guys a day offered me everything from wedding rings to highly specific pornographic solicitations. Sometimes I got weirder offers, too. While I'd been dating Donatello, I'd agreed to be an extra in his student film. This had entailed a 4:30 A.M. walk to a bar on Avenue D, during which I'd heard, from behind me, a mysterious chirpy sound. It had turned out to be the inhabitant of an aluminum bagel cart, trying to get my attention in order to gift me with a cream cheese schmear. I'd crossed the street to evade him, but he'd chased me, waving a bag of bagels.

"Baby doll! Baby doll! My coffee is the best in New York! I wanna give you a present! You don't need a present? I got bialys, you don't like the bagels! I got danishes, sweetheart!"

"I'm not actually hungry," I'd said, walking faster.

"Baby doll! You can't turn down my pastry," he'd yelled, his bagel cart teetering as it built up speed.

"Yeah, I can," I'd said, and then sprinted to the bar, barely escaping him.

It seemed that I exuded some sort of pheromone that caused strangers to stop whatever they were doing and follow me home. As far as looks went, I was nothing compared to New York City's Aphrodite-quality women, but I got hit on a lot. I attributed this to several factors.

(1) I was five foot three, which put me at the right height to enable all men, whether sitting or standing, to grab various unwilling parts of me.

(2) I had a big, uncontrollable smile, which I couldn't keep from bestowing on strangers. No matter how hard I tried, I was unable to master the Look of Frigid Death that most New York City girls could turn on at will. My best attempt, judging from the feedback that was forever getting shouted at me, seemed to be the Look of Absolute Willingness.

(3) I was curvy, and the men of New York seemed, for the most part, to approve. In Idaho, my curves had been yet another indication of my inappropriateness. In second grade, I'd started imitating my mom's sexy sashay. A snot-nosed boy named Jimmy (who would, a few years later, knock up my best friend) had crept up behind me in the lunch line and hysterically shrilled:

"Why does your butt wiggle when you walk? Wiggly-butt! Wiggly-butt!"

The other second graders had been roused into a mob.

"Wiggly-butt! Wiggly-butt," they'd chanted, the sloppy joes on their sectioned trays shifting precariously.

I'd grabbed Jimmy's grubby hand and bitten it savagely, then spun on my heel and departed the cafeteria, my bottom emphatically twitching my disapproval all the way to the playground, where I'd crawled beneath the tire pyramid. Too bad for them if they couldn't appreciate a spectacular walk when they saw one.

It'd been the beginning of a bad thing. As I'd gotten older, the walk I'd imitated had, by virtue of genetics, become my own. My butt did wiggle when I walked. I couldn't help it. It was something about the width of my hip bones juxtaposed with the small size of my feet. And the butt in question had inarguably become curvaceous. It was always getting grabbed. My mom complained about the same thing, her most memorable story involving a youthful trip to the Leaning Tower of Pisa, a long ascent up the twirling staircase, her appalled bottom cupped by the hands of an Italian stranger for the entire 294 steps. My slender dancer sister had, for years, been traumatized by a boyfriend dubbing her round and muscular ass Shelfie. He'd shared with her his revolutionary feeling that her derriere should be used as a kind of knickknack ledge, and brokered ass grabs to his friends in exchange for pot. His band had collaborated on an ode to the ass, entitled "She's a Shelf," which, years later, still echoes through the post-grunge clubs of Seattle. At least, living in New York, most of the comments about the family rump were positive. And if it incited men to ask me out, who was I to judge them? Maybe they liked me for my ass, I thought, but surely they'd like me for other reasons once they got to know me. They'd like me for my capacity to quote from *The Canterbury Tales*, for my ability to sew them a quilted toga, for the entirety of my personality. Of course they would.

RESOLVED, I MARCHED INTO THE KITCHEN, WHERE VICTORIA AND ZAK WERE PRETENDING NOT TO BE SHARING THE TABLE. Vic was wearing headphones to block out Zak's muttering. Zak was wearing an expression straight out of Edvard Munch. Taken as a trio, Zak (half–African American, half–Caucasian), Vic (Chinese), and I (Northern European mishmash) had the look of a multicultural *Three's Company*. I got along with both of my roommates, but they didn't care for each other.

Vic had been born in Taiwan and had spoken only Chinese until she was five, at which point her family had moved to Lafayette, Louisiana. She had a fascinating accent—slightly Chinese, slightly Southern—and her cooking accommodated both fried chicken and thousand-year-old eggs. She also had a pierced tongue, which, with extreme difficulty, she had so far managed to keep hidden from her mother. Vic was an interesting compendium of personality traits: both hypercritical (she'd been known to wail, in the manner of a flaming gay fashion critic, after seeing a large woman dressed in a tube top, "Oh *no*, she didnnnn't!") and maternal. She could be counted on to wrap blankets around you and feed you soup when you were sick, and hug you and feed you ice cream when you were crying over some bad boyfriend. She'd also be clicking her tongue in annoyance that you'd been so dumb as to get your heart broken in the first place, but nobody was perfect.

I'd met Zak on the first day of classes. He had curly, close-cropped black hair, big glasses, and a brain that never stopped. Zak was almost ridiculously Berkeley, the child of a wayward Vietnam vet and a lesbian. He was stunningly bright and incredibly well-read, and, for these traits, as well as for his enormous, though unpredictable, generosity, I had promptly developed a crush on him. The crush had ended midway through the year, when he'd bleached his hair yellow. I'd found Vic, and shallowly announced: "I'm over him. He looks like a duckling."

I'd had the crush reprieve for about a month and a half while the duckling grew out, and then summer hit, and I'd moved to a sublet in a sketchy bit of south Williamsburg, Brooklyn. At the end of three months, Vic had returned from her sister's house in New Orleans, and she and I had set about trying to find an apartment. One day we'd been walking through Washington Square Park, and had stumbled over Zak sitting with his back against a wall, meditating on his lack of living space. We'd offered him a slot in our undetermined home-to-be. Though my crush was on hold, I'd been excited to imagine that we could potentially become best of best friends by sharing a bathroom. I'd never had a male roommate before.

Now that Zak and I lived together, I was constantly on the verge of falling madly and idiotically in love with him. Considering that he insisted he didn't want me, I pretended a similar disinterest. To our mutual best friend, Griffin, I maintained that Zak and I were soul mates, but Zak denied it. Ha, I said, though quietly. We had chemistry, damn it. Since we'd moved in together, we'd stayed up late every night discussing the meaning of life. Who did this but people who were meant to fall in love? When we both fell hard for Denis Johnson's difficult, gorgeous novel *Already Dead*, it was confirmed. We were meant to spend the rest of eternity together. Victoria did not think that this was true. She circled the edges of our friendship, justifiably declaring us pretentious, but jealous of our communion. She'd been my best friend in New York until Zak had moved in.

It was fitting that the only time they'd really gotten along had been the day that our toilet had mysteriously exploded. The two of them (I had blessedly not been home) had been forced to fight the toilet monster together, and had, after two and a half hours of fierce plunging, slain their enemy. By the time I'd come home from work, they'd been sitting together at the kitchen table, drinking beers, and recounting choice moments from their war. The next day, Vic had gifted Zak with a *Star Wars* pillowcase, as a reward for his courage in the face of her repulsion. Their camaraderie had, unfortunately, lasted only as long as it took for the mops to dry, and then they'd gone back to mutual irritation, which was constantly aggravated by our too-small apartment.

Victoria had won the bedroom lottery, as a result of her disregard for the enormous power cables that ran inches from her window. Her room had space for a dresser, a queen-size futon, and hell, even a Shetland pony, had she so desired. Zak was paranoid about electricity too close to his brain, and hadn't even tried to claim the room, but this didn't keep him from feeling bitter about the fact that his own room was four by six feet, just large enough for a mattress, a television, and a significant collection of comic books and pornography.

I had needed their rent checks too desperately to challenge either one of them, and had therefore ended up with the only space left: a single mattress in the corner of the living room, inside a rickety hut I'd constructed of a neighbor's pruned tree branches and some brown paper grocery sacks. This was a bummer, of course: no privacy, no escape from the noise of the television, no door to shut against the nocturnal malfeasance of Big White Cat, who liked to sneak up and drool into my sleeping ear. I generally tried to pretend that my hut was a yurt, and that I was living a romantic, vagabond adventure. I'd pull shut the doorway drape I'd engineered out of half a skirt, and imagine myself in a cloud of mosquito netting, on my way to a secret assignation with my lover, something like Ondaatje's *The English Patient*, minus, of course, the dying in a desert cave.

AS I MADE MY WAY INTO THE KITCHEN, ZAK RAISED HIS ENOR-MOUS COFFEE MUG to me in weary salute, then sighed heavily and put his head down. Clearly, the night had not been kind to him, either.

"Too much vodka," he muttered. "I tripped over my arm and rolled down a flight of stairs, in front of Brittany and all her friends."

He turned his head to display a rug burn on his cheek.

"How exactly did you trip over your arm?" Not that I was

surprised. Zak and I were both left-handed, and we theorized that the difficulties of living in a right-handed world had made us prone to bizarre injury. We were thinking of investing our meager funds in Band-Aid stock.

"Caveman lapse. Thought I was upright. Wasn't. Massive humiliation."

"Are you okay?"

"Severe emotional damage," he said. "But I, my friend, am a survivor. Who called?"

"I just got an offer to make out to NPR," I replied.

"I told you to stop answering the phone. You complain about every guy who calls."

I collapsed dramatically onto the third-hand coffee table we pretended was a couch.

"I'm changing my ways," I informed him. "The intellectuals aren't doing it for me, and I've rejected everyone else. I'm gonna start saying yes, to everyone. Who am I to judge who's appropriate? Just because a guy might be sleeping in a cardboard box doesn't mean he isn't worthy of me."

"It might," said Zak.

"*I'm* sleeping in a cardboard box," I said, and pointed at my hut.

"What're you talking about?" Vic asked, plucking the headphones off, and giving me the look that said she'd interrupted deep thoughts in order to tend to my perennially tortured love life.

"The men I meet are emotionally crippled, arrogant, scum-sucking lowlifes, pretending to be evolved. I can't deal with them anymore," I said. It was necessary to exaggerate, or Vic wouldn't take me seriously.

"Some were hot, though," said Vic. She pointed at a photo above the stove, which depicted one of the good-looking, vapid ones. I kept it there to remind me not to be deceived by beauty.

"For the next year, I'm going out with every man who asks me. Like on the subway, on the street, whatever. I've been too picky, and it's making my life suck. I'm going to stop saying no."

Somewhere, a gong was rung. Somewhere, lightning struck.

In our kitchen, Vic and Zak were rendered speechless. "No" had been my theme song, my mantra, my favorite word. A whole year without no?

"Yes," I said. "Yes, yes, yes, yes, yes."

"Whoa," said Zak. "I so wish all girls were like you."

"Where do you think we live?" said Vic. "You're going to date dog walkers."

"If a man is good with animals, he might be good with me."

Zak eyed me, clearly considering some sort of comeback, then thought better of it and went back to his caffeine.

"I'm going to leave that alone," he said. "Say thank you. You owe me."

"Thank you, that's very kind," I said.

"Dog walkers from New Jersey," said Vic.

"Parts of New Jersey are attractive."

"Dog walkers from New Jersey who keep severed heads in their freezers."

"Not all serial killers are from Jersey," I told her. Many were from the Northwest, where I was from. I felt safer in New York, frankly.

"I could be missing really cool people, just because I don't think they're cool enough for me," I continued. "Maybe I'm meant to be with a taxi driver."

Vic looked skeptical.

"You'll only date the hot ones. And you'll end up with the same guys you always date. Actors. Writers. It's your destiny. They like you, you like them. Stop complaining."

"I cannot fucking wait to see what you bring home," said Zak. "*If* you really do this," he added. "Because you won't."

"I will," I said.

"Swear," he said.

"On my future happiness, on all matters of the heart, on true love, and on satisfaction. If I don't say yes, let me die alone," I said, and stuck out my hand. Zak nodded in approval of my melodrama. We shook.

"Oh my God," said Zak. "This is fucking great."

"Big fun," said Vic. "Just don't give our number to any more weirdos."

She had a point. In the past, I'd been somewhat too generous with our phone number. Victoria had tried to tutor me in the brush-off, but it did no good. I'd end up cringing in the corner, as Vic answered the phone and told whoever was on the other end that I had food poisoning/schizophrenia/moved back to Idaho/died tragically.

"I won't give anyone our number," I said, suspecting that I was lying already.

"And are you planning to sleep with all of them?" Vic made no bones about the fact that she believed that if a girl slept with more than nine guys total, she was automatically a slut. She called this the Double-Digit Rule. By her definition, I might as well have invested in a few pairs of platform vinyl boots and some Lycra hot pants, because I was past the point of no return. I, on the other hand, believed in dividing the number of men by the number of years on the market. Looked at that way, my number was minuscule.

"Obviously not," I said.

"Really," said Zak, raising one eyebrow.

"Why would I sleep with someone I didn't like?" Never mind that I'd done it before. Hadn't everyone? Sometimes you just didn't know you didn't like someone until it was too late.

"Antonio, Judah . . ." Vic started to count on her fingers. "Martyrman for two years!" I headed her off.

"Yes to conversation, yes to dinner, yes maybe to a movie, yes to a bar. That's it. No other guaranteed affirmatives." Big White Cat nipped my ankle. He liked to sit in strange men's laps. So did I. It was a problem. Obviously, though, sleeping with everyone I went out with would be a colossally dumb thing to do.

Vic and Zak were still looking skeptical, but I was resolved.

I felt intrepid, like an explorer setting forth into the frozen wilderness with a few snorting sled dogs, a parka, and some pemmican. Revise. No pemmican. Unless there was such a thing as vegetarian pemmican. Revise again. Dating was supposed to be the opposite of the Arctic. My adventurer's uniform, then, would include a push-up bra, a pair of stiletto heels, and some lipstick. Not too difficult. This was my usual uniform anyway. I couldn't help it. I liked being a girl. And provisions? I turned to Zak.

"Where's my hardtack?"

Zak looked at me blankly.

"I *so* have no idea what you're talking about," he said.

"For my adventure." Zak hadn't read as much Jack London as I had, apparently, but I would have thought he'd have read some Joseph Conrad. I decided not to think about Conrad. *Heart of Darkness* was an inappropriate reference for this, my Year of Yes.

Zak grinned in understanding, and handed me a pen.

"Eat your words," he said. "Live on love."

"Funny," I said. "Woman cannot live on love alone."

"If anyone could," he said, "it'd be you."

I was excited. I was ready. I was going to force open my heart and make myself willing. It wasn't that I was lowering my standards. Just the opposite. I was expanding my faith in humanity. I was going to say yes, not just to a different kind of man, but to a different kind of life.

MR. HANDYMAN, BRING ME A DREAM

IN WHICH
OUR HEROINE
PLAYS COWBOYS
AND NATIVE
COLOMBIANS . . .

MY FIRST DAY OF YES WAS, IN MY BRAIN ANYWAY, going to involve me going to the West Village and planting myself at a sidewalk café, where I'd pose nonchalantly in a cleavage-enhancing white sundress, my dark red tresses tossing in a balmy breeze, and a copy of *One Hundred Years of Solitude* in my perfectly manicured hand. Ideal Man Number One, preferably in possession of a pair of piercing blue eyes and some endearing, but nonemotionally disabled shyness, would approach. He would be straight, despite our location in the West Village. He'd sit down at the table next to me, steal a few glances, and then, over-come, he'd rummage through his worn, leather bookbag until he found a scrap of paper. Make that a scrap of paper with a few lines of Rilke already written on it. He'd scribble a note and get the waiter to bring it to me with my cappuccino. I wasn't dictating what it should say, but whatever it was, it'd be Pulitzer-worthy. I'd flip the slip of pa-per over, write the word "yes" on it, and send it back over. He'd smile at me. I'd smile back. My teeth, by some miracle, would be free of lipstick. He'd move to my table, we'd both be smitten, and we'd live happily ever after. Or, at least, for the rest of the night, which would, by the way, not require any rudimentary lesson in female anatomy from me.

Things did not work out quite the way I'd planned.

There were several initial difficulties with my scenario. Some of them, like the fact that it was thirty degrees outside, I could do nothing about. I could, however, address the fact that my hair was not red. Brown hair. Brown eyes. Skin a strange shade of sagebrush. I was, overall, the color of drought. My entire childhood had been spent being mistaken for a tiny, transient farm worker. Since moving to New York, I'd been taken for Puerto Rican, Polish, Russian, Hun-garian, and Colombian. I'd been Israeli, Armenian, Italian, and Turkish. In actuality, my ancestry was appallingly blue-blooded. William Bradford had sailed in on the *Mayflower* in 1620, become the governor of the Plymouth Colony, and begat a variety of dimin-ishingly Puritanical descendants until, a few hundred years later, his bloodline reached its nadir with me. Had I wanted to, I could've joined the Mayflower Society or the Daughters of the American Rev-olution. I was not inclined. There was one pleasing exception to the whiteness: an ancestor who'd fallen off the rails and married a Mohi-can Indian. Very plausible, in my opinion, was the notion that the merger with my family had taken the whole tribe down. Further down the chain was Elizabeth Barrett Browning, whose *Sonnets from the Portuguese* I'd learned to loathe as bad pillow talk. My dad's side was a string of blacksmiths, a couple hundred years of guys who pounded molten steel for a living, and came out only rarely into daylight. Family photos showed a lot of men with blackened skin and pale eyes. On that side, as well, in none-too-distant memory, was a woman who went by Bobo, because her name had been forgotten by everyone, including herself. The mixture of lines had resulted in me, looking, apparently, like everyone's ex-wife, lost love, or childhood baby-sitter. On the street, I was routinely entrusted with whispered confidences in a variety of languages. There seemed to be nothing to be done.

I'D RESERVED THIS SATURDAY MORNING FOR STAINING THE BATHROOM FLOOR, my ears, my hands, and theoretically my hair, with henna, a hashish-scented paste resembling, when I was in a good mood, creamed spinach. When I was in a bad mood, it looked regrettably like the maggot-filled mud puddle my sister and I had, as children, once stationed my younger brother in for "spa treatments." Because my hair was long, almost to my waist, the hennaing was a foul process of several hours. Length was not advantageous in New York City. I'd once felt a mysterious tugging while on the subway, only to turn and discover a man blissfully stuffing my ponytail down his pants. Now I usually wore it in a pile, dubiously secured with whatever bobby pins and takeout utensils I could unearth. I suspected that I looked like a small swami, carrying a coil of miserable infant cobras on my head. I convinced myself that this wouldn't matter. I'd get that sidewalk table, and morph into the self I wasn't. The reddened hair, I was certain, would make all the difference. Happiness would be mine!

However, within seconds of my starting to rinse the henna, the shower plugged up, and Pierre LaValle's version of Morse code started shaking the floor. Whenever Pierre heard something disagreeable from our apartment, he immediately began a militant march around his kitchen, banging his broomstick against the ceiling like a bayonet. This was supposed to signal that we should cease and desist. Unfortunately for Pierre, his banging had created a karmic perforation in his ceiling. I stomped on the floor of the shower a few times to signal that I was aware of the problem, then wrapped myself in a hand towel as Pierre grumbled up the stairs and pounded on our door.

Though he had a sexy exterior, tall, dark, handsome, and extensively tattooed, Pierre's personality was that of a snapping turtle. Despite his French name, he was a Puerto Rican boy from Miami. We speculated that he'd been raised not by wolves, but by retirees, playing canasta and developing a way with melba toast. He was twenty-five, but acted seventy. He was a chef, and going to business school on the side. Vic had a semisecret Scorpio-Scorpio crush on him, but I thought he was a pain in the ass. Pierre believed in shoe polish and expensive hair pomade. My muddied locks were twisted into stalagmites, and a glance in the tiny mirror had confirmed that I looked very swamp mummy. I didn't think Pierre deserved pretty.

I flung open the door, mud dripping down my face. Pierre, his trousers neatly creased, his hair perfectly spiky, blinked several times.

"Can I help you?" I prompted.

"Maria?" Pierre managed.

"Yeah?"

"Leak. I thought it was Zak, blowing up the toilet again," he said, averting his eyes from the horror of my appearance. Zak and Pierre had hated each other on sight. Pierre believed that Zak was an anarchist, and Zak believed that Pierre was a pod person. Added to this, Zak typically ascended the stairs at 3:00 or 4:00 in the morning, roaringly drunk and stomping his combat boots. Pierre's bedroom was just below Zak's. He was regularly rudely awakened, which was his justification for vacuuming in the dead of night. Revenge.

Pierre's eyes flitted to my towel, then back to my aboriginal head. Henna had a distinctively contraband odor. He probably thought I was stoned.

"Sorry," I said. "Bo told me he replaced a valve." Bo was the middle-aged, possibly mentally handicapped son of Gamma. His only claim to maintenance man status was his tritely sagging waistband. He used things like masking tape to fix broken pipes.

"What's up?" Pierre said. "I haven't seen you for a while."

What was his problem? Couldn't he see that I was fully involved in glamorizing myself for my meeting with Mr. Right? I tried to radiate go-away vibes. Pierre shuffled his feet and gave me an attempt at a smile. My go-away vibes were never very successful. I relented.

"Wanna come in, Pierre?"

"That'd be great," he said. I was instantly suspicious. Hanging with a hostile neighbor was akin to hanging with a vampire. You'd end up drained of blood, and it would be your own fault for inviting them across the threshold. I thought he might be trying to case my apartment for violations that would get me kicked out.

Pierre sat down at our kitchen table, crossed his legs, and prissily plucked a strand of Big White Cat's fur from his knee. I couldn't turn my back on him, because the towel gapped. My clothes were in my hut. Granted, this was supposed to be the Year of Yes, but I hadn't planned on beginning it this way. At least I could count on Pierre not to ask me out. According to Vic, he was "utterly unattracted" to me.

"Want coffee?" Maybe I could placate him before he reported the fact that my floor tiles were stapled down, and my kitchen was illegally painted with a mural, the centerpiece of which was Zak's contribution, a villainous comic book creature, and a morbid quote by Nietzsche: "Of all that is written, I love only that which is written in blood."

"So. You're pretty much naked," said Pierre.

"That's pretty much true," I said. I eased myself onto the other kitchen chair. Big White eyeballed Pierre, gave an ecstatic chirp, and then hopped into his lap and wallowed whorishly. So much for my guard cat.

"That's an interesting thing you're doing with your hair," Pierre continued politely. I'd grabbed a box of plastic wrap and was twisting it around my head like a turban. The henna box had said that heat would help the dye to set. At least, I was reasoning, the plastic wrap would keep it from dyeing my entire face. My ears were already a lost cause.

. . .

JUST THEN, MY BUZZER EMITTED A MUFFLED QUACK. Who was
ringing at my door? No one was supposed to be coming over. I
stayed put. There was no way I was going to answer it. Probably one
of the twins, prank buzzing.

Pierre stood up and proceeded to admit whoever it was into
the building.

"It's Mario," he explained, flashing me a triumphant grin. I was
instantly pissed off.

"I'm not dressed!"

"I called his pager before I came up. I knew you wouldn't let
him in, so I came upstairs to do it for you. I mean, your shower's
leaking into my copper pans. Everything tastes like soap. I can't take
it anymore."

Bastard. Bastard, bastard, bastard. Every day I found new reasons to dislike Pierre.

Mario was the handyman that Bo usually brought in as a savior
after he'd electrocuted himself a few times. He was a tall, skinny,
Colombian guy in his early forties, with a crest of black hair, a motorcycle jacket, jeans, and cowboy boots. He rode a Harley around
the neighborhood. His only tools seemed to be a screwdriver and a
hammer, and with these, he worked miracles.

This did not mean that I wanted him to see me dressed in a
hand towel.

It was, however, too late. The Handyman walked in the door,
looked me up and down, and gave a low whistle. I gave Pierre a glare
that, if directed at any normal guy, would have induced internal
bleeding. In Pierre, though, it only induced a smirk.

"Hola," said someone at about knee level. I looked down. A little girl was holding the Handyman's free hand.

"This is Carmela," he said.

Carmela was six. She had two haphazard black pigtails, and a
small suitcase in one hand. I felt my stomach drop. As a result of a
couple of kids' plays I'd written, I'd developed a horror of small

children. I would've taken an entire audience of *New York Times* reviewers over one critic dressed in OshKosh. The little girls were like Elizabethan audiences: They tended to boo and throw things. Had they rotten tomatoes at their disposal, we would have been pelted. The little boys typically slept through entire performances, only to surge forth, weeping, during the quietest scenes.

Carmela dropped the Handyman's hand, marched to the corner, sat down Indian style, and opened her suitcase. Something in her manner gave me the impression that she was carrying a disassembled sniper rifle. I allowed myself a fantasy. Maybe she'd take out the twins. Or the feral cats that hissed for hot dogs every time I passed through the courtyard. Or Pierre. Especially Pierre.

"Later," he said, spinning on his polished heel. The Handyman and I listened to him dancing his way down the stairs, and then turned to each other.

"You gotta leak, mami? You need me to fix you up?"

In fact, no. I just liked having strange men over to my apartment when I was looking like the Creature from the Black Lagoon. The Handyman must have seen the frustration on my face, because he jerked a thumb at the bathroom and departed. I fled into my hut for clothing and a newsboy cap to stuff my plastic head into.

I could hear the Handyman banging about and swearing. Our bathroom was three feet by three feet and boasted a triangular sink the size of a measuring cup, and a shower stall constructed of what seemed to be cellophane. The water had only two temperature options: Vesuvius and Siberia.

I cringed inside my hut, having severe second thoughts about the yes policy. The Handyman had asked me out before. In fact, the Handyman asked me out every time I saw him. He was that kind of guy. He was, indeed, a handyman, in both the usual sense and in the two-fisted-ass-grabbing sense. He hadn't actually grabbed my ass, but I felt that that was only because I'd never turned my back on him.

Did I really have the balls to do this? Was it insane? Maybe I needed to be hospitalized. I had a brief fantasy of abdicating responsibility à la Blanche DuBois, deep-ending on the kindness of strangers. Attendants to bring me juice, and hold my straw while I sipped. Someone else to do my laundry. A white-sheeted bed with a real box spring. It had been years since I'd had a box spring. Unfortunately, Zak and I had recently watched the filmed version of *Marat/Sade*, the Peter Weiss play set in the asylum at Charenton. All those crazed inmates, flinging themselves about, babbling and scrabbling, speaking in Brechtian tongues. I'd been traumatized. *Marat/Sade* was appallingly similar to my own life.

"Chica!" The Handyman came into the room, wrench in hand. "Chica, chica, chica, you gotta problem, but I'm gonna fix it for you no charge, 'cause you're sexy."

Let it be said that I had a severe allergy to the metaphoric conceit that women were as easy to (ful)fill as a hole in drywall. James Taylor's "Handyman," and the oft-covered gagger "If I Were a Carpenter," were two of my most-loathed songs of all time. "Handyman" had verses talking about how not only would he fix *your* broken heart, you ought to refer him to your girlfriends, too. Obviously, all women wanted a man who could do double duty as a power drill. I found "If I Were a Carpenter" just as appalling. What kind of carpenter was this guy, proposing marriage and babies? How did that have anything to do with woodworking? Well. I'd once worked for two unsuccessful days in a theater set shop. There, "woodworking" had been a favored euphemism for "screwing" and/or "nailing" a chick. With your "tool." In the company of men, many sex-related things developed a *This Old House* component. But really, if he were an actual carpenter, he'd knock up some bookshelves, not me. This carpenter seemed to just be a dude with a superficial hammer. I had my own superficial hammer.

Carmela removed a bright purple walrus, a packet of crayons, and a mystery sandwich from her suitcase. When I asked the Handyman what it was, he told me that it was her favorite, mustard and marshmallow fluff. I slid a few pieces of paper across the floor toward her, and then went to my computer, thinking that at least I could do my homework. I was thigh-deep in a class called Image of the Other, and was supposed to be writing an essay on Josephine Baker's subjugation via a miniskirt made of bananas. I'd been more inclined to write a comparative of Baker and Carmen Miranda. Why were these women wearing fruit, anyway? The class was largely composed of privileged white kids, and most of it was spent watching things like *Cabin in the Sky* and *Imitation of Life,* and listening to the frustrated sighs of the professor, a big name in the field of race and media studies. Classes like these were making me wonder why the hell I was paying an obscene amount of borrowed money for knowledge that I would never be able to apply to the real world. Sure, I'd seen *Birth of a Nation* in its twelve-hour entirety, but it wasn't the kind of thing that caused a human resources manager to hire you on the spot.

When the Handyman finally emerged, Carmela repacked her case, handed me her drawings, which were, somewhat traumatically, portraits of me, and marched out the door.

"Everything fixed?" I asked the Handyman. My head was itching wickedly. I hoped I wasn't going to remove my newsboy hat to discover all my hair fallen out.

"The shower's good, but I'm not," said the Handyman.

"How come?" I asked.

"'Cause you're not walking out of here with me." He winked. Clearly, he was blind. I was hideous. Maybe the wink was the result of something in his eye. Pierre arrived to check the progress of the leak, and was just in time to smirk at this.

I'd show him. Day one of the Year of Yes, not quite like the fantasy version, but what the hell. Wasn't that the point?

"Absolutely," I said. "Yes."

"Yes, what?" said the Handyman.

"Yes, I'm walking out of here with you. As long as you're inviting me."

I had the satisfaction of seeing Pierre's eyes bulge, and his tattooed koi flip their tails.

"Let's go, then, mamita," said the Handyman, who did not even seem surprised, but instead offered me a cigarette, and put his arm around me as though we'd been together forever.

"Give me a minute," I said, and went to wash my hair. It had turned out, unsurprisingly, not at all red. Some of it was orange. Some of it was blackish. Some of it was green. It hung in long, straight, hideous strands. I squinted at myself for a moment in the mirror, and decided that I'd had enough. I got out my dull scissors, pulled a hank of hair over my shoulder, and hacked it off. Two feet of tresses dropped onto the bathroom floor. My head felt thrillingly light. I continued to chop, ending up just above my shoulders, and then, in one of those bad impulses you can never afterward explain, I cut myself some Bettie Page bangs. Crooked. Of course.

As the result of a crippling first-grade year, which the teacher spent trying to make me a rightie, I'd never properly learned how to use scissors. Usually, when people saw me cutting, they thought I had cerebral palsy. I had to cut the bangs shorter. And shorter. The last time I'd had a haircut this bad, I'd been five, and my mom had gone away for the weekend, leaving my sister and me with our father. She'd come home to find my dad looking sheepish, and my sister and I sporting super-short, slanted bangs that made us look like we were recovering from brain surgery. Screw it. I kept snipping.

I maneuvered my face into the one expression that made them look even: one eyebrow raised high, and the other crunched down. There. That was not so bad. I fluffed it up to the best of my ability, smeared on some red lipstick, and went outside to meet the first man of my new life.

The Handyman didn't comment on the haircut. Maybe it looked good. On the way out of the building, however, we encountered Zak.

"What the fuck did you do to your hair?" he said.

"Cut it," I said.

"Why?" he said.

"Because," I said, getting defensive. "I should be able to cut my hair if I want to."

"It looks completely weird," said Zak. He had never been

known for his delicacy regarding feminine beauty and lack thereof. "And the front is crooked. Did you know that?"

I rearranged my face into the expression.

"How about now?"

"Now your face looks weird."

The Handyman cleared his throat. I'd forgotten about him.

"You know Mario," I said.

"Mario, the handyman," Zak said, suspiciously. I could see the memory of the exploding toilet flashing before his eyes. "Why are you here?"

"Mario the cowboy," the Handyman corrected. "I'm taking your girl to dinner, amigo."

Zak looked as though he was going to choke on suppressed laughter.

"My girl?" he said. "I'm just going inside."

"I'm just going out," I said, only partially believing what I was saying.

CARMELA WALKED TEN FEET IN FRONT OF US, pretending, no doubt, that she was a princess being attended by a couple of servants far below her station. She didn't even look back to see if we were behind her. The Handyman seemed to know everyone on every street corner. He greeted women ranging from seventeen-year-old Polish girls to their gray-haired grandmothers. He donated a buck to the yellow-eyed Kielbasa Dude, a career drunk who perpetually hung out on Greenpoint Avenue clutching a booze-filled brown paper sack and a sausage. He waved at the proprietors of the bodegas. He nodded at the waitresses in the Thai Café, which, despite its unlikely location deep in Polish Brooklyn, made the best green papaya salad in the city. It was as though we were traversing a *Mister Rogers' Neighborhood* arranged specifically for the Handyman.

I walked next to him, and wondered how I'd managed to live in Greenpoint for as many months as I had without getting to know anyone. I recognized the cast of characters, of course, but the

Handyman knew them by name. I'd been pretending I didn't really live in my neighborhood. Most of my time, by necessity, was spent in Manhattan anyway. Greenpoint was where I slept. When I slept. The neighborhood had, in my opinion, very little to recommend it. Greenpoint, obviously named early in an optimistic century, had nothing green to boast of, unless you counted the complexions of its residents, upon catching a whiff of the famous Greenpoint Sewage Treatment Plant. Or, perhaps, the neighborhood's moniker referred to Newton Creek, which divided the northernmost tip of our neighborhood from Queens, and which was euphemistically classified as "precluded for aquatic life" due to the massive Exxon oil leak that had, for years, been drooling into the creek's already sewage-contaminated waters. This did not keep certain neighborhood eccentrics and teenagers from cannonballing off the disintegrating India Street pier, and dog-paddling in the slurry. The Handyman seemed to thrive in this neighborhood. For the first time, I thought that maybe I could, too. I'd been rejecting my new home. If I was giving up on no, it was time to give up on that, too.

In between yelling hellos at hipsters, bums, and babies, the Handyman conducted a running monologue of his history.

"So, mamita, it used to be heroin for me, but I got clean of the devil, and now I'm here. Montana was where I came straight from Colombia, three wives ago. Her mamá, we never got married, 'cause I got smart."

I was alone amongst my friends in thinking that dating recovering addicts was actually not the worst thing in the world. They always told you their story, right up front. It was a refreshing change from persons addicted to other things: emotional warfare, codependence, Harold Pinter plays. At this point in my life, it seemed worth dealing with the addict's night sweats, sievelike memory, and "bad liver and broken heart," as Tom Waits put it, in order to get to his stories. Where else could I hear tales of piano bars and mystery scars, ballads of long-dead cronies named Mac, stories of jonesing for a hit of something or other and somehow ending up married to a waitress, and buried alive in a diner Dumpster by fried egg sand-wiches? Stories like the Handyman's.

Carmela dropped back to listen.

"Daddy also had a big mess with cocaine," she told me.

"I was getting to that, baby," the Handyman called after her, but she had resumed her place in front of us.

"Montana?" I asked. I was feeling pleased with myself for re-maining unfazed in the face of the Handyman's story. He was twirling his hammer with the panache of a marching band vixen. The zippers on his motorcycle jacket flashed in the sun. His spurs, yes, *spurs*, jingled. His teeth were white, and his skin was tanned, and it seemed that, even though he was a walking contradiction, a motorcycle-riding Colombian cowboy, nothing bad had ever hap-pened to him.

"Dude ranch. The Flying Bull. We called it the Flying Bullshit, mamita, but it was not a bad place to be. First I was the dishwasher, then I was the cook. And Montana! Baby, you gotta get your sweet ass to Montana!"

Carmela led us to a restaurant called the Manhattan Triple Decker. It was neither in Manhattan, nor three stories high. One story and a lot of eggs. She greeted the aged Polish man behind the counter, and then graciously accepted his lift onto a bar stool. Without being asked, he brought her a strawberry milkshake. Clearly, she was a regular.

"I was bringing the powder to the cowboys, baby, and they were out there, on their horses, high, high, high, and all because of me, their dishwasher. Man. Those days are dead and gone now, dead and gone."

The Handyman ordered a hamburger. I got a grilled cheese.

"Couple of the guys, they were the real thing, and the rest were the guests from everywhere, everybody who wanted to ride horses and pretend they were in a Western movie. Everybody liked the coke, though; man, *mi amigo* in the kitchen got me hooked up and before you knew it, we were selling the shit to the whole town. I could ride, back then, mamita, as good as the guys who were out there year-round. I had a horse I liked, and I used to ride all over the ranch, high out of my mind! And shit, baby! Did I tell you I could lasso? I lassoed whatever I felt like. One time, I put a loop around this chica in jeans and cowboy boots, and damn, damn, damn, mami!"

He paused for a moment, lost in the memory of a girl I pictured as a lot like the big-haired Rodeo Queens of my high school. There'd been one who'd been famous for the constantly visible outline of a Trojan in the back pocket of her skin-tight Wranglers.

"So, what happened? How'd you end up here?"

"He got busted," said Carmela, turning to give me the first smile I'd seen from her. A bewitching, missing-toothed grin. She slurped her milkshake. "And then he got my mommy."

"I met her in jail," said the Handyman. "I was in for only five months. They busted me, but they busted me on the wrong day. I didn't have shit. They wanted to put me away forever, but instead, they had to put me away for no time at all. She was my cellmate Victor's wife. Fool wouldn't see her, got pissed over some small shit, thought she was fucking his brother, so I went out and there she was."

"The most beautiful woman my daddy had ever seen," said Carmela, happily.

"Her name was Maria," said the Handyman.

I was enchanted. I'd started writing a tragic motherless-child-and-widower story in my head. Death in childbirth. Grieving widower, scarred by a criminal past, trying to hack out a living through fix-it gigs, little daughter raising herself on mustard-and-marshmallow sandwiches. Horrible as it was, it appealed to my drama-saturated nature. I was already considering how I'd adapt it into a hybrid of Tennessee Williams, Eugene O'Neill, and Sam Shepard. I was envisioning my Pulitzer. My Tony. My Oscar! The trifecta, balanced on the bookshelves I'd finally be able to afford.

"What happened to her?" I asked softly, ready to comfort him. He started laughing. Laughing hard. Slapping his knee at my apparent stupidity. Carmela drew some milkshake up in her straw. She shot it, with perfect accuracy, at the Handyman's cheek.

"Damn, mamita, whadda you think?" The Handyman wiped his face, still laughing.

I protested that I didn't know. How could they laugh about something as tragic as this? What kind of people were they? Had they no compassion?

"She ran off on the back of a motorcycle with some fucker she met in the 7-Eleven. Left me with this one, still a baby. I had to raise her on a bottle, yeah, Carmela?"

"Yuck," Carmela confirmed.

"And now, we gotta go. Somebody on Eagle Street has a busted buzzer. I'm coming by your place tomorrow afternoon, to fix yours, 'cause it's fucked, right, mamita?"

"It quacks," I told him.

"Yeah, I didn't like the people who lived there before you," said the Handyman, grinning. "I gave 'em a joke buzzer."

And with that, they were gone. I moved to a booth and ate my sandwich. I wasn't sure what to think of what had just happened. It was starting to be clear to me that, though I knew plenty about Greek tragedies, I knew almost nothing about real life. As if that were not enough, I could see my reflection in the window and it looked like an obsessive-compulsive bird had built a nest on my head.

I ONLY HAD A COUPLE OF MINUTES TO FEEL SORRY FOR MYSELF, before I noticed a guy pressing his face against the outside of the glass. He was tall and pale, with lank blond hair, and looked to be somewhere in his forties. He came inside, walked straight to my booth, ordered a beer in Polish, and without any warning, started sobbing. I signaled urgently to the waitress. She shrugged.

"Are you okay? Do you need a doctor?" I asked.

He let loose with a snot-drenched stream of Polish.

"He says you look like his ex-wife," the beautiful teenage waitress translated, rolling her eyes, and then went to get him another bottle of Tyskie beer. He opened it with his teeth. Normally, I would have moved to another table, or left the restaurant altogether. I could smell the crazy on him. But that day, I was willing to admit that maybe I was a little crazy, too. And here we were, in a diner in Brooklyn, crazy, at the same moment.

The scene in *King Lear* that I'd always liked best involved Lear, gone mad, wandering the beach in the storm to end all storms, running into his old friend Gloucester, who has been blinded. There they are: these two people who've known each other forever, in the middle of a rainstorm, at the end of their reigns. For a little while, they save each other.

And so, I stayed where I was. I ate my sandwich. He drank his beers. He talked, and talked, and talked, a monologue of Zs and Ks. I smiled. I nodded. He grabbed my hand and squeezed it hard.

When he left, it was dark outside. The day was over. My true love, whoever he was, hadn't shown up. For some reason, I was happy anyway.

THE NEXT DAY, THE HANDYMAN APPEARED AT MY APARTMENT and wired me a buzzer that turned out to be louder than the entire neighborhood combined. Its bleat registered equivalent to my teenage idiotic episodes of leaning against the speakers at grunge-era rock shows.

"So you always know when someone's coming," said the Handyman. I protested that the buzzer was likely to make me have a heart attack.

"Nobody wants to be safe," he grumbled.

"Obviously not," I said. "I just want to be happy." I thought I was being lighthearted. The Handyman disagreed.

"Fuck it," he said. "Fuck everyone." His eyes blazed.

The disadvantage of addicts, recovering and otherwise: mood swings. The Handyman stormed out of the apartment. A moment later, my buzzer screamed. And again. He rang it for an hour. Finally, I went outside to give him a piece of my mind.

"What are you doing?"

"You weren't supposed to answer that, mamita," he said. He was sitting on my stoop, looking calm and dejected. "I'm a crazy motherfucker, but you're one stupid girl."

"Probably true," I agreed. "Don't do that again, or I'll call the police."

"No charge for the buzzer. It'll keep you safe from people like me, and shit, mami, you look like you need it. You're too young for me, mamita, young and dumb, just like I was when I was in Montana."

Carmela materialized, suitcase in hand, followed by a troupe of three neighborhood mutts, and a lagging older woman in worn-down red stilettos.

"You were late, Daddy," she said, reprovingly. The old lady said something pissed off in Polish. The Handyman replied, also in Polish. She left, grumbling.

"Daddy's got problems," said Carmela, looking at me solemnly. "But I love him."

There was no one in my life that I could say that about. Besides myself, that is. I envied Carmela her capacity for the unconditional. Part of me wanted to be like her, to be able to accept everyone I met. To forgive them their trespasses, their buzzer ringings, their vacuuming. Obviously, I wasn't there yet. I wasn't sure I'd ever be.

"See you," I said to the Handyman.

"Next time something breaks, baby," he replied.

He swung Carmela up, and she scrambled onto his shoulders like a monkey. I watched them as they walked into the sunset, their two bodies becoming a silhouette of something bigger than both of them.

Zak sat down next to me with a bottle of beer in hand.

"Brittany?" I asked.

"Catastrophe," he said. "Debacle, disaster, horror, nightmare. You?"

"How about I sing a little bit of 'Handyman' for you? *I fix broken hearts . . .* "

"No. You know how I feel about easy listening."

"He was as broken as me, is the bottom line."

"That'd be life, yes," said Zak. "And the things that compensate for emotional instability aren't constant, either, that's the problem."

"What would those things be?"

"Things that eventually sag," he said, sadly.

I put my head on Zak's shoulder as the sun went down. Maybe love was like Godot. You spent the whole play talking about it, but it never actually made it onstage. You waited anyway. Of course you did.

"Wanna go play video games?" asked Zak.

"Desperately," I said.

And so, in lieu of love, we went out into the night to kill a few monsters.

JACK THE STRIPPER

IN WHICH OUR
HEROINE MEETS A
WUSS IN CREEP'S
CLOTHING . . .

THE NEXT FEW WEEKS WERE SPENT IN A STATE OF CON-TROLLED CHAOS. I went out with guys I met on the subway, guys I met in the bookstore, guys I met in line for stupidly expensive espresso. Varying degrees of dates. Mostly coffee, sometimes a drink in a bar. I went out with a couple of PhD-holding taxi drivers (one was an Indian surgeon, the other an Egyptian psychoanalyst); a Metropolitan Museum security guard who offered to take me home to meet his family in Sicily; a couple of construction workers; a Vietnam vet who was missing three fingers (alas, he had plenty to say about what he could do with the remaining digits); a Long Island City carpet salesman who asked if I wanted to "shag," and then laughed for a long, long time, pointing hysterically at a section of fluffy carpets. I had a glass of Rioja with a Spanish-accented painter who, in an ill-conceived effort to impress me, told me that the only medium worth painting in was your own viscera. He then gave a long diatribe about people who held down day jobs instead of "doing their art." The next day, I happened to go into Pearl Paint to buy latex for my living room, and there he was, working behind the counter, holding a bottle of glitter glue, and sounding very much like he was from New Jersey. I went out with a goatee-wearing psychic, who told me I was from Nebraska (no), a Capricorn (no), and about to find Big Love (hopefully). Then he spent forty-five minutes reading my palm, and found a line on it that clearly said I was going to sleep with him (hell no). I went out with one of the annoying New York guys who runs up to girls on the street, telling them they have great hair, and then tries to sell them salon gift certificates. I went out with a matchstick-skinny photographer, who came up to me in a café and told me he was looking for models to pose for his "tasteful and artistic nude series." Much to his sorrow, I didn't take my clothes off, but I regret to say that there's a picture out there somewhere in which there is not only far too much leg, there's a dyed-pink lapdog and a maraschino cherry.

Despite all these dates, I still hadn't gone out with anyone from my program at NYU. And I was glad. Dating in the Dramatic Writing Program was incestuous, on a Greek tragedy level. One mistake made at a party could find you putting out your eyes during your next playwriting workshop. Anything you did was destined to trail humiliatingly behind you, like toilet paper attached to your shoe, for the next four years. Even if you didn't remember it, everyone else was writing it down. It'd appear in the classroom the next week, translated into a scene in someone else's play. You'd end up sitting around the workshop table, impotently explaining why it was not good dramatic logic to include the scene in which the character based on you made out with the character based on the most flamingly gay boy in the program. Why were you making out? You were a girl. Yes, *okay*, he was a boy, but a boy who, if not for the joint influence of controlled substances and pure desperation, would've had no interest in girls. Not **that** you could even comment directly. All the people in my **program** were repression made flesh. We sublimated all our vitriol into pages, becoming not just backbiters, but backwriters. I'd dated a bunch of other NYU students, both during the months of my yes policy, and prior, but thus far I'd evaded any of the messes in my daily classes.

However, if someone from my program asked me out now, I couldn't say no. When I'd put my yes policy into effect, I'd neglected to think about that. Post-Handyman, I'd felt somewhat virtuous. A foray into the nonintellectually bound male. Hadn't turned out terribly well, but that wasn't really his fault. I felt comfortable taking the blame for that particular failure, whereas, if I was going to date a classmate, I felt that he should take equal responsibility for any tragedy. He, after all, would have the same frames of reference I did. *A Doll's House* and *The Three Sisters, The Misanthrope* and *Long Day's Journey into Night*. A shared vocabulary of this kind of material seemed to me to be a recipe for disaster.

There were several categories of male to be met in the Dramatic Writing Program, and, with the exception of the last two, I was critical of them all:

1. **THE RAINBOW BULLETS.** As in, gay like Liberace. One of these was writing a response to Eve Ensler's *The Vagina Monologues*, entitled *The Penis Monologues*. He claimed that the penis had been marginalized, too.
2. **THE GAYTS.** Gay-straight men. Obviously gay, but in denial. Usually, these guys would spend their time at NYU writing five or six scripts featuring characters that everyone knew were gay, except the playwright, who'd finish things up with a hetero wedding.

3. THE STRAYS. Straight-gay men. Dated girls, but used hair products that made girls suspicious of them. Always prettier than any woman in the department.

4. THE COMEDIANS. Interested only in fart jokes. No one ever got a good look at them, because they never removed their scraggly baseball caps. Traveled in packs. Deadly serious.

5. THE TRAGEDIANS. Usually strikingly handsome, and in possession of appealingly troubled souls, and extensive knowledge of French new wave cinema. Interested only in making experimental, Warhol-esque films consisting of five hours of footage of the Empire State Building. At night.

6. THE CULT OF PERSONALITY. Generally, slam poets. They paired wildly mismatched 1970s shirts with nylon workout pants and Converse high-tops, and vacillated between above-it-all silence and rabid ironic monologue. Asexual.

7. THE DO-OVERS. The thirty-something guys who were happily beginning their youth again, this time as the only "real men" in a program full of hot eighteen-year-olds.

8. THE GURUS. The thirty-something guys who didn't notice the eighteen-year-olds, and therefore were fervently desired by all of them. Usually yoga teachers on the side.

9. THE PROFESSORS. Though there were rules against dating one's students, they were not well enforced. A side effect of writerly repression was that several people in the program were obsessed with scripting sadomasochistic onstage sex. The rest of the unlucky workshop participants would have to pretend to be actors, and read the scenes aloud. "Ohh, ahh, yesssssss. Pleeease, plunge my head into a bucket of pee." Nothing could have been more unappealing.

Except for the semifamous professor in charge, lecherously informing my friend Elise that she looked as though she'd been really turned on during her reading of a rape scene.

10. **ZAK**. Lovable, but not dateable, given the roommate situation. Zak had his own in-program dating woes. He'd had a brief interlude with the blonde Russian babe that all the straight boys in the program followed around. Something undisclosed had gone wrong. Now he was forced to hide every time he saw her.

11. **GRIFFIN**. Lovable, but not dateable, given that, other than Zak, he was my only male friend in the department. He, Zak, and I formed a triumvirate of late-night intellectual obnoxiousness. When Griffin was in our kitchen, Zak and I were allowed to be as loud as we wanted to be, because he'd charmed Vic and could do no wrong. Griffin was a small Greek guy from Indiana, and in possession of a talent for making anyone, in any room he walked into, fall instantly in love with him. All of his female friends had tried to sleep with him at some point, and I was no exception. In my case, I'd hung out with him one night until 4:00 A.M., eating his trademark bad pasta and drinking wine. When it was too late for me to go home, he'd given me his bed.

"You can stay in here with me, you know," I'd said.

Griffin had taken a couple steps toward the bed, then a couple back.

"I can't. I'm from Indiana," he'd finally said, and flew from the room, his pillow clutched to his chest. It wasn't that he was confused about his sexuality. It was that he was one of the last men on the planet who believed in sleeping only with people you loved. He'd later revealed that he'd spent the remainder of the night conflicted. We were close friends. It was possible that we might really get along. Should he go back in? Should he not? What was really being offered?

"Yes," I'd told him. "It was what you thought."

"Damn it, damn it, damn it," he'd replied, but the moment had passed, and we'd never been inclined to get naked again. Soon after, I'd hooked Griffin up with Elise, who'd conquered his resistance through a combination of sexy ankles, fishnet stockings, and braless stirring of pumpkin risotto. Now, she was taking him shopping for small, soft sweaters in the women's department, and introducing him to the joys of high-thread-count sheets. He was slightly ashamed of how much he loved this, and worried that he'd be recategorized into a Stray. He wasn't. He was his own thing. There was no one on earth like Griffin, and that was half of why I adored him.

THE ABOVE CATEGORIES, COMBINED WITH MY WORK OVERLOAD, caused me to keep my head down whenever I had to make an appearance on the seventh floor of 721 Broadway. The boys of the DWP weren't even on my radar. Therefore, the first time I met the Boxer, I was dismissive. He was part of the Do-Over category, and in the grad program. Not bad looking. None too tall, but making up for it with great arm and chest muscles, due to the fact that he worked out at a boxing gym. Blondish, close-cropped hair. Sexily broken pugilist's nose. It did not occur to me to be interested in him. The thing that made me reconsider the Boxer was his voice. I heard this great, raspy boom echoing across a crowded classroom, and I looked around in spite of myself.

The class was taught by a famous avant-garde playwright. He'd assigned us the first page of Kafka's *The Castle*, not a play, mind you, an unfinished novel about a poor guy trying in vain to get into a very low-rent heaven. We were supposed to do we knew not what with it. The playwright sat in the back of the house, grimacing his trademark sexy grimace. We were not experimental enough for him. His plays involved dreamlike realities and absurdist dialogue seeded with spectacular one-liners. He was a superstar for a select audience. I pretended I'd read the play the teacher was known for, but I lied. I was only interested in Sam Shepard, and I had too many day jobs to spend any time on my homework. I was getting by solely on my smile, which I spread indiscriminately around the department, hoping it would get me forgiven for not working up to my potential. When my turn came around to show my interpretation of *The Castle*, I sent the Boxer into the booth, to speak over the God mic, and flung all the other men in the class onstage, where they opposed my friend Ruby in her quest for a place to sleep. It was a sort of no-room-at-the-inn situation, which went surprisingly well the first time around, and heinously the second, when the professor made me repeat what I'd improvised. After class, the Boxer came up to me and told me he thought it had been "not bad."

We shared other classes, it turned out. One was with my most beloved professor, Martin, a Guru in his own right, who always carried about twenty-five pounds of obscure and wonderful books in a beaten-up leather bag and delivered his lectures in a distinctive growl. Martin and I were close cohorts, often drinking wine after class and trading volumes. He had a pack of young male acolytes, who could usually be found trailing behind him, hoping that some of his elusive combination of brilliance, eccentricity, and badass sense of humor would rub off on them. In one of Martin's classes, I read aloud a prose piece about the ridiculous loss of my virginity, and the Boxer laughed so hard I thought he might have a coronary. He asked for my phone number, and though Vic had again admonished me for giving it out, I did. He'd laughed at my jokes, goddamn it. My ego was enamored. Also, even though I'd seen him carrying a well-thumbed paperback of Raymond Carver stories, never a very good sign in a prospective boyfriend, I thought that the boxing made up for it. It gave him a certain working-class appeal, a grounding in the physical that convinced me that he'd never try to knock me out with references to Rushdie.

We went out to a sports bar (a sports bar! I rejoiced. It was so not my taste, and since I thought my taste had historically sucked, anything in opposition to it seemed like a great idea) and watched baseball. He had another friend with him, who was possibly there to evaluate me. I was wearing the wrong thing. Red dress. Far too sexy for a bar full of televisions and beer. I feared that my dress made me look desperate, and so I spent the entire evening tugging at it, trying to make it less bombshell and more windbreaker. Not possible. The Boxer said almost nothing to me the whole night, and I went home, feeling dweeby.

When the Boxer called me later that week, and asked if I wanted to meet up that night, I was surprised, but pleased.

"Meet me at six," he said, and gave me an address on Broadway. Maybe he liked me after all. I could see myself liking him. He was intelligent, funny, and a gentleman! He hadn't even tried to kiss me on the first date! I revised my opinions of him, and decided that he was just old-fashioned. Nothing wrong with old-fashioned.

LATER THAT NIGHT, I WALKED DOWN THE STREET IN SEARCH OF OUR MEETING PLACE, expecting dinner, and maybe a play, given that we were roughly in the theater district. The neighborhood got less and less likely as I walked. I checked the address. Maybe I'd gotten something wrong. There was nothing on this corner. Nothing, that is, but something called Flashdancers, A Gentleman's Club. I'd seen this place advertised on the tops of taxis, a busty blonde in four sequins and a smile, offering herself up to traffic. Despite the fact that the sign was neon, I deluded myself into thinking that "gentleman's club" meant the sort of dark, oak-paneled bar where you might find F. Scott Fitzgerald and Hemingway drinking expensive scotch and smoking tobacco peddled by cigarette girls. I didn't think I could just walk in. Probably, I thought, I wasn't even allowed. I walked up to the big, bald guy standing outside, and nervously asked him if I had the right address.

"You wanna go inside?" He grinned at me. Gold tooth.

"I'm supposed to meet someone. But is there a restaurant? I think I might be lost."

"Yeah," he said. "We have an all-you-can-eat buffet." He winked, in a friendly manner. I looked at a sign posted next to the door, advertising the buffet. I felt happier. This was good news. Maybe it was one of those secret New York places. There was a club downtown, for example, that you had to access through a tunnel that started in the storage room of a grocery store. The clammy, dark passageway was the epitome of creepy, but if you had enough faith to get through the vault door at the end, you hit paradise: an old speakeasy, with swing music, velvet couches, and great martinis. I couldn't imagine that the Boxer would actually take me somewhere sleazy. We had to go to school together, after all, and it'd be too embarrassing. I peered into the dark hallway beyond the door, but couldn't see anything.

"Do you think he's inside already?"

"Shit, I don't know. You wanna go in, or you wanna stay out?" The bouncer was looking impatient.

"I guess I'll go in."

"That's twenty bucks." He stuck out a palm as big as my face.

I'd never been to a bar that had such a big cover charge before. I dug in my purse, but I only had eight dollars.

"Only because you're a chick. Get in before I change my mind," said the bouncer, waving me in for free. I wadded my money into my purse and ducked through a curtain.

AT THE END OF A SHORT HALLWAY I FOUND A HOLIDAY INN DIN-ING ROOM: metal chairs with wipe-clean burgundy upholstery, small fake-marble tables, and little fake-crystal vases with fake flowers in them. A steam table against one wall, loaded with metal trays of anonymous fried objects. It would've been the kind of place I'd often ended up at during family vacations, had it not been for the fact that it was strewn with naked women.

Freaked out, I looked around for the Boxer. No sign of him. I went and got a dangerously bargain-priced glass of wine, averting my eyes from a woman who was sitting with her essentially bare bottom on the bar. I surreptitiously wiped my glass with a cocktail napkin, drank it down, ordered another, and fled to a table for two, hoping that the Boxer would appear quickly. Maybe he'd misunderstood what kind of place this was.

I'd only been to one strip club, and it had been in Idaho. I'd been dragged by some vagabond acting intern who'd thought it was local color. He'd neglected to understand that I, too, was local color, that these were my people, and if those things were immaterial, that I'd also been drastically underage. The strip club had been converted from a finger steak restaurant, but the vinyl booths and sawdust floor remained intact. The strippers had gyrated piteously around a PVC pole in the middle of the room. "Gyrated," though, was too strong a word. Most of them had looked to be on serious drugs. They'd alternated between nodding off and racing about like wild ferrets. Sometimes they'd served as waitresses, bringing paper baskets of finger steaks. People ordered them. People ate them. People went to this place on purpose. There was a prominent sign posted: THE TORCH LOUNGE ASSUMES NO RESPONSIBILITY FOR CONSEQUENCES OF VIEWING. I didn't blame them.

The only other stripping I'd seen had been with Zak, at a downtown cabaret that had been wildly, briefly hip. There'd been a woman dressed in a couple of plastic holly leaves and a tutu, shaking her thing to an Ani DiFranco song. Another woman had dripped hot candle wax all over herself while chanting Hail Marys. A woman dressed all in white feathers had brought out a guitar and sung a country-western ballad entitled "Did I Shave My Vagina for This?" Most bizarrely, there'd been a woman who'd billed herself as the Last Burlesque Show. ("Oh no," Zak had whispered. "Oh no, oh no, oh God no.") She was in her eighties, and fully dressed, at first, in a Dale Evans cowgirl suit. The Last Burlesque Show did scary things with a baton. By the time she'd gotten down to her tasseled pasties and spun them in opposite directions, Zak and I were both paralyzed, I with wonder, he with horror. The next act had been a belligerent woman who'd held a flashlight beneath her chin, campfire-ghost story–style, angrily reciting Sylvia Plath's "Daddy." When she'd finished, she'd trolled the audience for tips, and, discovering Zak, shone her flashlight on him, and demanded his wallet, yelling that she'd noticed he was cheap. We'd fled into the night, Zak fumbling for his asthma inhaler as we hit the street, me suspecting that it had been the last time he'd trust me to take him anywhere.

My glass stuck to my table. My ass stuck to my chair. I didn't want to stand up and walk out because I was hoping that I'd become invisible. I was completely embarrassed. If this was not just a miscommunication, if this was intentional, it was because the Boxer had assumed me to be wilder than I really was. I regretted that red dress. He probably thought that I was this kind of girl. What kind of girl was this, though? I had no idea. I was on my third, desperate glass of wine, and I'd graduated to drinking it with a straw to avoid touching my mouth to the glass.

I was the only woman in the room who wasn't a stripper. Not that the strippers were really stripping. They were dangling from poles, looking bored. They all had boob jobs. Breasts the size of cannonballs. My imagination launched to images of enormous false bosoms being shot at enemies. Civil War–era costumes. Screaming men. I squinched my eyes shut and tried not to think about exploding tits.

BEHIND ME, THERE WAS SOME ACTIVITY, and it didn't take long to figure out that it was a table full of kids, daring each other to approach me. School uniforms, like beacons shining out of the dark. Faces scarred by inept shaving. No one in their right mind would think these prep-school boys were done with puberty. I could hear them poking each other, trying to get up their courage. I was wearing a white wrap-around sweater and jeans, and I couldn't imagine they really thought I was a stripper. The strippers looked to have been allotted three inches of cloth each. That, and as much silicone as their hearts desired.

A skinny, freckled kid plunked himself down at my table. He blinked at me for a moment, then suddenly grabbed my glass of wine and slugged a sip. He looked triumphant. He weighed ninety pounds, at most. I grabbed it back, imagining my arrest for providing alcohol to a minor.

"Who are you?" I said.

"Peter."

"Peter what?"

"VanHeu . . ." He reconsidered. "You wish."

"Peter YouWish," I said, "you're too young to be here."

"My friends want to know if you're . . ." He dissolved into stammering giggles.

I gave him the best evil eye I could muster. Not so hot, considering my lower lip was starting to tremble.

"They want to know if you're wearing a bra."

"None of your business." A lacy bra that had cost too much money. I'd bought it that afternoon, and put it on in the dressing room, full of optimism for the evening.

"Like, would you, like, give my friend Matt a lap dance?" he blurted, shoving a wad of ones at me. I shoved them back, but not before I noticed that there was a platinum card tucked into the cash.

"No. Never. Absolutely not." I decided then that the yes policy definitely did not include the underage. I hadn't realized that I'd needed to make a rule about ninth graders.

"The girls won't. They say they'll get arrested. We're only allowed to sit quietly and drink soda."

"I don't even know how you got in here."

"Bribed the bouncer. Duh."

I could see one of the kids doing homework at the table. Maybe this was what you did after school, if you were a kid in New York City.

They were all clustered around my table now, sweating and shuffling their feet. Being surrounded by adolescent boys is like being surrounded by a flock of seriously awkward hummingbirds, and discovering, belatedly, that you are the feeder.

"What'd she say?" they clamored.

"She'll do it," said Peter YouWish.

"She won't," I said. "Move it."

"I have my allowance," offered another kid.

"Me too," said another.

I wondered blurrily if there was a niche market in stripping for schoolboys. You'd travel from private school to private school, disguised as a substitute teacher. Four-inch-long plaid skirts and knee socks would hold no appeal for these kids. They saw them all the time. A Sexy Substitute, though, could make a killing.

Finally, the Boxer arrived, holding a beer. The kids scattered like marbles. He looked at them, bemused, and then leaned across the table.

"Need a drink?" The kids had managed to siphon my entire glass. The Boxer, for some reason, acted like this was perfectly normal. My pride hurt. If this was a test, if he thought I couldn't deal with this, he was wrong. I was brave. And maybe he was going to apologize. And maybe he was going to morph suddenly into someone he wasn't. In a foolish little corner of my mind, I still had hope. The alternative was too depressing.

"Wine," I said. I was already half-drunk. I might as well keep going.

A stripper in a neon pink G-string had started to twirl, sensing the arrival of someone who might actually tip her. Over the God mic, a voice informed us that this girl was a stockbroker during the day and a stripper at night. Cannonballs. Or bowling balls. My brain dragged me to a bowling alley, where a guy in an embroidered shirt and rented shoes was hooking his fingers into the stripper's breast, and tossing it, girl and all, down the lane. Strike! I cringed.

"Are you okay?"

"Fine. Terrific!" I nodded like a convert. "Great stripper!" Great was a misnomer. She had rigor mortits, and looked maybe seventeen. I felt like my wine might have poisoned me.

"**MIND IF I GO GET A LAP DANCE?** There's this Russian girl here, Masha . . ."

The Boxer thumped me on the back, like I was a buddy.

My mind flipped forcibly to Chekhov. Moscow! Moscow! I yanked it back.

"Not at all," I said, much too loudly.

Why would I mind? We were on a date. Sure, go and get some unknown Masha to squirm in your lap, and I'll just sit here and fight off the fourteen-year-olds. Great! Exactly how I wanted to spend my evening! Unless, it suddenly occurred to me, we weren't on a date? Maybe he really *did* want to be buddies. Maybe he wasn't attracted to me at all! I could feel myself turning red. Oh God. I'd completely misinterpreted everything. He didn't like me. Obviously. Anyone who liked me would not leave me sitting at a wobbly little table in a room full of pubescents on the prowl.

I watched the Boxer put his arm around the tattooed shoulder of a girl I'd noticed before, a skinny girl, with long black hair and iridescent blue eyes. She smiled, fake adoration appearing on her face. I could see the Boxer grinning. I could see him believing her.

I put a handful of ice cubes in my mouth and crunched them until they melted away. I put my face down onto the sticky table and let my eyes overflow.

SOME UNFORTUNATE SIDE EFFECTS OF HUMILIATION: Three drinks later, I lost my senses and went home with the Boxer. I climbed five flights of his stairs, and ended up in his bedroom, participating in some truly awful sex. The Boxer, startlingly, ended up crying on my neck. I thought I knew why. Who wanted this to be their life? Not me, and apparently not him, either.

I thumped him on the shoulder. We were buddies, after all. But we weren't. We were two people making a naked mistake. I called a car service at 5:00 A.M. Some knight came in a shining white car and took me home.

I dabbed at my eyes the whole time I dressed for work. Things already sucked, and they got even suckier. I went looking for Vic, but she wasn't in her bedroom. Her diary was open on her bed, though, and I glimpsed my name. I couldn't help myself. I didn't pick the book up, but I read what was on the page, and it wasn't pretty. I knew Vic was annoyed at my yes policy, but I hadn't known she thought I was an irredeemable, arrogant slut. Apparently so. I walked to the train, sleepless and sad.

That afternoon in class, the Boxer acted perfectly normal, and I was relieved. I thought maybe I'd been wrong about him. Afterward, however, the whole class went to the basement bar, ordered drinks, and got down to bitching about the state of the universe. Suddenly, the Boxer slammed his glass down and announced, in his booming voice, "Do I have a story for you."

I cringed. Somehow, I knew what was coming.

"So, I was having sex with *this girl* last night, who actually came home with me after we went to a strip club . . ."

Here's the thing about sitting at a table where someone is telling a story about you, in the third person. It sucks. Not that I'd never done it, but I'd never done it in a kiss-and-tell vein. It had only been eight hours.

Pause for a short discussion with the male members of the group about strip clubs in New York City, advantages and disadvantages of going to same, and a small story from an otherwise shy member of the group about the broken finger suffered by his brother-in-law while attempting to stuff dollar bills down the G-string of a stripper in New Orleans during a bachelor party. Pause for a short discussion with the female members of the group about feminism versus stripping, G-strings, comfortable or not, and, "What the hell kind of girl goes with a guy to a strip club, anyway? None of us! Where do you find your girls?"

Pause for me, unnoticed, turning purple, drowning my misery in Maker's Mark and wondering if there was any way to make a graceful exit without everyone figuring out what was going on.

And back to the point, the Boxer declaiming like William Jennings Bryan.

"It just wasn't happening, no matter how much I wanted it to. I was on top of her, and she was looking at me like she didn't really know me, which she didn't. And halfway through, I looked at her and it hit me. I actually wasn't even into her. What was I doing there? I was in love with Masha. This girl, there's nothing wrong with her, per se, but she's not Masha. I mean, this girl, she's pretty and smart, but not like Masha."

For a moment, I clung to the fact that at least he'd said that I was pretty and smart. Unfortunately, there was the rest of the sentence to consider. I wanted to scream nasty things, statistics on the small size of both his penis and his soul, but I didn't. It wasn't like I was blameless. I'd gone home with him. It was me who'd made that stupid choice, and now I was getting a little bit of just reward. I stayed silent.

People had been cruel before, but it'd rolled off my back. For some reason, this one hurt. Maybe it was because the Boxer was a writer, too, and my brain had granted him automatic comrade status. This was friendly fire. No dignity to getting shot by one of your own. I don't even think he meant to be cruel. I think he was embarrassed himself, and trying to excuse his behavior. No one wants to start crying in bed. There was plenty I didn't know about him, and likewise, but that didn't really matter in the moment. I still felt like I was bleeding all over the bar. And that was seriously uncool. I wanted to be the kind of girl who could tolerate her heart being translated into a story the morning after, the kind of girl who didn't care so damned much. I was not that person. I never had been.

The Boxer was sitting next to me, and he started to grope my thigh. I didn't get it. He was telling all these people he wasn't attracted to me, and his fingers were kneading me like bread. And people were sympathetic. I could see on their faces the fear that maybe the Boxer would never find love. If the Boxer remained alone and miserable forever, so too might they. I agreed. Love was looking less and less likely to me. I'd been saying yes for three months, and though I'd met some nice people, I hadn't even come close to meeting anyone I wanted to spend much of the rest of my life with.

I swatted the Boxer's fingers away. He was onto a discussion of boxing: the macho factor, how he'd had his nose broken a few times. I was thinking about athlete's foot, willing fungus and jock itch upon him.

I BELATEDLY NOTICED THAT TWO OF MY CLASSMATES HAD BEEN WATCHING ME DURING THE BOXER'S MONOLOGUE. The Princelings, so called for their extreme family-bestowed affluence, were not only rich, but good looking, too. They unexpectedly offered to buy me a drink at the bar. Though I'd never really talked with either of them before, I was glad to escape. Much more of this, and I was liable to either sob, or try to throttle the Boxer. I was thinking that maybe I could compensate for my lack of muscles with a series of swift jabs to his throat. Then I could bake him into a pie, à la *Titus Andronicus*, and serve him to Masha.

I was competitive with a stripper. How sad was that?

The Princelings asked if the story had been about me. They'd been watching me during the exchange and were "interested in the dynamic."

"Yes," I whispered, applying Kleenex to my eyes.

"What an asshole," said Princeling One.

"Dickhead," agreed Princeling Two.

I instantly became their friend. I hoped that the Princelings, in the grand tradition of the Dramatic Writing Program, would write a seven-hour play about the Boxer, and how he was scum.

Over the next few weeks, the Boxer and I saw each other in class every couple of days, and he acted as though he'd done nothing wrong. Of course, I refused to discuss the things I thought he'd done wrong. I had no intention of giving him the satisfaction of knowing that he'd messed me up.

I banished my heart to Baden-Baden, where I directed her to wear a bright bathing costume, take the waters, and read peacefully plodding, romantic novels by E. M. Forster. Instead, she lurked sarcastically in a cabana, savagely pinching the pool boys when they were too slow in bringing the refreshments she incessantly rang for. She clutched dog-eared copies of *The Stranger, Death in Venice,* and *The Last Temptation of Christ* (look where love got *him*), and spent the entire day meticulously decrying everything on earth. She refused to shed her dark glasses, slugged down pitchers of stiff drinks, and occasionally laughed in sardonic barks. In the evenings, she'd get herself up in bugle-beaded, bias-cut satin. She'd languish delicately on a fainting couch, until some man was fool enough to ask her to dance, at which point she'd eviscerate him with her smile, fling his entrails to the spaniels, and request that the band play a tango. She was Joan Crawford, Bette Davis, Marlene Dietrich, and Dorothy Parker rolled into one. If, however, I accidentally allowed her to take the dark glasses off, she turned without warning into the post-lobotomy Frances Farmer, and I had to dash from the room. She wasn't healed. Not by a long shot. I had hurt feelings, but I pretended I cared nothing about anything.

To bolster that notion, I went with the Princelings to Japanese restaurants, ate raw fish, and engaged in a sort of bizarre verbal ménage à trois. I flirted openly with them during class, while the Boxer watched with slitted eyes. It seemed he was jealous. He'd been attracted to me, after all. One of the boys? Ha! I was *so* not a boy. Never mind that Princeling Two was gayt. Never mind that Princeling One was stray, and too good looking for his height of roughly five foot four.

PRINCELING ONE WAS NINETEEN, WHICH MEANT THAT HE CALLED ME AN "OLDER WOMAN." I was still young enough that I thought that was funny. He had black hair, blue eyes, and a constant tan. He was from Florida.

Princeling Two was from a Kansas family furniture empire, and so deep in the closet that he was basically a cashmere sweater. He looked like a slimmer hybrid of the Campbell's Soup Kid and Bob's Big Boy, his hair combed into a hipster pompadour. His parents had bought him an apartment in the West Village, where he lived blissfully (and bafflingly) on deliveries of French food and cocaine.

I was a prude when it came to drugs. I'd never even taken a drag off a cigarette. I had an idea that persons who snorted things off of hand mirrors would automatically be punished by looking like Jeremy Irons. My time with the Princelings was spent with them high and me sober. I hadn't been around people with expensive habits before. Idaho had topped out at marijuana, and so I was both familiar with, and annoyed by, the lugubrious hilarity of the pothead. The coked-up dialogue of the Princelings wasn't irritating to me, because I talked that fast naturally. I'd just assumed that I'd found two other people like me, at least until I learned that their hyperactivity was chemical, not innate.

Princeling One's parents had been drug smugglers, until his father had fallen off a sailboat and disappeared into the Atlantic. Now he had a millionaire stepfather, and owned a significant portion of Miami. I studied him as one would study a strange and somewhat rare bird, the kind of bird whose females are dusky brown and whose own plumage is sparkling and gaudy. Princeling One had slept with everyone, including Zak's current girlfriend. He wore sexy button-down shirts and expensive pants that looked like old jeans, but were really replicas. He was beautiful, beautiful enough that one day, when Vic and I were walking down the street and ran into him, Vic deigned to be amazed, although she said, "Why do you want to sleep with a tiny gay guy?"

Princeling One wasn't gay. Just well-groomed. He had a defiant unibrow, but it didn't matter. His self-confidence transcended his facial hair. I'd been lured into his bedroom by this point. We'd sat on his bed and watched a DVD of *Walkabout*. It'd been strange foreplay, this movie about an Aborigine kid on his vision quest, meeting up with a couple of stranded Australian kids, but when the movie had ended, Princeling One had turned to me, put his callous-free hand on my breast, and said, "So. Are you going to put me in one of your plays as a fucked-up cowboy?"

Um. No. The boy did not radiate open range. He radiated martini lounge.

"Do you *want* me to write about you?" I'd asked.

"Yes, because whatever it is, it'll be famous." Well. Flattering, anyway.

"You probably won't be a cowboy," I'd said. He was a psychoanalyzed rich boy. But whatever. He was a good kisser. And what they said about the stamina of nineteen-year-old boys was true. I outweighed him by fifteen pounds, and so I felt like Jocasta, but he didn't seem to care. There were no crying fits. There were no buddy slaps. Good enough for me.

"Superfun," he'd declare, postcoitus, and then we'd discuss *Picnic at Hanging Rock* or *Chinatown*, or go to Princeling Two's apartment, where, to my amazement, the Princelings had only to make a quick call to summon a delivery guy with a backpack full of every drug imaginable. They'd take their drugs, and I'd sit there, rapturously listening to them talk five thousand words a minute. I was their groupie. I felt like I was going back to the parts of teenage life I'd missed out on by being my deeply unsexy self and living in the library. It was kind of great to act my age. It could have gone on indefinitely, had they not had the other problem of nineteen-year-old boys. Acute immaturity.

"Our generation is way cooler than our parents' generation," said Princeling One one afternoon as the three of us sat eating sashimi.

"Totally," said Princeling Two.

I knew what was coming. A version of the thing that young men had been saying since young men started speaking.

"Nothing from the past has any relevance beyond entertainment," they'd say.

"Live in a hut, write a tortured manifesto, and then eat it," I wanted to reply. "You're at the stupid age."

Princeling One gave equal cultural impact to the Zapruder JFK film footage and *Pulp Fiction*. Never mind that the Zapruder film was real-life horror and *Pulp Fiction* was, well, fiction. The Princelings were the kind of people who watch *Faces of Death* while eating foie gras.

"We can look at something like . . . okay . . . perfect example:

the Zapruder film, and since we weren't around, since these things don't mean anything to us, we can say, 'Look, there's the gun, there's the hit, wait, wait, *yeah*! There's the brain, there's Jackie's hat flying off!' Rewind! Or we can make fun of Hitler's mustache, I mean, Hitler looked so stupid. Our parents get all upset; they can't be objective about anything, because they're thinking about genocide, or where they were when they heard about Kennedy. Whatever."

I put my head under the table.

"Why do you have your head under the table?" he asked me and I could give no coherent answer. The conversation continued above me. The Princelings argued semantics for a while, and then Princeling Two's face appeared, bending down to check on me.

"She's still under the table," he noted. "Is she epileptic?"

"I think she has PMS," said Princeling One.

I put my head back above the table, ready to lecture on the merits of empathy.

"Were you checking me out?" asked Princeling One.

"Yes," I said. "You're very small." Maybe I didn't have any compassion, either. Maybe I wanted something that no longer existed. The Princelings slapped hands.

"I told you she had PMS," said Princeling One, unoffended. "Good one. Okay. New topic. Would you rather be seen as a winner or as a hero?"

I didn't understand the question.

"Like, do you live your life to be seen as the culturally acceptable winner, or to be seen for a moment as a hero?"

"Neither. I just live my life," I said. "Why would you want to live like that?"

"Like, do you want to be immortal, but maybe tragic, or do you want to be successful and make lots of money, but maybe have no one remember your name?"

My existential crisis was tapping at my eyeballs again.

"I wonder what happened to Hitler's teeth," said Princeling One. "It'd be so cool to have them. On display? Like, get them . . . fuck, yeah! Bronzed! Or, Dude! Make them into a windup toy."

"Totally," said Princeling Two.

"They're holding your screenplay together," I said from beneath the table, where I'd retreated again.

"You're so cool," said Princeling One. "Even if we don't really get you. I'm writing a horror-western. Hitler wouldn't understand it."

"He wouldn't, huh?" I said and laughed a terrible little laugh that turned into a terrible little sob halfway out. I'd been having sense of humor problems. When men on the street said obscene things to me, I had visions of how awful it would be to be a female dog, genitals forever exposed to the scrutiny of panting male dogs. I wondered if female dogs had the same problem I did: They saw an attractive male dog, walked closer, closer, only to witness the male dog suddenly shitting all over himself. Maybe it was just that they were high, and I was not. Maybe if I'd been high, too, I wouldn't have noticed the glaring lack of compassion that the Princelings displayed as part of their daily routine. But I was me.

I didn't like anyone enough to come out from under the table, and so I started to crawl. I stood up when I got out from under, and walked to the door. I turned around.

Princeling One, applauded by Princeling Two, was trying his thesis on some other girl. They gave me a wave. "Later," said Princeling One.

"Later," I said. In about twenty years, I thought that the Princelings might have enough empathy to be around other humans. Until then, though, I had better things to do.

I WAS SCHEDULED TO GO THE NEXT DAY TO A PLAYWRIGHTS' CONFERENCE AT THE KENNEDY CENTER. I'd been looking forward to this for months, not because I was plotting to acquire any dates while in D.C., but because a writer whose work I was crazy about was supposed to be there, too. I was hoping to pick his brain about the business. As far as the Year of Yes was concerned, I was planning on keeping to myself.

After the last few NYU-related traumas, I wasn't keen to throw myself into the fray at a writers' conference. I'd been very open for three months, walking around New York, consciously making eye contact with everyone, and smiling even more than usual. I'd decided that I'd just turn it off. No eye contact. No smiles. And I damn well would not flirt. It wasn't saying no, exactly. It was just putting up a force field. This conference would be a pool of people I already knew I shouldn't date. Writers and actors: my downfall. The last time I'd been to a thing like this, I'd fluttered wildly around from attractive actor to attractive actor, looking at their scrapbooks of laminated reviews. Never again. I didn't need to see Ophelia in black leather bondage gear, nor Hamlet in a rumpled T-shirt and dilated pupils. I didn't need a man who was so uninhibited that he could urinate fearlessly in front of an audience. Public peeing was not a virtue.

I'd acquired the infamous Martyrman at the Sundance Playlab. I'd gone to all his rehearsals, because I'd had a crush on the playwright whose play he was in. My perfect attendance had caused Martyrman to believe that I'd had a crush on him. The writer had been impervious to my charms, but Martyrman had flattered me into his single bed, thus beginning two years of disaster. Actors were notoriously hard to break up with. They tended to filibuster with dramatic monologues.

At the same conference, a crotchety composer had sung me a short experimental song, comparing my breasts to "two shining harvest moons," and then tried for a lunar landing. A famous producer had given me a ride up the mountain during a rainstorm and told me that if I ever wanted to get a play produced, I'd need to start screwing producers. A female Wiccan had invited me to a naked celebration on the mountaintop, and then put a curse on me for failing to show up. All in all, writers' conferences were dangerous places to be friendly to anyone.

Hence, my force field. If someone asked me out, I'd go, but I'd do whatever I could not to attract anyone. I'd radiate professionalism, and work rabidly on my children's play. That was the other thing. It was a children's play conference. How bad could it be?

I WAS TAKING MY PLAY, *THE INCREDIBLE DISAPPEARING LADY,* which every artistic director in the country would shortly reject as "too dark." So what if it had a mother running away from her children to join the circus? It was a musical, damn it! There was a torch song–singing lion, and he sang a catchy ditty about being lonely as a piece of liver. My favorite song had the mother taking "a single banana inside of her bandanna . . . she's gone to Havana, or maybe to Berlin. She shouldn't go anywhere, showing so much skin . . ."

I got grief about the symbolism of the banana.

"No child thinks that way," I said. "Only adults do." To no avail.

I was quickly informed that, in children's theater, mothers were not allowed to leave. Only fathers were. And if the mothers left, they were very emphatically not allowed to take anything resembling a banana with them as provisions. As usual, I was mystified by the muck of sexual politics, what women were and were not allowed to do.

Mostly, though, I was happy to be at the conference, because my idolized playwright had indeed shown up, and the conference was small enough that I knew I'd be able to meet him. I'd read his play—rather, his cycle of ten short plays—years before, on a family vacation, while sitting on the beach at the Oregon Coast. I'd gotten lost for hours in the two-hundred-year epic of love, land, and family, becoming so enamored that I'd promptly gone home and tried to write my own version. Obviously, I'd foundered, 'round about play two. *The Kentucky Cycle* was, in my opinion, a masterpiece of American mythology. The Playwright had won a Pulitzer for it.

I'd never met a Pulitzer winner before, and contrary to my fantasies, the Playwright was not nine feet tall and decked in intimidating robes and a crown. He was a handsome, shockingly approachable-looking guy in his mid-forties, with silvering blond hair and beard, bright blue eyes, a plaid shirt, and a worn-in leather bag, full of what? Pages upon pages of genius, I was certain.

It turned out that we were sharing a cast. Both of our plays needed four actors, and they needed the same four actors. In fact, we'd written basically the same play. He'd been smarter than I, however, given that his had a missing father, not mother. And no bananas. The actors told me he was a nice guy and that I should just say hello, but I was too starstruck. I skittered around the edges of rooms, eyeballing him from various corners for a couple of days, attempting to learn how to pronounce his last name. He didn't seem to be arrogant. His brain was not swollen out and hidden beneath a hat. That put him in the minority. Children's play authors were, on the whole, an odd-looking bunch, the sort of people whose childhood misfit status echoed into the present. I was right at home, in other words. To my good fortune, a group gathered for dinner at a Japanese restaurant, and I finally got up the nerve to seat myself across from him. I immediately started name-dropping. We had mutual acquaintances. I'd researched.

I WAS SHOCKED TO DISCOVER THAT WHEN THE PLAYWRIGHT LIS-TENED, he listened with absolute focus. None of the men I'd met lately had had this quality. Revise. None of the men I'd *ever* met had had this quality, at least not so intensely. He made me so nervous that I managed to use my chopsticks backward, but he also had a big, raucous laugh, a brilliant smile, and something else. I couldn't put my finger on it. He was perfectly sociable, but there was a certain restraint beneath the surface. I spent the evening trying to figure out what he wasn't saying. When he thought no one was watching him, something arrived in his eyes. It seemed to be sadness, though I felt that this was implausible. What did he have to be sad about? I could only imagine having a life as fantastic as the Playwright's was. He wrote for a living, screenplays as well as plays. And he wasn't just hoping to be discovered in the slush pile—the Schwab's drugstore of screenwriters—as everyone I knew at NYU was. He wrote for Hollywood, which, to my mind, gave him a golden glow. He owned a house, with a view of a lake. He had his very own *Pulitzer*, for God's sake, and short of a Nobel, that was as good as it got. The man had the perfect life.

I decided that I was wrong about the sadness. Maybe he was just tired. He caught me staring, and gave me the smile again.

"Sorry, what? I was drifting," he said.

"Thinking about your play?"

"Yeah," he said, after a moment. "You, too?"

"Yeah," I lied. "It's all I ever think about."

He handed me my fortune cookie. "The journey of a thousand miles begins with a single step." Typical. The universe was sending me an inappropriate message. What step? The Playwright was wearing a wedding ring. *That* step was not going to happen.

We drank our tea. We talked until everyone else was ready to leave, and then we talked some more as we walked home. I was still starstruck, and I was happy to discover that I had reason to be. The Playwright was not only a wonderful writer, he seemed to be a wonderful person.

It figured that the only wonderful person I'd met in months was someone I had no prayer of ever dating. He'd never ask, and even if he did, I'd never be able to say yes. Married. Kids. I wasn't in the market for that particular disaster, and my yes policy, without question, didn't include cheaters. Oh well. I didn't need to worry about it anyway, because he showed no sign of being interested in me. Which, I reminded myself, was a really good thing.

"SO, WHAT'RE YOU LOOKING FOR, MARIA HEADLEY?" The Playwright and I were leaning up against a ballroom wall, sick of working the room during the conference's final cocktail party. I'd seen him edging toward the door. Since I'd been doing the same thing, I'd joined him. "What's your life missing?"

"A better class of man," I said, without thinking, and then regretted it. I sounded stupid. Of course my life needed things other than a man—what was I, the heroine of a 1930s pulp romance?—but somehow, alas, that was what had come out. Had I a brain at all, I might have said something along the lines of "an air conditioner," or "enough money to pay my rent this month."

"What do you mean? I can't imagine you have a hard time getting a date. . . ?" He seemed genuinely amazed. I was flattered, but certainly, it was possible for me to imagine myself forever dateless, and forever loveless seemed even more plausible. Look at what had happened with the Boxer. Look at the Princelings. The Handyman. Martyrman. Zak, the only one I really cared about. Look at everything. I could see plenty of my flaws, and it was very likely that there were more flaws just waiting to be discovered. I talked too fast, and listened badly. I had a weird haircut, getting weirder every day, and a tendency to fall up subway staircases, like a fish trying and failing to evolve. All my clothes came from the Salvation Army. And according to Vic's calculations, I was a slut.

"I mean, I can't find one I really want. I guess. That's all. Or one who really wants me, either, actually. I don't mean to sound arrogant."

"Hell, darlin', it's a tall order to find one that measures up to you," he said, and grinned. I was stymied.

I reminded myself that he was just being nice. He had, after all, been an actor before he'd been a writer. He was *acting*. Acting! I must have looked pretty pitiful, if he felt the need to buffer my self-confidence in such a way. I reminded myself that this man was not just a writer, not just an actor, but a *writer-actor*. Both of my nemesis professions, rolled into one. I repeated "writer-actor" seventeen times in my head, talking myself out of having any form of a crush on the Playwright. I took a deep breath and searched for a new topic. A depressing, unromantic one. Eugene O'Neill, how about? *The Iceman Cometh*?

"I'm going to bed," he said. "Early flight tomorrow. It was nice to meet you." And then he shook my hand.

Thank God.

I wasn't hitting on the Playwright, and he wasn't hitting on me. I wasn't the kind of person who wanted to steal someone else's man. It was bad form, and though much of my life was an exercise in bad form, that particular thing was outside my limits.

Besides, I didn't want a man with that much baggage. I had my own baggage: five or six broken-zippered duffel bags crammed full of anvils. The last thing I needed was a man who wanted a lackey to lug his overstuffed set of Samsonite. And kids! No thank you. Me, a stepmother? Almost as implausible as me getting elected president of the United States. Being a stepmother required mothering skills, and it was up for debate whether or not I could even take care of myself. I alternated between adult and child on a daily basis. And then there was the age difference. When he was thirty-five, I'd still been on training wheels. Sure, he was my kind of guy, but it was becoming clearer every day that my kind of guy was *not* the kind of guy I should be with.

So, I frog-marched my attraction to the Playwright into a barricaded vault in the corner of my brain. I knew myself well enough to know that, despite all of my objections to him being a writer and actor, despite my horror of his children, had the Playwright been single, I would've thrown myself at him. With the reality as it was, though, the man was nothing I wanted to deal with. Unavailable. End of story.

I congratulated myself on my newfound maturity. I hadn't fallen ridiculously for something I couldn't have, just because he possessed a few traits that seemed ideal. I could be friends with him, and that would be great. I'd send him a letter, a puritanical letter that would absolve me of my embarrassing comment about a better class of men.

I got on the train the next morning and went back home to deal with the rest of my year. Maybe the next day, I'd meet the man I'd been waiting for. Or maybe not. I had nine months to go. Something better could happen at any moment. It couldn't get any worse.

I was so, so wrong.

LE PETIT CORNICHON

IN WHICH OUR
HEROINE LEARNS
THAT NOTHING IS
GREENER ON THE
OTHER SIDE OF THE
POND . . .

"CAN I ASK YOU A FAVOR?" Baler leaned over the café table, a movie-star grin on his handsome, weathered face. I'd met him in line at the grocery store, forty-five minutes before, and now we were drinking espresso and eating sandwiches. He was from Cyprus. I'd never met anyone from Cyprus before, not too surprising, considering that they usually introduced themselves, as Baler had, as either Turkish or Greek. They assumed that, being an ignorant American, you wouldn't know where Cyprus was. Not that he was wrong. I had only the vaguest notion of his home island floating in a romantic glittering sea. From the age of fourteen on, he told me, he'd gone to boarding school in Paris. The Eiffel Tower! Baguettes! The Sorbonne! All promising. And his name!

"A man made of honey," he'd translated. Could it be any more appealing? Add the man made of honey to the homemade croissants I envisioned every time the word "Paris" was spoken, and I was ready to dine with Baler forever.

I envisioned French men—or really, any man not from the U.S.—as uber-romantic, evolved to the point of near-sainthood. Again, I was denying certain parts of world literature. Jean Genet, anyone? Not exactly known for his love stories. But never mind him.

Baler was a competitive bicyclist, so he was in terrific shape. He had black hair, and sea green eyes, and enough charisma to induce me to leave my grocery shopping behind and follow him to a coffee shop. Which was saying something. I'd been scavenging for lunch. The only food in my apartment was the remains of a roasted chicken belonging to Zak. Every few weeks, he'd come home with a couple of grocery bags and a smug look on his face. He'd spend the next several hours chortling to himself as he wedged a lemon into the chicken's nether regions and inserted herbs beneath its skin.

"My chicken," he'd sigh, blissed out. Vic preferred her chicken fried. I preferred my chicken inviolate.

Baler was giving me a questioning look. Well, whatever. A favor, to me, meant something minor.

"Of course I can," I said, and then leaned in to see what I'd agreed to. Maybe it would be something wonderful, like, "Would you please sunbathe upon the deck of my boat, as we sail to Cyprus?" Or "Would you wear a black bikini and movie-star sunglasses, would you drink ouzo and eat olives, would you be embraced by my loving and nondysfunctional family?" Yes, I was ready to say. Yes, yes, yes! *Yes*, I'd ramble with the goats on picturesque hillsides. *Yes*, I'd dance on the tables, jingling my tambourine, and *YES*, I'd embrace the Mediterranean ancestry I didn't have. I was ready to go.

These things, however, were not what Baler wanted. At all.

"DO YOU THINK THAT YOU COULD BITE MY PENIS?" BALER
ASKED.

My vision of rambling with the goats short-circuited and became something not so appealing: bedding down with a satyr. I suddenly remembered other examples of the proclivities of foreign guys. Roman Polanski and his much-reviled film, *Bitter Moon*, for example. There'd been a notorious sex scene in that movie, involving a gorgeous French actress hopping around in a pig mask for the titillation of Peter Coyote. And what about *Last Tango in Paris*? Why had I thought that Americans had a monopoly on perversity? Bite his penis?

"I don't think that I could, actually," I said.

"You mean you won't."

"That, too."

What kind of man wanted a woman to bite his penis on a first date? What kind of man wanted a woman to bite his penis *ever*?

Zak had a high-school horror story involving his girlfriend Rayna's grandmother coming to the bedroom door to offer Zak and Rayna an after-school snack. She'd been a little late, considering that Rayna had already been engaged in giving Zak his very first experience with fellatio, on a set of bunk beds. When the door had opened, Zak, in terror, had lost his balance and fallen backward off the top bunk. Later, Rayna had told him he was lucky. When he, bruised and blue-balled, had asked why, she'd told him that her first impulse had been to hold on. *With her teeth.* Even years later, the retelling of this story still turned Zak green.

Baler was intelligent, no doubt about it. In the short time I'd known him, we'd had a conversation that had touched on Thomas Pynchon, Shakespeare, and string theory. I was bewildered. He'd seemed much too erudite for this kind of uber-visceral request. Not that there was any class of population known for their custom of genital mastication. It wasn't a thing that you often found, for example, in the South. Or Latin America. Cockfighting, yes. Cockbiting, no.

Most men were terrified of teeth. They preferred to imagine you as some sort of Gummy Girl. Not that they wanted you in dentures. No. They wanted you hot. But they wanted the teeth to dematerialize the moment the mouth opened on the member.

"Hire a dominatrix," I advised. "Or hit on someone who's just had a bad divorce."

"It's not about that," said Baler, his tone matter-of-fact. "When boys turn fourteen on Cyprus, their fathers take them to the Island of the Prostitutes."

Island of the Prostitutes? Yeah, right.

"Here, we just give them a copy of *Playboy*, a thump on the back, and a good luck," I said. "Most people lose their virginity in car backseats, or in rumpus rooms."

"What's a rumpus room? A brothel? A strip club?"

"A basement. Belonging to someone's parents."

Baler looked disappointed.

"What's the use of that? On Cyprus, everyone acknowledges that the male sex drive is superior. Women have to be protected. If they have sexual relations before marriage, they get emotionally attached. It's biology."

Ha. In my experience, men were much more likely than women to become enslaved to their emotions. And they were creative. In high school, my friend/nemesis Ira had written me a love letter on a roll of toilet paper, and delivered it to me during drama class. It had, essentially, been a single-ply litany of the ways I'd made him feel like crap. The note had concluded with an attempt to persuade me to show him my breasts, which Ira had been obsessed with basically since I'd grown them. (He continued to be, in fact, and I continued, somewhat out of habit, to deny him.) Not that I was immune to the unrequited crush. I'd had some hangdog moments in which the toy I'd been fetching had been thrown into the forest, and I'd emerged, panting happily, only to see the guy I'd been playing with leap into his car and drive away. In fact, usually, if I liked someone at all, that was exactly what happened. If I wasn't into them, they invariably wanted to play fetch for the rest of our lives.

"All the girls of Cyprus are virgins until marriage, and their mothers guard the doors to make sure they stay that way. The prostitutes all wear black dresses, because they're disgraced. Our fathers buy us each a day with one of them, and then leave us on the island without a boat, like *Lord of the Flies*."

"Lord of the Zipper-Flies."

"You're funny, for an American. Which is to say, not very." Baler paused to give me a grin that managed to radiate both charm and machismo. Dangerous.

One of my girlfriends had, years before, been involved in a brief marriage to a Greek guy. She'd met him on a ship. He hadn't spoken English, and she hadn't spoken Greek. In all other aspects of her life, she was a very intelligent woman, but this man had won her, with absolutely no effort. "It was his arm hair and his ego," she'd explained, sheepishly. "That was all I liked about him. Six wasted weeks."

"My prostitute was . . . shall we say . . . volatile," said Baler, and put his hand on my knee. I could suddenly feel hormones conga-ing through my bloodstream. I shut my eyes. He was sexy, yes, but this was obviously not a good idea. Experience had taught me that if a man asked you to do something extreme this early on, it would only get worse. Men retained the scars of puberty. If something terrible happened to them between the ages of about twelve to fourteen, they tended to repeat versions of it ever after.

For example. My friend Taylor had, at the age of twelve, accompanied his father, a vehement born-again Christian, to Vegas. It'd been a happy father-son trip into Sin City, and Taylor had been pleased to be considered mature enough to tag along. Until, as they walked down the street, Taylor's dad had spotted a sequin-bedecked hooker.

"Hang on a sec, son," he'd said, and then grabbed the girl, pulled up her Lycra miniskirt, bent her over backward, and stuck his tongue down her throat. Taylor had watched, wide-eyed. His father had, at the time, still been married to his mother. Was this what normal people did? Taylor was uncertain. The experience had left Taylor with a confused fetish for women naked beneath their drugstore pantyhose. However, a fetish for hosiery was one thing. A fetish for having your penis chewed was another.

"Did she bite you?" I asked Baler. "That's awful. You were so young!"

"You're overreacting. It's just something I like."

"You mean gently. You mean, like, run my teeth *gently* across it."

"No. I mean really bite it. The harder the better."

Part of me wanted to try it. I certainly had some rage I'd been holding in reserve. What woman didn't? Just that morning, I'd over-heard a tense sidewalk conversation in which a guy had been saying, "Why do you always have to emasculate me in public?"

"Because I just can't help myself," his girlfriend had replied, resignation in her voice.

Sometimes I felt the same way. I was pretty sure, though, that biting didn't count as safe sex.

It was like we'd gone back in time. In every high school, there's that guy who wants you to punch him in the guts. It's supposed to show you what a big, strong King Kong he is. You're supposed to be Fay Wray. Invariably, it turns out more like Houdini. You punch him before he's ready. He dies shortly thereafter, tangled in the chains he himself has requested. You are left trying to flatter him back to life. Usually this means you have to let him get to third base.

I looked at Baler, and I wanted to drool. O, that stubble! O, that testosterone! O, those white teeth! A real man! But. What if he wanted to bite *me*? I didn't want to be bitten. I could envision a very unhappy bedroom scenario, the whole thing disintegrating from art-film passion into a horror movie/denture commercial. Not sexy. Not sexy at all. I was confused.

YES, I UNDERSTOOD THAT THERE WAS SUCH A THING AS MASO-CHISM. As usual, though, everything I knew, I knew from reading. During my second week in New York, I'd run across a disturbing ar-ticle about fetish spanking in the *Village Voice*. This was not the cutesy endeavor I'd assumed it to be. It apparently required a variety of props: schoolgirl attire, rulers, and the occasional tennis racquet. I'd been baffled.

My grade school had had a public paddling policy. At least once a week, the entire student body was called into the cafeteria to watch a sinner being dragged forth. Sometimes the spankee would be tearful, sometimes defiant, but it didn't matter. That paddle was coming down, and that bottom would be bare beneath that paddle, regardless of whether or not the perpetrator had actually *meant* malevolence when he was dribbling rubber cement down the pants of his female classmate. Watching spankings had been like watching an execution. The eros in the equation was not evident to me.

It seemed, however, that most of New York City was fully cognizant of the pleasure/pain principle. Shortly after my education in spanking, Taylor had taken me shopping for clubwear. I'd been naïve. Clubwear, to me, meant nice clothing. Clubwear, to Taylor, meant a rubber suit. Taylor was emphatically straight, though anyone who saw him dressed in his usual party outfit of leather hot pants, roller skates, and a smile, would have thought differently. He was an actor and had a weakness for costumes. Luckily for him, his girlfriend, Janet, was an actor, too, and understood his yen to borrow her clothes.

Taylor had led me into a cave deep in the West Village. The walls had been hung with various vinyl and latex items, buckles and bows, topless tops and bottomless bottoms. Taylor'd been in the dressing room, entangled in his rubber shirt, yowling as it yanked out his chest hairs, when I'd glanced toward a darkened back room and noticed a faint, appealing glow. I'd drifted toward it, entranced. What was it? A shrine, maybe, or one of those lights in which a plastic Jesus stands in the middle of fiber-optic stars. Or a lava lamp?

Or a room entirely studded with glow-in-the-dark dildos.

They'd protruded proudly from the plaster, like handgrips on a climbing wall. And they'd been large. Large enough to serve as baseball bat stand-ins in the event of an apartment burglary. Large enough to be labeled blue-ribbon zucchini in a roadside produce stand. Large enough to be trotted out on leashes, wearing clothing marketed for lapdogs. When I'd fled the dark room, I could've sworn I'd seen one of them bending to watch me go, like a periscope rising from a Russian submarine.

"Taylor!" I'd whispered, peering into his dressing room, only to find him panting in exertion, his arms in knots over his head and his rubber shirt become a tourniquet.

"I'm just taking a little break," he'd replied.

"Have you been in the other room?"

"Why?"

"There are big *things* all over the walls. I think we should leave. It's creepy."

"You mean the dildos? Welcome to New York, baby!" He'd screamed as he'd torn the shirt the rest of the way off, and then looked down at his soon-to-be-denuded legs.

"I'll need your help with these pants," he'd said, sorrowfully.

"No pain, no gain," he'd explained later, as we left the store, having purchased the depilatory suit. I was sure, though, that even Taylor would have balked at the idea of getting his private parts gnawed.

"LIKE THIS?" I ASKED BALER, BITING MY PICKLE IN HALF. HE NODDED.

"I like a woman with strong jaws," he said, and then put his hand up to feel mine.

"Explain. How in the name of God can you like that?"

He shook his head, woefully.

"I really thought you were an open-minded girl," he said. "But you're . . . how do you say? A Puritan. It was nice to meet you, but it'll never work. Always good to find out quickly, don't you think?"

"What's the point of being with a person who can't give you what you need?" I said. I agreed with him, at least on this subject. If the man needed to be bitten, he needed to be bitten. Who was I to stand in the way of his happiness? However, I was also adding some categories to my "never in a million years" list.

"Have a good life, Maria," Baler said, unlocking his racing bicycle from the rack, mounting it, and riding fearlessly into traffic. I could only speculate that all those years bound up in bike shorts had resulted in a lack of penile sensitivity. But really, I was completely dumbfounded.

Could biting count as love? The last time I'd bitten someone, it'd been on the fourth grade playground, and it'd been about alienation. I'd been unclear on the rules for the game called Chase, and therefore I'd had a grand old time sprinting around the playground, flinging myself wholesale upon the boys, and biting and pinching them until they'd begged for mercy. After a few recesses of this, a knot of tight-lipped girls had informed me that only boys were allowed to chase. Girls were supposed to *run slowly*, and then be thrown to the ground and *kissed*. Not bitten. Run slowly? I hadn't cared for the contradiction. If I was running, I'd wanted to win, and who wanted to be kissed anyway? Disgusting. I'd kept playing Chase my way, even when it'd landed me in Special Ed for observation. Eventually, though, I'd gotten bored with pursuing a pack of screaming ninnies while the rest of the girls watched irritably from the jungle gym. I'd spent the rest of grade school bosom buddies with one outcast girl who wasn't allowed to wear pants, and another whose family raised bull terriers in a double-wide trailer. Screw fitting in.

My yes policy was getting a similar kind of response from my current female friends. They told me that what I was doing would mess up the balance of the universe. Women were supposed to say no, and men were supposed to chase them. When a woman finally said yes, it'd be such a big deal that trumpets would sound and men would fall down in gratitude. This balance felt like something out of *Lysistrata*, in which the women swore off sex in order to force their husbands to stop going to war. It made for amusing theater: a bunch of stammering actors staggering around, weighed down by four-foot phalluses, and a chorus of imperious women yelling "no!" But if that was what real life had to be, I was unimpressed. I didn't like the thought that a woman's only power was in her ability to deny. As for balance, it wasn't like there were millions of joyful people populating the streets. It seemed like there were far more rejected and disappointed people. The more I said yes, the more I realized that I'd never wanted to play by the rules anyway. Why had I even tried? I wasn't built that way.

LATER THAT NIGHT, I RAN THE SCENARIO BY ZAK AND GRIFFIN.

"He asked you to *bite* him?" Griffin was aghast.

"BITE?!" Zak was even more aghast.

"Bite! Bite! Bite!" Griffin moaned. "Oh God. I'm going to throw up. You *do* know that's abnormal, right?"

"More than abnormal," said Zak. "Insane. On a Marquis de Sade level. The guy needs to be locked up."

"He was an interesting guy. Maybe I should have done it."

"You could meet an interesting guy in the middle of the Sahara," said Zak. "That's nothing new."

"There you'd be, on your camel, and some guy would appear in the distance, asking you to kindly bite his penis," said Griffin.

"And she would," said Zak. "That's the thing about her. They're not wrong."

"It'd depend," I said.

"On what, exactly?"

"Whether or not I was thirsty."

There was a shout of horror from both Griffin and Zak. I went back to drinking my coffee mug of jug wine, and pretending that I wasn't stressed out by the way things were going. What if only weirdos wanted me? Historically, that had certainly been true. Part of my heart, the part I was in denial of, suspected that no acceptable man would ever be interested. In Idaho, I'd been too fat, too brunette, too smart, and though there'd certainly been guys who'd chased me, most of them—with the exception of my first pseudoboyfriend, Ira, with whom I continued to engage in drama—had been creepy. Ira, despite being somewhat acceptable, had met with my no policy for years. When he'd heard about my new yes policy, he was very excited, at least until I informed him that the yes he had in mind was not what I was practicing. Nevertheless, he still called me every couple of months, just to check.

IRA WAS A SPECIAL KIND OF STRANGE: A SARCASTIC, BELLIGER-ENT COMRADE-ENEMY. He loved me, but throughout high school he'd also written a newspaper column for the sole purpose of mocking me. Our two columns were published on the same page, Ira going so far as to post a leering headshot that spoofed my smiling one. We'd been dueling clowns, and the attraction/repulsion of this dynamic explained why Ira had never officially been acknowledged as my boyfriend. We'd gone to two proms together, but we'd never even kissed.

When I'd met Ira, I was in a blood-red velvet phase, and given to wearing a necklace made of a roach clip, which I'd inherited from my mother's wild period. Having no idea what a roach clip actually was, and thinking cheery thoughts of Gregor Samsa's cockroach transformation, I'd felt my roach clip gave me a Kafka-esque cool. Early on, Ira had informed me that I was the "freakiest thing" he'd ever seen, but that he liked the necklace. Ira was a flushed, freckled redhead who had been born looking like a forty-year-old Orson Welles. He'd had stubble from the age of nine, and he spoke in the howling bellow of an accordion. I'd met him sophomore year of high school. He was a transfer student, and he'd made his situation even more wretched by tumbling off the stage on the first day of drama class. I'd taken pity on him. A few days later, I'd brought him home to meet my family.

My mom had gone pale when Ira had shambled in, grinning and twisting a lock of his long red hair. She'd grabbed me by the arm, pulled me into the pantry, and whispered, "You can't date him."

"Why not?"

"He's a dog. You have to trust me. I know some things, and this is one of them."

"He's not a dog. He's Ira."

"He's a dachshund," she'd said, vehemently. "A redheaded dachshund."

Okay. Whatever. Ira had neither been short-legged nor particularly long in the torso. I'd figured that my mom, somewhat kooky already (we all were), had just been exhibiting a repressed rage against men in general, but then at dinner she'd seen fit to tell a certain story. As follows.

ONCE UPON A TIME, IN THE 1970S, WHEN MY MOM WAS twenty-one, she was living happily in a haunted A-frame in the Oregon woods with her dog Buddha, an enormous Great Dane–wolf–Labrador mix. Buddha was the size of a horse, but very charming and a good protector. My mom lived with the ghost, two cats, and Buddha in relative harmony, despite occasional paranormal episodes.

Until one fateful day.

My mom was driving home from a trip to the grocery store when she suddenly heard the sounds of violent car sickness coming from the backseat. Freaked out, she pulled her maroon Datsun over to the side of the road and opened the back door. There, in the middle of a half-eaten flat of strawberries, was a puking dachshund. The dog had apparently snuck into the car as she'd been loading her groceries. He had no collar, but the scraggly pink bows on each ear told her that he was an escaped lapdog. A refugee, thought my mom, taking pity on the fugitive.

"What's your name?" she asked the dog.

"I-Rah!" the dog yipped. "I-Rah! I-Rah! I-Raaaaaaaaaaaaaaaah!"

"Hello, Ira. It's very nice to meet you," my mom said, and brought him home.

Though she posted flyers, no one claimed ownership of Ira. The reason for this soon became clear. Ira was a demon masquerading as a dachshund. The moment he skittered into the A-frame, his fur stood on end, and his long ears stuck out from his head like coffin planks. He raced hysterically across the wood floors, chasing the ghost, which, offended, began a campaign of malicious acts. Ira never slept. His eyes rolled wildly in his head, and he panted rabidly, charging through the house twenty-four hours a day, shrieking his war cry: "I-Rah! I-Rah! I-Rah! I-RAAAAAAAAAAAAAAAAAAAAAAAAAAAAHHHHHH!"

Shortly after Ira moved in, both cats moved out. Soon, Buddha started running miserably through the house, too, Ira nipping in pursuit. My mom was reduced to a completely sleepless existence, listening to dog cries, searching the house for Ira, and finding him snarling in corners, teeth bared. She had thought the ghost was benevolent, but Ira gave her the impression that it was a murderous wraith. She was terrified, and spent most of her time cringing in her bed, hiding under the covers as Ira trembled and screamed his way through the house, and the ghost spilled milk and banged pots and pans in the kitchen.

After six months of living in complete stress, my mom was near a nervous breakdown. She decided that, in order to survive, she would have to get rid of Ira. She couldn't give him to the Portland pound, because they'd euthanize him. She didn't want that to happen. She just wanted Ira to move out. He was not her dog. He was a hitchhiker who wouldn't leave. She brushed Ira's fur and gave him new pink ear bows. She coaxed him into the Datsun. They drove to a park in a fancy neighborhood. Mansion windows looked down onto the manicured greens. It was exactly the right place for a sweet, pampered little dachshund to find a new owner. My mom put Ira down in the middle of the grass.

"I-Rah!" he commented.

"I'm very sorry about this, Ira, but you and I are not a good match. I know you'll find a happy home," said my mom, and then she sprinted to her car. The last time she saw Ira, he was lifting his leg at a rosebush. When she got home, the ghost and Buddha were peaceable again. The cats moved back in. Everything was happily ever after, at least for another couple of years, until she met my dad.

My mom never saw Ira again. That is, not until twenty years later, when I brought him home with me.

"I don't mean to act weird around you," my mom told human Ira. "But wouldn't you act weird if a reincarnated dachshund came home with *your* daughter?" She paused, a look of revelation on her face.

"I just realized something. That's why you like that old necklace. You liked it in 1972, too. You liked to chew it. You also liked to chew the *roaches*."

My dad became suddenly engaged, and directed a threatening glare at Ira. I could date a dachshund, apparently, but not a pothead.

"You abandoned me in a park?" Ira asked, stunned.

"I'm very sorry," said my mom, "but I'm sure you found a nice family."

"You put pink bows on my ears?"

"I thought you'd appeal to a little girl."

"I need a minute," said Ira, and left the room to hyperventilate.

He got significant mileage out of the event, spending the next several years reminding me and everyone else of the trauma he'd endured when the mother of his first love had informed him that he was a reincarnated dachshund. Whenever Ira did something bad, out the story would come, as an excuse. He'd roll his sad eyes, and moan: "I can't help it. I'm a dachshund. A *destitute* dachshund. I'm supposed to be a lapdog, and instead, I'm a scavenger. You should feel sorry for me."

A year after I met him, Ira came to pick me up for the junior prom. By this point, my dad had decided that a pothead dachshund was better than nothing, and he'd pulled Ira aside and informed him that he had his blessing to marry me. Not that marriage was on the table at all. We were talking about desperation: two people who were enough at odds (largely due to me repeatedly refusing to kiss Ira) that Ira had vindictively given me a giant sausage instead of a corsage, and told me to use it to conquer my frigidity. My dad had informed Ira that he should marry me because "no one else will want her." Obviously, my dad had been mistaken. Plenty of people seemed to want me, or, at least, want part of me. It was just that I was having a hard time wanting them. I was bummed about Baler. He'd been so appealing until he'd brought up his fetish.

My list of nos was growing. No masochists. No addicts. No one who moaned over NPR. It would have been nice to know what, exactly, I wanted, but at least I knew more every day about what I didn't. I'd thought things couldn't get worse after the strip club debacle. Ha! Still more proof that there were more things in heaven and earth, or, in this case, hell, than had hitherto been dreamt of in my philosophy.

A FEW DAYS LATER, I FOUND MYSELF IN THE ASTOR PLACE BARNES & NOBLE CHECKOUT LINE, eyeballing the selections of the short, balding guy standing in front of me. I was unimpressed. He had a stack of self-help books, and several generic CDs of Mendelssohn-Bartholdy and Bach, played by television network orchestras.

"What ees the things that you are purchasing?" he asked, reaching uninvited into my arms and plucking out my Patti Smith CD. *"Hmmmph,"* he commented, in his French accent. "I am not interested in zis thing."

I picked up one of his books, a guide to losing weight through Feng Shui. Stop judging him, I thought to myself. Stop it. This was not as easy as it sounded. I had to physically hit myself upside the head, not the most discreet thing to do. He looked at me oddly.

"That's fine," I said politely, having shaken myself into submission. "I'm not interested in your things, either."

"I am Jarzhe," he declared.

"George?"

"Yes, Jarzhe." He grandly pounced forward and kissed me on both cheeks. I'd never gotten used to the European method of greeting. It still seemed to me as though it was more a way to get a cheap feel than to say hello. Maybe it was his fingers fluttering at hip level. He seemed seconds away from a grab.

Suspicious as I was, as long as a guy didn't introduce himself by groping me against my will, the yes policy remained in effect, and so I agreed to go to Starbucks with him.

.   .   .

LATER, he was on his third 105-degree, nonfat-half-shot of caramel, foam-free latte, and shaking like a leaf. Something bad seemed to happen to foreigners living in America. They'd become poster children for all the worst parts of our society. Jarzhe had loudly and piteously rejected two attempts at his drink of choice, as "scalding to my mouth." He had also, to my horror, clandestinely nibbled a biscotti and then put it back, saying, "*Pffft*. That is not biscotti."

"I will take you to France to meet my family tomorrow," Jarzhe said casually. "You will meet my mother tonight. You like escargot, yes?"

Something went wrong in my brain, and Jarzhe's question provoked a frightening image of a chic Frenchwoman living as a snail. I could see Jarzhe proffering a silver spoon, in which was the butter-sopped matriarch of his family. Unfortunately, I had no idea how to extract Jarzhe's mother from her exoskeleton, and this was aside from the fact that I didn't want to eat her anyway.

"*Oui! S'il vous plaît!*" she shouted furiously from her place on my spoon. "*Crème brûlée! Kir royale! Louvre! Merde! Madeleines! Café! Merci! Oui! Oui!*"

It was not as though I spoke French. I knew only the names of desserts, drinks, and shit. In the mouth of Jarzhe's bitch mother, though, these words were plenty. I did not like her, particularly when she used the silk scarf tied around her neck as an impromptu noose to strangle my fingertip.

I began to use my CD case to pry at her shell.

"*Non! Non! Non! NON!*" she said, and I muffled her in my napkin.

Obviously, this date was not going well.

We'd been discussing marriage. I'd told him that I wasn't sure I wanted to get married, ever. He'd pooh-poohed this. According to Jarzhe, every woman wanted to get married. Particularly once they hit the old maid age of twenty-one.

I'd speedily become convinced that Jarzhe was a pathological liar. He'd shown me an Apple ID card, claiming to have worked in high-level management for fifteen years and recently retired, at the age of thirty-five. He was dressed in a costume of "office-casual" clothing: a windbreaker over a sports jacket, a polo shirt, and khakis. There were Montblanc pens arranged in his pocket and a Rolex displayed on his furry wrist. I suspected that all this was smoke and mirrors.

I had ideas about Jarzhe, and they did not include self-made corporate millions. They included filthy rich parents and Jarzhe being raised from birth by a disturbed nanny. Meeting Jarzhe felt similar to the way it might have felt to meet Howard Hughes. It was a disaster waiting to happen, but it was a fascinating disaster.

"Do you know the film *Pretty Woman*?" Jarzhe asked. "That film is my existence. Women in this country offer me only beauty. And that is not enough for a person like I am. They offer me beauty and want me to support them financially. They rent me a space beside them! It offends me deeply, to be wanted only for my money. I want a wife who looks up to me! That is what I deserve for myself."

I pulled out a notebook. "Would you repeat that?" I asked. Maybe I could use his character for a playwriting assignment.

He was happy to.

"We will be married in less than one year, with our first child on the way," he continued.

"I can't marry you, Jarzhe." I felt that this was an important point.

"Why not?"

"Because I don't know you. Because I don't love you."

"*Pfffft*. Let me tell you something about yourself: You will. I saw it in my dreams last night. It ees the truth. I have a talent for these things. Let me tell you something about yourself. You are born in April? No? October? No? I am a Libra on the cusp of Scorpio. Scorpios are known for their passion, yes? I have a talent for guessing the names of people. Sometimes I walk into rooms, and I am not giving you the joke, I know the names without asking. I will call you Maaaaawhrie."

People often tried to use Marie instead of my name, saying that it was "more elegant" and that I shouldn't mind being addressed that way. Also Maya. Marian. Mhari. Mary. The occasional telemarketer calling me Murray. Murray? I was relatively resigned, but that didn't mean it made me happy.

"That's not my name," I said.

"It was written in my soul." Jarzhe's eyes flickered sideways, possibly guiltily, possibly due to excess caffeine.

I looked down at my notebook. My name was on the cover. About half of everyone I met attempted to sing *I just met a girl named Maria* when I introduced myself, and the other half made me suffer through "They Call the Wind Mariah." Who exactly called the wind Mariah? No one I wanted to know. I'd been forced to befriend a bedraggled hippie child named Mariah when I was a kid, and our names were always being mixed together. I'd never really gotten over my egomaniacal fury at being confused with someone else. Particularly someone who believed that dried fruit and carob were "just like candy."

"I will fall in love with you now. But first, I must introduce you to God," Jarzhe said, banging his empty cup down on the table. His eyes were frighteningly earnest. I'd envisioned my punishment for my teenage attempts to tempt Mormon missionaries as something more along the lines of being forced to hand out pamphlets outside the Pearly Gates for a few millennia. Apparently, I was getting my just reward while still on earth. Month four of my Year of Yes, and I was on a date with a horny zealot.

Jarzhe opened a small box of chocolate-covered cherries and began eating them swiftly, one after another. Pinkish syrup dribbled from the corner of his mouth. He stood up and flagged a taxi.

Was he really religious? I couldn't tell. I'd seen a St. Christopher medal tangled in his chest hair. He'd prayed briefly prior to each cherry. He'd told me he was Catholic, but I was unused to encountering religious people in New York City.

"We will go uptown to get the blessing of my mother."

"Where does your mother live?"

"Our apartment is on Eighty-fifth Street."

Our apartment? He lived with his mother? This was a new one.
"I'm not sure I want to go with you . . ."

"*Pffft.* You are just young and do not know what is the right thing for you. Let me to lead you." Jarzhe put his hand on the small of my back, and ushered me into the cab.

I got in. I couldn't help myself. The yes was done, I thought, I'd already had coffee with him, but I was too curious to depart. I figured that if things got weird, I could always open the door and jump out at an intersection. Jarzhe turned to me.

"I have been with two women on three separate occasions, and on one occasion with two women and one man. This is a most interesting story of how this occurred, which I will tell you soon. You look as though you could deep throat ten inches cock. True? Let me tell you something about yourself. You like it most doggie style, and you trim your bush with the scissors. True? Your breasts are average sized with small nipples. You like to have your head massaged when you are sucking the cock."

This qualified as weird. I heard the driver snort from the front seat. I moved back as Jarzhe's tongue approached, pink and wet as a puppy's. My eyes were, alas, open as he licked my eyeball. I blinked frantically, contact lens displaced, and put my hand on the door.

"I am French. I need no condiments. I lick the salt from your eyeball," Jarzhe said, by way of explanation. "You did not like that?"

I settled uneasily back into my seat. I couldn't help myself. I wanted to see if the apartment actually existed. A typical problem. Even when I disliked a book before I'd finished the first chapter, I felt compelled to keep reading all the way through. I always thought it would get better. The price wasn't so high: a little corneal lick now and then. However.

"I'm not going to sleep with you," I informed him. "I don't sleep with strangers." A lie, unfortunately, but a reasonably plausible one.

He looked offended.

"*Pffffffffft!!!* I am not wanting the sex. My mother is at home, I told you. We will make love for the first time on the wedding night. I am a Catholic!"

The cab pulled up in front of a very fancy building on Eighty-fifth Street and Fifth Avenue. I imagined Jarzhe's mother, again, oozing her snail self up to peer nearsightedly out the windows. I imagined the kind of havoc an enormous escargot would wreak on Persian carpets. However, it also occurred to me that it would be kind of nice to carry your bedroom on your back. Instead of my hut, I could curl up into my shell and be spared the noise of New York. During this imagining, Jarzhe somehow got me into the elevator. I vaguely registered the fact that the doorman greeted him by name.

"Which apartment is yours?"

"*Pfffftt!* Zee penthouse, of course, but I own the building," said Jarzhe, rapid-fire. "I have a house in Provence. It is in the middle of a lavender field. You like that, yes? You are one of the American . . . how do you say? The Francophiles. *Pffft.* You know nothing about France. Marcel Proust, yes? *Pffffftt*—ha! Let me tell you something about yourself. We will have four sons. I will sail around the world in my little boat. You will tend to our children. I will return home from time to time."

He paused to swallow his last chocolate-covered cherry whole. Before he could open his mouth again, I interrupted.

"I don't think we get along well enough to get married."

He pulled a photograph out of his wallet and pointed at it nervously.

"Steve Jobs has had me to his home as a participant in social events! I am a friend to persons well-known in the world!"

The photo showed Jarzhe with his arm around someone who looked very much like Apple's CEO. They were both grinning, and giving the thumbs-up sign in front of a melting ice sculpture. It had the look of a souvenir photo taken in, say, Colonial Williamsburg. Steve Jobs looked like a cardboard cutout, which was, in my opinion, very plausibly what he was. Jarzhe looked rapturous.

"Now I will introduce you to God," Jarzhe said.

. . .

SOMEWHERE, THERE WAS A PHANTOM DRUMROLL, AS JARZHE UNZIPPED HIS FLY. I backed myself into the corner, but really, there was no need. If this was God, it was more like one of the lesser gods. Why would a man cede higher power to his penis, anyway? Penises had terrible judgment. They were known for betraying their owners. Wouldn't Judas be a more appropriate name?

Jarzhe said, "You will suck on my cock a little bit?"

When my sister was in high school, she'd gone out with a devout Mormon guy named John. He'd been wracked with guilt over their heavy petting and had confessed his sins to his church, going so far as to drag Molly in for a joint consultation with a panel of church elders on the wickedness of tempting young men. John had then been referred to God, for a serious talk. Upon emerging from his powwow with the Heavenly Father, Molly's boyfriend had happily explained that, while he was not allowed to do anything that might give her any pleasure, God would look the other way if Molly wanted to give John a blow job. God was a guy himself, John had explained, and so he'd cut him a break.

Apparently, Jarzhe had a similar deal.

The elevator doors opened into a gilded foyer, just in time to save me from having to respond. Jarzhe zipped up.

"We will meet in the powder room after dinner," he said, patted my rump, and stepped out of the elevator. The apartment door was already swinging open. I glimpsed an unlucky young someone in a maid's outfit, holding a tray of champagne glasses and smiling a frozen smile, as the elevator doors closed again, me still inside.

The last thing I heard Jarzhe say, as the elevator descended, was, "I am a millionaiiiiiiiiiiirrrrrre! Where are you goooooooooooooooing?"

As I left Jarzhe's building, the doorman asked if I'd been crying. I looked at my reflection in the glass door. Jarzhe's lick had left mascara smeared from eyebrow to chin. I spit on my finger and tried in vain to scrub it off.

"He makes a lot of women react that way," the doorman said, handing me a tissue.

"I wasn't really going home with him," I said quickly, embarrassed. I *had* gone home with him, after all. If he was a pathological liar, I was a pathological story stealer.

"I'm not judging you," said the doorman. "I'm just the guy who opens the door."

And with that, he opened it, and ushered me out.

WHEN I GOT HOME, I LOOKED JARZHE UP ON THE INTERNET. He was both too good, in terms of finances, and too bad, in terms of personality, to be true. If not family wealth, I expected maybe an escaped lunatic with delusions of grandeur and friendships with doormen in high places. I called Vic into the room.

"I met an award-winning weirdo today," I told her.

"Shocker," she said. "You always do."

I'd thought that I might find a laundry list of psychiatric records for Jarzhe, but instead, I found the unbelievable. A photo and bio of Jarzhe, documenting him as, indeed, an Apple man. And here was his name funding charitable activities for the Catholic Church. And here was a photo of him on a sailboat. He'd been telling the truth.

"He doesn't look that weird," said Vic.

"Neither do I," I said. "Looks can be deceiving."

"Actually, you *do* look weird," said Vic. I was wearing a spangled gold cocktail dress and it was full daylight. "You need someone who's a little strange, or it won't work at all."

That hadn't occurred to me. Maybe the reason weirdos wanted me was that even when I was trying to look normal, they recognized one of their own. There were clearly plenty of men in New York who'd be happy to take me as I was: gnashing my teeth, hitting myself upside the head, and wearing a cocktail dress. Given that I wasn't sure I could change, this was yet another reason to love New York. I hadn't found anything spectacular with either Baler or Jarzhe, but I'd learned something. I wanted a man with passion, but

I also had some boundaries, no matter how open-minded I was. Greater knowledge, even if it was just greater knowledge of myself, was reason to celebrate.

I put Tom Waits on the stereo, picked up Big White Cat, and tangoed him around the room. Vic rolled her eyes a little, but she joined us. Maybe she'd forgiven me for my men. At least she was willing to have a good time. It was a triumph to have her happy with me again. The three of us dipped and twirled a while, and then Vic and I went out and gorged on ice cream. We bought Big White some kalamata olives, his addiction. Maybe we were freaks, but we were having a good time anyway.

TE AMO, CHUPA CHUPA

IN WHICH
OUR HEROINE
CONFRONTS
HER DIRTY
LAUNDRY . . .

A RICHARD GERE LOOK-ALIKE CRAWLED ACROSS THE FLOOR OF THE DOWNTOWN TRAIN. It was 11:00 P.M., and I'd been walking all over the boiling hot city for the entire day. My feet were black with grunge unknown, and there Pseudo-Gere was, down on his knees. Somehow, I didn't think he was about to propose. He trailed his fingers over the arch of my flip-flop–wearing foot, and I looked down at him. He looked up at me. His eyes were green and intelligent. He really didn't look like the kind of person I suspected he was.

"*Please* tell me you're not going to do that," I said, and Pseudo-Gere smiled. A great smile. A sexy smile. The smile of a man who knows exactly what he's doing.

And then, alas, he bent down and applied his lips to my toes. Very thoroughly. Another woman on the train looked over to me, and twirled her finger beside her ear, rolling her eyes. *Crazy.* I shrugged. Oh well. It was gross, and yes, he was maybe somewhat imbalanced, but he wasn't hurting me. My standards for what I would and would not allow had shifted considerably in the yes months.

"Thanks," said Pseudo-Gere. "I needed that."

"You're welcome," I replied. "But you should wash your mouth out with Listerine. You don't want to know where these toes have been today." Toe kissing was not, in my opinion, something people ought to do in a place where negligent dog owners lived.

"That's the point," he said, gave me a (literally) shit-eating grin, and got off the train.

"Eww," said the woman. "Why are the messed-up ones always so cute?"

"Why are the cute ones always so messed up?" I replied, thinking of Baler.

"Because this is New York in June," she said. "And I don't like it. How about you?"

"I *do* like a Gershwin tune, though," I said, pleased to meet someone witty.

"Life is *never* as good as Gershwin," she said, assuredly. "The Gershwins didn't even write that song. George and Ira would never have written about liking New York in the summer. They were smarter than that." She went back to reading her copy of *Variety*.

Such was the peril of the flippant reference. You were pretty much guaranteed to be talking to someone who knew a hell of a lot more than you, or at least felt that they did.

IT WAS TRUE THAT NEW YORK IN THE SUMMER WAS NOT THE BEST PLACE. The city smelled like four hundred bulls doing heavy exercise. The humidity made the air as thick as Play-Doh. Everywhere you looked, there were women wringing sweat from their sundresses. Vic debarked for her sister's house in New Orleans, where it was even hotter than in New York City. She didn't care. She liked the Southern manners the men displayed there, and she had a point. On my way to work one morning, I was groped not once, not twice, but *three times*. One grope on the rush-hour G from Greenpoint, one on the R under the East River, and the last on the 6 uptown. I'd elbowed the G groper, and given the R groper a growl and feral hiss that made him think I might be crazy. By the time I met the 6 groper, I'd reached my limit. When I turned around and saw that his Armani trousers were unzipped, and his penis entirely out of his pants, I screamed, somewhat hysterically, "Look! There it is! He wants you to see it!"

He inexplicably put his hands in the air. There were several black-clad old ladies on my train, and for a moment, we transited to Sicily. They all started pointing and cursing him. One bashed him with her enormous valise. The guy fled at the next stop. It was enormously satisfying, if somewhat surreal. Of course, it only made me more pissed off at all the men on the train who'd failed to defend me. They looked at me like I was a hooker turned rabid feminist. I had a recurrent fantasy of a Riot Grrrls–style project, in which cameras would be distributed to all female subway passengers. Then, when being groped against her will, a woman could turn around and snap an image of the offender. The photos would be blown up to poster size, and posted in the trains. This was the kind of master plan that always ended up dominating my thoughts when the weather was too warm.

THAT NIGHT, IN AN EFFORT TO COOL MY BLOOD BEFORE I KILLED SOMEONE, I purchased a twenty-nine-dollar piece-of-shit used air conditioner from the nearby junk store, Your Purveyor of Discontent. I'd gotten our seventies-era spontaneously defrosting refrigerator there the year before. The store did not offer delivery, and so I'd used a case of Pabst as a bribe to get three career alcoholics to help me carry it down the street and up the stairs. I hadn't really understood mortality until I found myself holding up the bottom end of the refrigerator, in collaboration with a skinny white guy named MoFo, whose fingers felt like noodles, and who kept murmuring, "Where . . . what? Beer? Fuck! Yo! Heavy!" I hadn't learned my lesson. Your Purveyor of Discontent was cheap. Frenzied with hope, I tied my new AC to a skateboard I'd bought at the Salvation Army and dragged it home to await Zak's assistance.

Zak, however, had gone to his girlfriend's apartment, and did not seem to be coming home. I lay in my bed, steaming like a dumpling. At 4:00 A.M., I brilliantly decided that I was fully capable of installing the AC by myself. Alas, I misjudged the weight of the unit versus the axis of the windowsill. The back neighbors, engaged in partying in their backyard, were very startled to watch the air conditioner tumble out my second-story window, nearly followed by me. The top two-thirds of my body hung out the window for a full two minutes, before I managed to right myself. I'd bitched about all the people in the neighborhood who stood naked in their windows, and now I was one of them, topless for all to see. Fortunately, the neighbors were too drunk to give a damn.

"Come down, girl! We're roasting the rooster!" one of them yelled.

"Die, you crowing motherfucker!" screamed someone else.

Both the rooster and the AC died. Chicken bones and AC parts were scattered across several lots. In the days that followed, I periodically looked down at my air conditioner's skeleton and whimpered. I started sleeping beneath wet towels, rising occasionally to wedge ice cubes into my cleavage, thinking I'd reached my lowest point, but then things got even worse.

NINE GUESTS FROM ALL OVER THE COUNTRY CONVERGED SIMULTANEOUSLY ON OUR APARTMENT. I was forced to surrender my hut to them. This meant that Zak and I had to sleep entwined on his single mattress. Despite the months of repressed sexual tension, there was nothing sexy about this. It was too hot to be titillated. It was too hot to exist. Everyone hated everyone else, and we were resolving the situation by drinking too much. Our living room was occupied by my sister, Molly, her friend Brynn, my friend Moon and her friend Kitty, Zak's friend Joe, and his girlfriend Maisie. Vic's room was occupied by my friend Leah, who was renting it for the summer, and her friends Jess and Nina. My friend Jack was sleeping on a pile of blankets in the kitchen, having come in from Idaho prior to his attendance at an acting workshop. He was a neurotic guy already, and New York City was making it worse. His first day in the city coincided with the Gay Pride Parade, and his first excursion was onto Sixth Avenue, into the heart of about five thousand topless lesbians wearing Band-Aids on their nipples. Everything was swathed in rainbow.

"Is this how New York is every day?" he asked, fearful.

Jack spent the rest of the night listening to Joni Mitchell and Fugazi, rocking sadly, and keeping an eye out for the creepy, and apparently jobless, new neighbor who'd moved in directly opposite our kitchen windows.

The neighbor liked to stand in his own kitchen window, dressed only in an undershirt, raising and lowering his penis via a peculiar system of cords he'd hooked to his wall. Jack never saw Pulley Guy, because whenever a male walked into the room, Pulley Guy dematerialized. As soon as a woman entered the kitchen alone, Pulley Guy would reappear, hoisting his thing like an overachieving kid assigned to flagpole duty. We'd never seen our onanist's face, because he pulled his blinds down to cover his head, but the rest of his body strongly resembled that of a rubber chicken. None of us could fathom what satisfaction he was deriving from the pulley.

This was the second summer that I'd lived in a building opposite an exhibitionist. The one before this had, at least, been insanely handsome: six foot something and the color of a piece of carved mahogany. Living across from him was like living within spitting distance of the David. Had I not known that he thought it was okay to get busy on his fire escape, both alone and with a variety of female companions, I might've gotten a crush on him. He'd been ridiculously well endowed, and watching his nightly show had been like a free trip to Amsterdam. Come 8:00 P.M., you'd find most of my building sitting on our own fire escapes, drinks in hand, some of us with binoculars. There'd been a betting pool in the building next to ours, involving just how long he could keep it up. The answer? *Forever*. Eventually, we'd all just get bored and go to bed. Nobody'd gotten laid that summer. Our Exhibitionist was too intimidating. Sometimes I'd see him at the grocery store. I'd know he was there, because of the mass exodus of neighborhood men, all ducking their heads in shame. The Exhibitionist would always grin and wink, place his Goya mango juice on the conveyor belt, and say, "Hey. How's your life?"

"Not as good as yours," I'd say, and we'd laugh, but I had no intention of following up on that particular flirtation. I'd seen the dude naked from twenty paces, and that had been close enough for me. Sleeping with him would have been like sleeping with a baguette. Besides, it was summer. Who wanted to get close to anything? It was too damned hot. All I wanted was to find a nice ice floe and drift away.

I WAS SITTING, DRAINED AND BEDRAGGLED, AT MY KITCHEN TABLE, trying to ignore the fact that Pulley Guy was frantically flipping his penis just ten feet away, when Taylor called to invite me to go dancing. The idea of going to a club and pressing my boiled body up against a bunch of other boiled bodies suddenly seemed brilliant, even though it was what I'd been complaining about the entire day.

"You have to wear a costume," he said. "We're going to this club called Mother. I'm going to read you the dress code. Got something to write with?"

"Come on. I'll remember."

"That's what you think. 'Cyberslut, gothic, classic fetish, dark fetish, vampire, trekkie, anime, sexy robot, imaginative head-to-toe-black, genderhacking, gothic erotica, Russ Meyer hot mama, dominatrix debutante, or access denied! No blue denim, no athletic wear, no white sneakers, no exceptions!' You have to dress up. Got it?"

"Could you repeat that?" I said meekly, having decided I needed a pencil after all. It wasn't like dressing up was a problem. I spent half my life in various weird costumes, particularly given that my budget ran to Early Salvation Army. But sexy robot? What exactly did that mean? C-3PO dressed in crotchless panties and a push-up bra?

I made a dubious attempt at breast cones before determining that wearing a costume made of tinfoil and Scotch tape was not just flirting with disaster, but sleeping with disaster on the first date. The next several hours were spent staring morosely at my pile of clothing. Taylor, of course, would be wearing rubber.

I gave up and put on a black miniskirt and high-heeled boots, and tied a transparent chiffon scarf around my chest. I moved the hand mirror around for forty-five minutes, neurotic and unable to get a full view. I was pretty sure I'd get past the bouncer (I'd *be* the bouncer), but what if no one else had visible breasts? Rudy Giuliani, our mayor, had recently expressed the opinion that dancing led to drug use, and so rabid police had been patrolling the nightclubs. What if I got arrested? Not to mention the fact that going topless in public was something I'd never done before. Bottomless, alas, yes. The previous summer, I'd inadvertently exposed my ass to rush-hour Grand Central Station, having somehow tucked the hem of my skirt into my G-string, and then, clueless, walked the length of the terminal, wondering why I was getting so many catcalls.

Finally, I went downstairs to consult Pierre's roommate, Annie, who was a dancer, and as such, always had ideas for how to keep from being obscene while in costume.

Pierre opened the door. I immediately crossed my arms over my chest.

"What?" said Pierre. He had a mixing bowl in his hand and was whisking furiously.

"Is Annie home?"

"Rehearsal. Taste this." He stuck a finger in his bowl, and offered it to me. I opened my mouth and let him put his finger in it. It would have been almost sexy, had whatever was in the bowl not involved a psychotic quantity of habañero peppers.

"It's too hot?" asked Pierre. I had stopped caring about exposed breasts and was bent over with my head in his kitchen sink, my mouth open under the faucet.

"Kind of spicy," I croaked.

"So, you were coming to show me your tits?" He had his usual confident smirk, but one of his hands was fiddling with his earring.

"No, but now you've seen them. So? Can I go out like this?"

"Are you choking?"

"I don't really need my trachea. What do you think?"

"Milk," he said, and handed me a glass of it. He was right, although it was disturbing to have him appraising my breasts while handing me dairy products. He looked me up and down for a moment, and then went back to whisking.

"I think . . . nice rack," said Pierre, his back to me.

I watched his shoulders for a moment. If he whisked any faster, he'd achieve liftoff.

"Thank you," I said. For some reason, I was blushing. Why, I couldn't tell. It was Pierre, for God's sake. I fled, wondering what the hell was wrong with me.

I WORE A SWEATSHIRT ON THE SUBWAY AND CAREFULLY AVOIDED EYE CONTACT as I made my way to the meatpacking district, which was, at that time, still very much about meat. I had to pick my way over cobblestones divided by runnels of blood, until I got to the end of Fourteenth Street and a crowd of what looked like circus refugees. Taylor and his girlfriend, Janet, were among them. He was wearing a pair of leather hot pants, Day-Glo–striped knee socks, and nothing else. Nothing else, that is, but flaming red paint. She was wearing a fishnet body stocking with a sequined halter dress, and a red wig that matched Taylor's paint.

"You didn't get dressed up," Taylor said, eyeing me with distinct annoyance.

I took off my sweatshirt. His eyes widened.

"What? You don't think they'll let me in?" He'd made me nervous.

Taylor grinned and slapped me on the back.

"That works," he said.

And it did. The breasts were like a secret password. The bouncer took one look, raised his eyebrows, and waved me through. Even in this crowd full of people ranging from guys in black leather harnesses to a trio of women dressed as geek-sirens (fishnets, thigh-high boots, Scotch-taped horn-rim glasses, tiny white shirts with pocket protectors), it seemed I'd gone off the deep end. Luckily for me, the deep end was where everyone wanted to swim. I got more compliments in ten minutes than I'd gotten in my entire life.

"Can I just say that your tits are completely subversive?" one man in leather chaps and sideburns told me.

"Because they're real!" his companion chimed in, from behind the unzipped mouth of his/her full-body black latex suit. "Nothing's real anymore!"

"Come dance with us," said Taylor, dragging me away from a transvestite who wanted to compare bra sizes.

The dance floor was a sauna of grinding, twisting, gorgeous people. Sweat hung in a mist over the room. Taylor, doing his own peculiar brand of the robot, shook us into the fray. Dancing with Taylor was never really dancing *with* him. You danced in the vicinity of Taylor, being careful to avoid his high-stepping knees. He always danced with his eyes shut, but he was also very kind in that he opened them every five minutes or so, to verify the safety of his female companions.

Marilyn Manson's song "The Beautiful People," a paean to freakiness, was inspiring everyone in the room to shout along. I wasn't that familiar with his music and I didn't know the words, but I shouted anyway. Someone danced up behind me and grabbed me around the waist. Long, silver fake fingernails on slender, pale hands. A wrist corsage. Pink roses and baby's breath. I had to turn around to see what the hell I was dancing with.

And it was shocking. At least, shocking for a girl from Idaho. Long, stick-straight black hair. Bicolored eyes, one ice blue, one dark. Skin pale as Wite-Out. A 1950s pink tulle strapless prom dress. Dark red lipstick. Six feet tall, rail thin, and definitely male.

"Hi," I said, taking a step back. "What's your name? I'm Maria. I've never been here before. Have you? It's kind of dark, don't you think? I like the music! I hate house music! But this isn't really house, is it? More, what would you say? Goth?" I had an unfortunate tendency to talk too much when I felt awkward. Also, when I felt comfortable. In fact, I talked too much all the time.

He said nothing. He just smiled. Vampire fangs. There was something vaguely familiar about him, but since I didn't recall ever meeting anyone so weird before, I decided that maybe it was just that he reminded me of the villainous stepmother, Maleficent, from Disney's *Sleeping Beauty*. The Prom Queen extended his hand to me and curtsied an invitation to dance. Well. Okay. Year of Yes. I gave him a bow, and then I danced with the man. Why the hell not? I was getting to twirl with the belle of the ball. I wasn't just lost in a fantasy. I speedily discovered that everyone else in the room wanted to dance with this guy, too. Taylor opened his eyes and squinted at me from behind the Prom Queen's shoulder. He mouthed "Are you okay?"

I nodded and shrugged. Taylor shut his eyes again. "The Beautiful People" continued to play. The entire room raised its fists in the air and rapturously tossed their heads.

I liked the song. I'd heard it before, but apparently never in the right context. The silver fingernails were groping my breasts. I let them. I'd put them on display, after all. I was trying to be liberated. Besides, when else was I going to be groped by a guy in a cotillion gown? It hadn't been on my list of life goals, admittedly, but it was the kind of thing that you didn't know you'd kind of like until you kind of did.

A neon redhead in black tulle came up beside us just then and shoved me. She'd been dancing next to us for a while, staring adoringly at the Prom Queen and jealously at me. In fact, there were several people who seemed to want to cut in. We were in the middle of the floor, and we were being circled by a bunch of dance club werewolves. I tried to ignore them, but it wasn't exactly easy, particularly as the woman had, by then, come up behind me, and was dancing with her arms reaching around my waist to grab my partner. For a while, the three of us danced uncomfortably in a mass of knees, tits, and netting.

Finally, just after the Prom Queen wrapped his pale hands around my neck and stuck his serpentine tongue down my throat, I retreated. It was one thing to dance with the devil. It was another thing to make out with him. The guy had bared his vampire teeth at me a few too many times, and, from the bumping and grinding he'd done against me, I could tell that he wasn't wearing underwear under his dress. I couldn't get into cross-dressers. I had visions of trying to make a life with a person like that, sharing a closet, finding my shoes stretched out and my clothing looking better on him. I didn't think I could take the competition. The girl behind me could have him. They matched, after all. All they needed was a vat of pig's blood, readily available in the neighborhood, and they could reenact *Carrie*.

The last I saw of the duo, the redhead was dragging him by his corsaged wrist onto one of the couches lining the walls and straddling him. His silver talons waved a vague good-bye, and then he stuck them up her skirt.

Someone nudged me. I turned to see a glitter-painted face and a gold Lurex wig.

"Do you know who that guy is?" yelled the glittered man, over the music.

"Random vampire in a pink dress," I said. Not a sentence I'd ever have imagined coming out of my mouth.

"You're kidding." He looked at me like I'd just arrived from a voyage with Shackleton.

"Is he famous or something?"

"Hello?" said the guy, and walked away, appalled by my ignorance. I racked my brain as to who I could have been dancing with, but I was clueless. (It wasn't until I saw a recent photo of Marilyn Manson, a few months later, that I understood what the ruckus had been about. My vampire was either Mr. Manson, or a very good look-alike.)

DISCONCERTED, I WENT TOWARD THE BATHROOM. There was a line. A long line. Apparently, the bathroom cam was on. This meant that one of the stalls was broadcasting live to a room in the club. The rest of the stalls were normal. The line was equal parts people who wanted to be filmed and people hopping with desperation to get out of their leotards.

After a while, I focused on the fact that the person in front of me was wearing a very credible Marie Antoinette costume. He was also about six foot five and shaped like a linebacker. The powdered wig gave him another foot of height. His skirts were silk brocade and crinolined. I'd worked for a summer in a Shakespeare festival costume shop, and I had to compliment him.

"I love your dress," I said.

"You wouldn't, if you had to pee," he said grimly. His voice was deep, booming, and weirdly, perfectly suited to his costume. "I've been waiting in this line for *years*. Fucking exhibitionists. Let me tell you, we've all seen enough ass to last us."

Marie Antoinette and I watched an obviously coked-up guy in three peacock feathers and a vinyl jockstrap shaking his skinny white rump at the door of the bathroom, and yelling out, "Don't wait for me! I'm going to be in there for*evah*!"

I didn't want to think about how those peacock feathers were staying in place.

"That's it," said Marie Antoinette. "That is just *the end*." He grabbed my hand, and pulled me through the line. People complained, but when they saw what they were being trampled by, they gave up. Marie Antoinette was a force of nature. As we reached the bathroom door, someone whined, halfheartedly, "Why does *she* get to go with you?"

I'd been wondering the same thing.

"SHE'S MY DRESSER, YOU IMBECILE," Marie Antoinette yelled. There was a collective nod of understanding. Apparently having a dresser, or an undresser, was completely normal. Marie maneuvered us into the stall with the bathroom cam.

"Thanks," I said. "I'd never have gotten in."

"Peons out there. Literally. Let them eat cake. Or let them snort coke, darling. Help me lift this motherfucking skirt."

Later, I ran into Taylor and Janet. Taylor's red paint was running. He raised an eyebrow at me.

"I saw you on the bathroom cam," he said. "Underneath a transvestite's skirt."

"Really?" I asked, as though I had no idea what he was referencing.

"Yes, really," he said. "But I'm not even going to ask you to explain. I don't know if I wanna know. It's six in the morning. We're going to go eat."

The whole restaurant was full of people like us, looking somewhat the worse for the wear, but happy anyway. There were uniformed cops sitting at the counter, having the same breakfast we were. Looking around the room, at all of us glittering under the neon lights, I felt an unexpected rush of tenderness. It wasn't for anyone in particular, but for the whole insane, spectacular city.

"I think I might love everyone," I announced.

"Drink your coffee," said Taylor, but he was smiling, too.

"WHERE'VE YOU BEEN?" mumbled Zak a couple hours later, after I tiptoed over the sleeping bodies of our guests, kicked off my shoes, and crawled into bed with him.

"Dancing."

"You smell like hellfire and brimstone."

"Lots of smokers there," I said. "And vampires, dead French queens, debutantes . . ."

Zak smiled blurrily at me.

"I think I'm dreaming," he said.

"Me, too." He put his arm around me, and we were out.

I GOT UP AROUND NOON TO DO MY LAUNDRY. It was a hundred degrees again, but I was happy enough that I actually danced my way down India Street, balancing my pink laundry sack on my head. My neighborhood Laundromat was called Lavadero Limpio, or Clean Laundry. The first syllable of the second Spanish word usually seemed more appropriate to me: limp. The night of dancing had made my thighs feel like jelly. I adjusted my bag and started to sing. The only way I'd actually make it to the Laundromat was if I wrote revisionist movie musicals in my head, and sang the lyrics out loud. Today, it was "Singing Through the Pain." It had been unwise to jiggle braless for seven hours. Everything hurt.

That was when I heard someone else singing, and snapping his fingers, too. Every once in a while there was a little shuffling sound, like someone practicing a soft-shoe.

"Chupa, chupa," sang the voice.

I was not sure what that meant.

"Chupa la paleta, chupa la, chupa la paleta, chupa la . . ."

I turned around. My serenader was five foot zero, white-haired, and Latino. He looked like a doll, costumed in a fancy pleated-and-embroidered guayabera shirt, pressed slacks, and a dapper straw hat. He twirled on his polished heel.

"Chupa, chupa!" he sang. I recognized the lyrics now. This was a song that had been broadcasting through Brooklyn for months, piercing my night with a tune akin to that of an ice-cream truck's solicitation. Though I was unclear on the translation, my impression

was that it had a sexy connotation, given that I had seen a herd of fourteen-year-old girls singing it a few days before, sucking lollipops and swinging their hips suggestively. The old man did a little solo salsa in the middle of the sidewalk. He grinned from ear to ear, like a demented, ancient child. I'd been told that my smile was demented, too. Maybe he was enjoying his day as much as I was enjoying mine. I smiled, and hoisted the laundry back onto my head.

"*Lavadero,*" I told him, shrugging. He tailed me the three blocks to the Laundromat. Unless he was planning on stripping, he was not carrying any laundry that needed to be done.

"*Chupa, chupa,*" he sang under his breath. He seemed harmless enough, grandfatherly even, and soon I'd almost forgotten him. He sat down in a chair, and quietly drank a bottle of juice, while watching the Spanish-channel soap operas that the Laundromat played all day. It wasn't until I was unloading my underwear from the dryer that my attention was drawn to the old man again. He came up next to me, and said, in English:

"You are pretty. Marry me, Louie."

"I don't actually want to get married, but thanks for the compliment," I responded, smiling politely at him.

"*Qué?*" he said. "*Un momento.*" He dashed from the Laundromat.

I tried, with little success, to stuff all my remaining laundry into one machine. This was a period of time during which I often ended up with strangely colored lumps of clothing. I hated spending my whole afternoon waiting for the dryer to beep, but if you didn't stay there, people would steal your clothes. I usually read three or four *New Yorkers*, or stared stupidly at the soap operas I didn't understand. Not that there was much to understand. They were the same in every language. I was deeply involved in a doctor/nurse drama when the bell on the door jingled, and Señor Chupa reappeared, dragging another old man by the arm.

"Marco," he said, and made a Vanna White–esque gesture of presentation. Marco was about the same age as Señor Chupa, but not as well turned out. His skin was lined with deep furrows and he was missing some teeth. He had a brown paper bag in his hand, with a straw protruding from it. His tie was loosened. I'd seen him before, hanging out at the neighborhood bodega, but he'd never spoken to me.

"Louie asks will you go to a dance with him," Marco said, and sighed deeply.

Señor Chupa gave a little hop and stuck his hand out toward me for a shake. Amused, I gave him my hand, and he kissed it. Anything was possible, I reminded myself. Okay. Maybe not anything. This man was clearly too old for me, and he also seemed to be mildly mentally retarded, but what the hell, maybe he had a grandson.

"Yeah," I said. "Sure."

Marco looked flabbergasted. He conferred with Señor Chupa.

"Louie will pick you up here, tonight, at seven-thirty," said Marco, his voice wavering, clearly giving me an opportunity to say that I had misunderstood.

"*Chupa, chupa,*" trilled my elderly datesman, sashaying his way out the door. The women of the Laundromat rolled their eyes. I would need to find out what that word meant.

"Louie," said the head Laundromat lady, her lips pursed disapprovingly.

"Yeah?"

"*Está loco.*" She nodded meaningfully. I had a piddling grasp of Spanish gleaned over two years of required high school classes. I proudly constructed my response.

"*Es él malo?*" I wasn't sure what the word for "dangerous" was, so I tried to ask if he was bad.

"*Él es un niño,*" she responded, and shook her head. He was a child, I thought that meant. Well, that wasn't terrible. Had she told me he was a child molester, it would have been different. Hopefully I hadn't missed anything.

"*Qué es 'chupa'?*"

"*Chupa!*" she chortled and went to the jawbreaker machine in the corner and put a dime in it. She brought the jawbreaker back to me, and displayed it between thumb and forefinger. It was enormous, and speckled with Jackson Pollock splatters. I hoped she didn't want me to swallow it. Big as my mouth was, that would not be possible.

The Laundromat lady put the jawbreaker into her mouth and sucked it furiously. She pointed at her mouth. She exaggerated the sucking. She took it out.

"*Chupa,*" she explained.

I'd been followed around with a sound track of "suck, suck." I tried not to think that that was appropriate.

"*Gracias. Qué es 'paleta'?*" I might as well get the rest of the meaning.

She went to the Laundromat's freezer case (due to lack of air-conditioning, all the Laundromats in the area also sold ice cream), and pulled out a popsicle.

Chupa la paleta. Suck the popsicle.

Why was I even surprised?

THAT NIGHT, SEÑOR CHUPA AND I WALKED TOGETHER TO SOUTH WILLIAMSBURG. I had to keep slowing down, because his legs weren't long enough to keep up with mine. Without Marco, it was difficult to converse, but he managed to tell me several things which I partially understood, one of which seemed to be a declaration of his love for young girls. He informed me that he was seventy. I asked if he had children, and he said yes, eleven, though I wasn't sure I understood that correctly.

"*Te amo,*" he said. "*Chupa, chupa.*"

I love you. Suck, suck. It was the perfect phrase. Everything you needed to know about relationships. No. No, no, no. I wouldn't think that way anymore. Things could be worse. I could be kissing a vampire. I could be on my way to France with a psychopathic millionaire, or stripping for schoolboys. Instead, I was going dancing with a relatively polite old man. My life was pretty good, all things considered.

. . .

THE CLUB WAS LOUD, DARK, AND UNMARKED. I'd passed it a million times when I'd lived in the neighborhood. It normally boasted a couple of old guys playing dominoes outside, but tonight, it had a band wedged into the corner, playing salsa music. A bunch of people were spinning and stomping, shaking everything they had. These were the parties that had once kept me awake. Now I was one of the guests. I got into it. I spun and kicked up my heels. I shook every bit of my rump. Finally, something that would put it to good use!

Señor Chupa looked at me skeptically, and waved some people over to watch me. It was very quickly clear that almost everyone in the room was related to him. It was also very clear that my dancing was the most horrifying thing any of them had ever witnessed. Señor Chupa looked put upon. He held out his arms, patiently, in the universal gesture for "Let Me Teach You, You Idiot." I wasn't an idiot! I shook it some more. Now people were laughing. I hadn't really understood that salsa was something that had to be learned. I thought you just naturally knew how. Not so. Counting was required. Precise placement of arms and elbows and, most importantly, knees.

Señor Chupa handed me off, groaning, to another old man. This one was confident, until I stepped hard on his tiny, shiny foot. Another old man cut in, and spun me twice, before I whirled the wrong way and dislocated his shoulder. I was willing, but willing wasn't enough. Finally, an old woman, who'd been giving me a dirty look for a while, waved the men aside and stomped over to me in her spike heels. She looked like a prison guard. If anyone could lead the unleadable, it was her.

"*Soy esposa de Louie,*" she informed me, tersely.

No wonder she'd been pissed off. Chupa had lied. He was married, and this was his wife. Fortunately, my Spanish was good enough to apologize.

"*Soy embarazada.*" I put my hands up in a gesture of supplication.

"*Embarazada?*" She looked enraged. "*EMBARAZADA?!*"

"*Sí, soy embarazada.*" Maybe she didn't think I was sorry enough. "*Muy embarazada!!*"

It wasn't until several people were screaming at Señor Chupa that it dawned on me.

Embarazada did not mean embarrassed.

It meant pregnant.

"*NO! No soy embarazada! No! No!*" I couldn't think of any other words, so I pressed the fabric of my dress against my stomach. I mimed holding a baby, and then mimed throwing it, which in my mind showed that it had never existed. There were gasps of horror. Oops. Charades. The deathmatch version.

"No?" Two women patted my stomach suspiciously.

"No!" I said. They motioned Señor Chupa's wife over and conferred with her. Whatever they said made her shrug and gesture around at all the people, in a way that suggested perhaps some of them were themselves the result of Señor Chupa's dalliances. Señor Chupa grinned, and winked at me. His wife clicked her tongue warningly at him, and he went back to his beer.

"*Bien,*" said Louie's wife, and then took my hands to dance with me. People started clapping in rhythm. I had a terrifying feeling that I was about to become a piñata, spilling not candy, but all the stories I'd been collecting my whole life. I imagined the people looking at a big pile of my miscellaneous sentences all over the floor, then picking them up to suck on. Why not? Eat my words. Swallow me whole.

Then I was spinning like a dreidel, going too fast to think.

"*Uno, dos, tres,*" chanted Señor Chupa's wife, her feet tapping. The band was playing loud. The room was full of people I didn't understand. Señor Chupa was clapping from the corner. His children were all around us. No doubt someone was making fun of me in Spanish, and I, well, I was *dancing*. Señor Chupa's wife was leading, and I was going wherever she wanted to take me. She had her hand in the small of my back, and she pinched me whenever I got it wrong.

"*Gracias,*" I yelled.

"*De nada,*" she said, and spun me until I was too dizzy to stand.

. . .

SEÑOR CHUPA'S TWELVE-YEAR-OLD GRANDSON rode my blister-footed self home at 3:00 A.M. He stood and pedaled his bicycle furiously through the streets of Brooklyn, whistling. The temperature had dropped, and there were four bright stars out. There was a breeze in the trees of McCarren Park. All the lights were green.

Maybe it was me, but it seemed like we were flying.

INNOCENCE, A BROAD

IN WHICH OUR
HEROINE STICKS
WITH WHAT SHE
THINKS SHE
KNOWS . . .

WONDERWOMAN TOOK OFF HER GLASSES AND COVERED HER FACE WITH HER HANDS. "Sorry," she said. "This is completely embarrassing. I like to make a regular meal of my feet. Sometimes I swallow both at once, and I have to just roll, like Ouroboros."

"It's okay," I said. "I'm not gay right now, but give me a second."

I was questioning something that it had never occurred to me to question. I'd never been asked out by a woman before. It seemed that I radiated straightness. Apparently something had changed, though, because here we were, sitting in a white-tableclothed restaurant, and Clara—aka Wonderwoman, for her distinct resemblance to Lynda Carter, my television idol for all of the 1980s, and for her occasional donning of a covetable pair of red stiletto boots—had asked me to have dinner with her. I'd thought the meal was an attempt to hire me away from my temp agency. I was flattered. Something must have shifted in my demeanor. Maybe it was dancing with the Prom Queen, who was admittedly male, but was not dressed like any straight man I'd ever met, or maybe it was hitching up Marie Antoinette's skirt. Most likely it was salsaing with Señor Chupa's wife. My life was getting bigger and I liked it.

Maybe I liked Wonderwoman, too. It wasn't everyone who could drop Ouroboros, an ancient symbol of either eternal renewal or mistakes made ad infinitum, into casual conversation. Ouroboros was depicted as a serpent biting its own tail. I felt very Ouroboros, very often. Maybe this would get my tail out of my teeth.

I'd been cutting half the population out, just because I had this silly idea that I was straight. What if the person who could make me happy happened to be in the half I'd discounted? Besides which, I was in college. Wasn't it accepted policy that you were supposed to have a lesbian period? Maybe I was, in fact, a lesbian, and I just didn't know it. What if Wonderwoman had seen something in me that I couldn't see in myself?

Yes, yes, yes. I knew that you were supposed to know you were gay for as long as you could remember, that it was supposed to be the reason you'd never gotten invited to the prom, that it was supposed to be the explanation for your kickball skills, but I thought maybe I'd been brainwashed into heterosexuality. If I just opened my mind, and informed it that dating women was much less confusing, suddenly there it'd be: a revelation. Girls! It'd be such a relief. I understood women! We liked expressing our emotions, and we liked pretty shoes! We liked to listen to female singer-songwriters, and we liked to read Alice Munro short stories. Surely, these commonalities were enough to build a stable relationship on. There were other things in my life that I'd thought would never appeal to me. Things like sushi, which, given Idaho's inland status, I'd never tried until I moved to New York. I'd been sure that I'd have to choke it down. Instead, I'd decided it was all I ever wanted to eat. I was suddenly sure that sushi could happen again. In a manner of speaking.

I'd had a little bit of experience with girls: a brief affair with Susan Sarandon. I thought that should count.

My dad had introduced us. He was a reader, among other things, most of them more difficult to explain. (For example: "Why does your dad have so many dogs?" "Why does he dress as a sad clown named Scruffy, and dance the shuffle?" "Why doesn't he go off to an office?" "What the hell is this implausible person, this thing you call your father, who is like no other fathers, who, at dusk, goes out with steaming buckets of dog porridge and a ladle, his hundred dogs whining at chain for his attention? What kind of life is this?" And later, in college, "Do you even have a dad? You don't mention him.") His books were bought at secondhand stores, discount aisles, estate sales. He had everything from H. G. Wells to Civil War histories, books on plague, cockroaches, and kayaks, *National Geographics* dating to 1913. A book on Trickster, the most appropriate thing in the collection. My dad was a connoisseur. And crazy, too, but that was ancillary. His shelves were worth climbing.

When I was about eight, I found, in his stash of *Field & Stream,* the *Playboy* section. Susan Sarandon was on the cover. She was wearing glasses. I wore glasses. She was brainy. I wanted to be brainy. She was described as universally beloved (except by the Republicans). I wanted to be universally beloved (whoever the Republicans were). Susan Sarandon was not nude. It was a special on smart, sexy women. The article said that her IQ was as large as her physical appeal. I wanted to be exactly like her. Shortly before my discovery of the *Playboy,* my mom had given me a "you are what you eat" lecture. It'd been in response to my rabid overconsumption of frozen bean burritos, but the message had stuck, and now it rattled around in my head, driving me toward a logical consummation.

I put my tongue out and licked Susan Sarandon, from top to bottom.

Susan Sarandon, in case anyone is wondering, tasted like paper, and alas, I hadn't become her.

I was clearly overdue for another go at girls. I could be a lesbian. I said it to myself. I said it to Wonderwoman.

"What?" she asked.

"I could be a lesbian!" I repeated, joyfully. No more men! No more confusion! No more falling in love with my roommate (unless by roommate, I meant Victoria). No more worries at all! I had a somewhat convoluted notion of what it meant to be gay.

"You have to be *attracted* to women," Wonderwoman said.

"I love women!" And I did. Women were beautiful, compassionate, and nothing I wanted to get naked next to, but why should that matter? So what if I wasn't inherently attracted to women? People said that love was more about the human being's soul than about what the human being looked like. Which was not to say that Wonderwoman looked bad. On the contrary. She was better looking than most of the men I'd gone out with: tall, dark, and handsome. Not equine, which is what handsome often meant when applied to women. Wonderwoman was more like a panther in human form. Not beautiful. Beautiful implied some level of vulnerability, and no matter Wonderwoman's sense of humor, it was pretty clear that she was made of steel. She wasn't vulnerable to kryptonite, either. If she didn't like you, it was pretty obvious that she'd have no problem throwing you into traffic.

I'd met her at my temp job at a publishing company, where she'd loaded me up with free books in the break room, free fruit from the delivery basket, and a free lunch on the day that she'd casually asked me what my girlfriend did.

"I don't have a girlfriend," I'd said.

"How is that possible?" she'd asked.

"Well, I'm not—"

She'd interrupted me. "Listen, would you like to have dinner with me?"

"—not a lesbian. Actually."

I hadn't been trying to be misleading. I hadn't known she was gay until that moment. Wonderwoman didn't fit my, admittedly narrow, picture of what real-world lesbians looked like. My lesbian friends in Boise complained that all lesbians in the West had their hair cut to resemble beavers. They said I could take that any way I wanted to, but that it was always depressing. Wonderwoman was the polar opposite. She wore high heels and tight skirts. She smiled like a very sexy, lipsticked shark.

"This isn't even my style," she said. "I'm just tired of doing it the normal way. It's not like I haven't been set up with every friend of a friend of a friend. I've dated every woman in the tristate area."

Despite her Prada suit and alligator pumps, it seemed that Wonderwoman was a lot like me. More like me than any of the men I'd met. And with Wonderwoman, it had just occurred to me, I'd be freed from the paranoia of pregnancy that took up most of my time, post any naked interaction. A huge bonus.

"Yes!" I announced.

Wonderwoman looked confused.

"Yes, what?"

"Let's go out!"

"This is weird," she said.

"I'm converted!" I said.

"Is this because you're straight, but sick of men? I've made this mistake before."

"I'm opening my mind!" I'd turned into a revivalist minister. I was about to shout "hallelujah" and speak in tongues.

In my defense, I'd gone out with a guy the night before, who had, in a show of support for a certain eighties hair-metal superstar we'd seen walking down the street, suddenly pumped his hands in the air and yelled, "Rock out with your cock out, muthafucka!"

I never wanted to hear anything like that again. Griffin had a story in a similar vein, told him by a girl he'd subsequently decided never, ever to sleep with. This girl, apparently, had even worse luck than I did, because one of her lovers, at the moment of orgasm, had screamed, "Yo, yo, yo, let's get this party started!"

Griffin felt sad for him, considering, as Griffin said, "the party was ending. People were going home. The beer was gone, and the lights were out, and there was this guy, standing on the street, yelling into the darkness, missing his car keys."

I'd felt the same way with my Rock Out guy, except that, thank God, we'd been clothed. He was a refugee from an earlier time, and he felt compelled to mention his genitals to strangers. I was sure that no woman would ever do such a thing.

"Okay," said Wonderwoman, with some definite trepidation. Then she grinned and said, "What the hell. People say I never do anything unpredictable."

She put her manicured hand on the table. I put my scraggly hand on top of hers. And there we were, for a moment. She ran her thumb under my wrist.

"Where do you want to go?" she asked.

"Meow Mix." How could I not? It was the premier lesbian bar in the city, and I'd never had balls enough to go there.

"Meow Mix?" Wonderwoman was grimacing.

"Why not?"

"Because it's trite. We could just go out to dinner," she said.

"Meow Mix." I was fixated. I loved the name. I didn't really notice that Wonderwoman looked worried, or maybe I just didn't care.

I went home and listened to k.d. lang and the Indigo Girls. I read Colette, Jeanette Winterson, and Gertrude Stein. Elise lent me the Adrienne Rich book she'd been given by an ex-boyfriend, who apparently hadn't been reading closely enough. He'd read sexy passages aloud, and she'd just looked at him, wondering why the hell he was referring to his vagina. I suspected he'd been trying to suggest a typical male fantasy.

Prior to Griffin, Elise had had a fairly long-standing relationship with a girl named April. They'd met while working at Williams-Sonoma, where April was using her employee discount to restock her gourmet kitchen with Le Creuset cookware. Somehow, they'd fallen into each other's arms. How did that work? I was uncertain. I was fuzzy enough on how attraction worked with men. When I'd met

Elise, she'd just been finishing up with April, who'd bought a bed-and-breakfast in Pennsylvania. The lesbian period had lent Elise a certain kind of glamorous, try-anything vibe. She was my guru.

The good news was that most of the lesbian reference materials were already in my possession. Maybe, I thought, I was already a lesbian and I didn't even know it. I picked up a few more things. A book of lesbian erotica that shocked the hell out of me. Videos of *Chasing Amy, Bound,* and *The Incredibly True Adventures of Two Girls in Love.* I held a pop-culture lesbian marathon.

I ASKED ZAK FOR POINTERS. His mom was a lesbian. Surely he'd know something. And he did:

"Exactly like everything else," he said. "If you don't find the right person, everything goes wrong."

I wasn't really paying attention. I was giddy on Sappho.

"It'll be fun," I said. "Should I dress femme or dyke?"

"I don't think you're gay," Zak said, taking off his glasses and rubbing his forehead.

"I might be bi," I said. "I'll try anything once."

"That's not fair," he said. "She probably doesn't want to be an experiment."

"Who are you?" I said. "What have you done with Zak?"

"I just think you have enough to deal with, without bringing in a whole new gender."

"Maybe you just don't know that I'm gay." I felt rebellious. Who was Zak to tell me what my sexual orientation was? What did he know? He'd only observed me through forty or fifty dates with men, and countless evenings over the kitchen table. "You don't know me that well," I said, pissily.

He just looked at me.

"I don't know why you think you need to sleep with women. You could sleep with anyone you want to."

"Not anyone."

This hung in the air for slightly longer than either of us wanted it to, and then we went our separate ways. Discomfort. Denial. Discomfort. Denial. I ate Thai food alone, and justified myself to myself. It was not very satisfying. I choked on my chopsticks and ended up spitting Pad Thai across half the restaurant.

THE NEXT NIGHT, DRESSED IN MEN'S TROUSERS AND A SKIMPY WHITE TANK TOP, I made my way to Meow Mix. Wonderwoman was there, looking out of place in her corporate drag. I'd already acquired phrases like "corporate drag." I rejoiced.

The place itself was the kind of place everyone knew, and no one had ever been to. It was small and divey, with a jukebox and a lot of teetery barstools. That night, there was a cover band playing exclusively Smiths and Morrissey songs. The singer was a ringer for Morrissey, albeit female. All the women in the bar seemed to know the words to every song. Particularly, disturbingly, the chorus of "November Spawned a Monster," which involved denying a kiss to an ugly girl.

Meow Mix, and much of its clientele, reminded me of a trucker bar. In the universe that exists in certain flesh films and comic books, all lesbians look like Brigitte Bardot. Sort of blowsy, sleepy, cushion-lipped, big-breasted, and wearing the ubiquitous wife-beater tank top with no brassiere. Also dying to sleep with men, naturally, or at least let them watch, while putting up a little token lesbian kicking, screaming, and arm wrestling. In real life, this was rarely the case.

I had only one friend who fit the myth. Zoë went to NYU with me. She'd been in the same class in which I'd met Zak and Griffin, and had arrived half an hour late on the first day. She'd undulated into the room, a native New Yorker, looking nine thousand times better than any of us. She'd perched her perfect ass at the circular table, taken off her jacket to reveal, yes, the accidentally see-through little boy's tank top, over the best tits anyone had ever seen. She dug into her purse for gloss to lubricate her unbelievably full lips, and said, in her husky, sexy voice,

"Oh my God, guys, am I late? I was at a callback for *RENT*."

Zoë had run the room for the rest of the year, and, indeed, ran most rooms she entered. Now she hosted parties at various clubs. I periodically ran across postcards advertising her hotness to the women of New York. Sometimes I dragged a friend to one of her parties, we halfheartedly drank martinis for an hour or so, felt tragically unhip, and galumphed into the night to hang out at some greasy spoon, eating what amounted to straight Crisco.

But all that was changing. I leaned back against the peeling paint and posters. I hooked my thumbs in my belt loops. Wonderwoman looked skeptical. Other women arrived, and embraced and kissed her. Other women arrived, and did not acknowledge my presence. In the bathroom, someone looked at me with slitted eyes, and said, "She's gonna knock you up, you know."

"I'm sorry?"

"She wants you for your womb. Otherwise, she'd never go out with someone your age. Just FYI." The woman shook her hands dry, and shoved her way out the door. I watched the thick chain around her waist shifting with her hips. A tattoo of Rosie the Riveter, fist upraised, was etched at the base of her spine.

I dried my hands slowly, and departed. She, I thought, was just jealous of my glowing future as a lesbian. Of course Wonderwoman didn't want me for my womb.

On the street, after we'd walked away from Meow Mix, Wonderwoman leaned in.

"So, I'm going to kiss you," she said.

"So do," I said, in what I hoped was a flirtatious tone. I was neurotic, though. Wonderwoman was so confident. It was beyond my power to take the first-kiss initiative. I never did. I spent a lot of time waiting in vain for people to kiss me, applying lipgloss, attempting languid gazes. ("You look sick," one of my prospective kissers had informed me, leaning in with concern. "Do you need to throw up?" I'd puckered my lips and continued the languid gaze. He'd run to get me a wastebasket.) What if I didn't actually know how to kiss? What if all the men I'd kissed had misled me and, really, I was a slobbery mass of eel teeth, a gnashing, dribbling monster-mouth? Historically, my first kisses had been disastrous. It never managed to be magical. Teeth always collided, noses always got smushed, and hands always flailed frantically. Sometimes it'd get better as the kissing went on. Sometimes it would get worse. Since this was my first with a girl, I was having to count it as my first, all over again. This was not a good thing.

The *first* first kiss had been when I was a very uncomfortable sixteen-year-old, spending the summer living with my grandparents and working for the Idaho Shakespeare Festival. I was playing Hermia in an apprentice production of *A Midsummer Night's Dream.* The director had decided that the production needed to be very, very sexy to distract from the fact that we were very, very bad actors. He figured that we were teenagers and that all we were thinking about was sex anyway. This was technically true, but it did not mean that we had any experience. By "we," I mean me. And I, of course, had been cast as the makeout queen of the production. I was costumed in a skintight pencil skirt, some tipsy high heels, and a pointy bra. The director gave me a breathless voice and an oversexed vibe. But I was not oversexed. I was under. Profoundly under.

All of my blocking involved writhing about the stage, crawling on my hands and knees, and wriggling my rump while reciting rhyming couplets. I invented excuses not to kiss in rehearsal (an obscure condition that caused me to need to breathe through my mouth, and to suffocate if smooched) because I'd become convinced that I wouldn't know how to do it. Have my first kiss with the guy playing Lysander? No thank you. He was repellent, a black-clad, Carmex-addicted tech guy who hadn't yet discovered deodorant. I imagined the kiss two million times, and had nightmares of battle cries and clashing tongues. The director got increasingly pissed off.

"You're young! You're horny! You're Hermia!" he barked.

"I might have a stomach bug," I whimpered. My only real acting skills were the ones I'd developed to get out of going to grade school. Maybe I couldn't shed salty tears in an emotional scene, but I *could* turn green on cue. And that vomit? Real! It was very Stanislavski.

"If you don't do it tomorrow, I'll personally slit your throat," the director told me, even as I quivered with fake fever tremors.

Beaten, I went out that night wearing a dress that was essentially a handkerchief. I stood, shivering, by a pay phone in downtown Boise, until a guy named Roger appeared out of the dark, asking me if I was lost.

"Not really," I said, eyeing him silhouetted against the streetlight, a vision of acceptable masculinity.

"Need a ride?"

"Okay."

"How old are you?"

"Eighteen," I lied.

"You look younger," he said, squinting.

"I am," I said accidentally, caught up in the cinematic nature of the conversation.

He laughed, and bought me a soda. He had self-designed tattoos all over his arms. Barbed wire interspersed with peace signs and dolphins. I convinced myself that this was cool. He had a ponytail. To his waist. I convinced myself that long hair on boys was fine with me, even though I was having decidedly unromantic thoughts about how "Roger" and "Rapunzel" began with the same letter. He talked about sweat lodges and peyote. I convinced myself that he was Native American.

"Huh-uh," he said, and then looked at me as though wondering why I'd asked him a question. I convinced myself that he was just trying not to intimidate me with his brilliance.

I gave him directions to my grandma's house, left him on the front lawn, and brought him a cherry Popsicle. Yes. A. Cherry. Popsicle. Devoid of irony. Phallic symbol? What? I sat down beside him and sucked my Popsicle. He chewed his. He lectured briefly on the lack of "real women" in Boise and said that I was the first one he'd met.

"Why?" I asked, fascinated that I'd managed to look like a real woman.

"You're wearing a dress," he said, tossing his Popsicle stick into the bushes. He then turned to me, and tried to turn me on. The first kiss was speedy and baffling. The second was worse. His tongue pried at my lips, which I hadn't known enough to open. Then, in an attempt to duplicate what I'd seen in movies, I opened my mouth wide, Muppet-style, and instantly gagged. Roger withdrew.

"I'm sorry," he said. "I just had to kiss you. You're, like, seriously hot."

"It's fine," I said, and then humiliated myself further by saying, "Could you just hold me for a moment?" This had been a line on a soap opera, and I knew very well that it didn't apply to kissing. It only applied to sex. Nevertheless, out it came, and so one of Roger's hands slithered up my dress

"You've done this before, right?" Roger said, and then buried his face in my breasts.

"Duh," I lied, trying to sound jaded and experienced, despite the taste of chemical cherry mixed with Roger's cigarette breath. Despite my grandparents' front lawn. "Roger? What's your last name?"

The answer was muffled by my dress getting caught on my ears as it went over my head. My grandparents' front lawn faced a busy street, and cars periodically drove up the hill, shining their lights all over us. We were essentially reclining on a raked stage, but were we performing *Romeo and Juliet* or *Measure for Measure*? I was lost.

"Don't you want to know *my* last name?" I said, with the pitiful optimism of the teenage girl, who, from the outside, looks like a grown woman, and on the inside is about six.

"All I know is that I really, *really* like you," Roger said, a look of the utmost sincerity on his face. I melted. He liked me, he really liked me! A boy! A twenty-six-year-old boy, in fact! I'd looked at his license while he'd been peeing in my grandparents' hedge. I sat up, eager to get him to document exactly what he found appealing, so that I could relay it to my girlfriends.

"I'm getting blue balls, baby," Roger continued, very tenderly.

"You don't even know me," I said, blushing furiously. What were blue balls? No boy had ever seen me naked before. No boy had ever called me "baby" before. I sucked in my stomach and pressed my knees together.

"Of course I do," he said, reassuringly stroking my cheek. "You're the pretty girl I met in the parking lot."

He thought I was pretty! The rapture!

And so, with a sensation like a cross between splinters and water balloons, I allowed Roger to divest me of my hymen. At least—I consoled myself for the balance of the night, after Roger referred to me as Jennifer—I now knew how to kiss. No matter that I'd accidentally lost my virginity, too. It was sometimes necessary to make certain sacrifices in order to get the things you needed.

The next day I bounced into rehearsal and jumped several lines in order to launch myself onto Lysander's lips. I sucked the air from his lungs. I whirled my tongue like a lawn mower blade. I grabbed his thigh. I stroked his chest. I put all my new moves to good use, and then pulled back, pleased with myself. Lysander gasped. The director gaped. I grinned.

Ha! I'd shown everyone exactly how experienced I was in the Art of Kissing. I was now officially ready for my title. French Kisser Extraordinaire. The Sultana of Smooch. I shook out my hair, and trotted gaily to my place at the edge of the stage.

"Wasn't that a little extreme?" the director hissed.

"I thought it was appropriate," I said, self-assuredly. "Hermia is very passionate!"

"I only meant a stage kiss," the director sputtered. "As in, fake!"

And then, he dashed off to minister to Lysander, who was turning blue.

Asthma attack. Severe asthma attack involving the summoning of paramedics. Lysander pointed at me in mute accusation as he was trundled away, a little mask on his face.

I had almost kissed him to death.

Kissing had retained a scary aura for me. Until now.

WONDERWOMAN HELD MY FACE IN HER HANDS AND KISSED ME, in the middle of the street. Her lips were big, soft, and warm. There was no stubble. She didn't drool like many of the men I'd kissed, who seemed to have been hybridized to bull mastiffs. And she didn't grab for an inhaler.

"So?" she said. "Give me a review."

"Who taught you to kiss?" I said.

"Practice," she said. "It's one of those things it's good to be good at. Come here, and I'll teach you a few more."

We went out a few more times, each time fantastic. We ate cupcakes at the Magnolia Bakery. We went shopping together and she advised me in dressing rooms. We danced in her living room to Crowded House. We did the *New York Times* crossword together one morning at brunch. Never mind that we hadn't wakened together, and were meeting in a manner much more friend than lover. I was enamored. And so what if I was enamored in a largely platonic kind of way? Maybe this was what lesbian relationships were really like. Maybe this would be another one of those things I'd missed out on for no good reason. Maybe we'd soon go out shopping for one of those "best friends forever" necklaces where each of you wears half of the heart.

"So, how do you feel about kids?" asked Wonderwoman, casually one night, over the top of her wineglass.

"Why?" I said. I felt too young to feel anything but fear about the topic of kids. "You don't have any, do you? I mean, I guess you wouldn't."

She arched an eyebrow.

"Lesbians can have kids, you know. I was just wondering what you thought."

"I don't want them."

"Really? I wouldn't have thought that."

I was strangely flattered. Did she mean that I seemed like I'd be a good parent? Which meant that I was a good person. Which meant that even now, she was falling in love with me. Never mind that I continued to feel vague on any real attraction. I still thought it might appear. I hoped it would.

I was feeling, however, a warped nostalgia for beard burn. I'd never noticed before how soft women's skin was. I'd always scoffed internally when men had said things about it, but now I realized that they weren't kidding. When I'd been working for that same Shakespeare festival, that same summer, there'd been a light board operator, about twenty-three, rail-skinny with long, scraggly blond hair and a bad attitude. He'd pulled me behind the light booth, reached out a hand to stroke my cheek, and said, with creepy lasciviousness, "It's like silk."

Shortly thereafter, he'd asked me if I knew why one of his biceps was so much more muscular than the other one. I had no idea. "Because I jerk off with that one," he'd whispered, and I'd run away in my corset and high heels, feeling dumb.

I was feeling dumb again. I was feeling like I was missing something vital to the conversation.

"Do *you* want to have kids?" I asked Wonderwoman, somewhat against my better judgment. The Tattooed Girl was strutting triumphantly across my field of vision, her Rosie the Riveter tattoo pumping its fist in the air and saying something about "Yo, yo, yo, let's get this party started!"

"Well, I'm on kind of a tight schedule," she said. "Career-wise."

Wonderwoman was thirty-five. I'd snuck her driver's license out of her purse when she was in the bathroom one night. I could feel my youthful womb hysterically rattling around like a maraca. There it was in my throat, then whacking against my liver. This thing, which to this point had only caused me cramps and discontent, had a purpose. Just like the breasts. Fertility. Something I didn't particularly want to think about.

"What do you mean?" I said, though I suspected I knew.

"Okay. Hear me out. I want to have a baby, but I don't have nine months to spare. So I was thinking that you could, well, I mean, we could—"

The familiar stomach drop. The uterus, flinging itself into my rib cage. I completely understood why, at the turn of the century, people had thought that feminine insanity was caused by the uterus detaching and floating unhinged. Had I been able to simply hand her my womb, I would have. I wasn't planning to use it.

I could feel my lesbian solution to birth control dribbling away. Back to the world of panicky trips to drugstores, of waiting for pink lines to appear, of dreading and praying and peeing onto test strips. Back to boys.

"I don't want to have a baby, and it takes more than nine months, anyway," I said. "It takes the rest of your life."

"I didn't mean to scare you," said Wonderwoman. "More wine?"

I had a sudden image of myself, reclining drunk and bleary on a mattress somewhere, while a turkey baster squirted something viscous in my direction.

"I have to go," I said, putting down my glass.

"Shit. Ouroboros syndrome. Pretend we never had this conversation."

"Am I only a womb?" Granted, this was melodramatic. I was twenty-one. There was only so much maturity in me, and, while it was enough to conduct a semiadult relationship (sort of, anyway), it was not enough to have anyone's baby. Suddenly, I wanted to clamp my hands over my crotch and hop in urgent circles, like a four-year-old who had to pee. That was all my nether regions were for! Not birth. Never. I wasn't going to show my cervix to anyone's video camera, and I wasn't planning to ever talk about how far I was dilated. I didn't want to know that I could stretch to extrude a cantaloupe. I didn't want to think about it. Not one bit.

"No, no, you're misunderstanding. You're more than a womb to me."

That was when the Bee Gees appeared, and did the hustle, right there, right in Wonderwoman's living room.

You're more than a womb! More than a woooo-ooomb to me!

"Why won't you look at me?" Wonderwoman put her hand on my chin, and turned my face in her direction. I looked at her for a moment, and she was beautiful and successful, and I got along with her better than I'd gotten along with any of the boys I'd been out with, and then Paul Anka arrived with a Casio keyboard under his arm, and began a command performance of "(You're) Having My Baby."

One of the serious disadvantages to having been born in the late seventies was the fact that whenever anything stressed me out, a mangled part of my brain would embark on a clock radio mélange of nightmarish soft rock.

"I'm sorry," I said. "I can't."

"You're so young. It wouldn't really affect you," said Wonder woman. "I make enough that you could just stay home and write while you're pregnant. It'd be perfect."

That wasn't really what I heard. What I heard was Sheena Easton trilling "Morning Train," a peppy song all about staying at home and doing nothing but eating bonbons while your man goes to work to support you.

What I saw was Wonderwoman, conquering the world, wearing a leopard print power suit and matching spike heels. What I saw was myself, conquering nothing, wearing a tattered minitoga, pabulum on my shoulder, pained expression on my face, and bundle of joy clutched like a bomb against my ridiculously swollen breasts. My mom had been an A cup until she'd gotten pregnant with me and had become a D. They'd never really gone down. The photos showed her pregnant like a torpedo. I was built like my mom. It'd be the same damn thing. Too young, too young, too young. And too selfish, too.

"I'm sorry. I have to go." And, like an asshole, I ran.

I thought the confusion between us was too large for anything to proceed. Maybe that wasn't true. Maybe I was just a coward. This was very possible. We should have been friends to start with. Now, though, I had the sense that she'd just been marketing the best parts of herself in order to gain access to my childbearing capabilities. I didn't stop to think that we were all marketing the best parts of ourselves, all the time. Anything real would have to contain both the best and the worst. Considering I'd never had a relationship I'd considered to be worth pursuing for more than a few months, I had no idea what that would be like. Maybe the Bee Gees would appear every night. Maybe I'd just have to get used to it. But for now, I was on the train, and I was going home to my tortured nonlove affair with Zak, who said, "I told you."

"It wasn't that she was a girl, it was that she wanted me to have a baby."

"You're. Not. Gay. Accept it, and move on."

"It was only about the baby," I said.

"You don't have a baby," said Zak, changing tacks. "He died this afternoon in a car accident."

But I was not in the mood to play *Who's Afraid of Virginia Woolf?* Who was afraid of Miss Woolf? Me. I had a feeling that a long and happy affair with someone like Vita Sackville-West was not necessarily in my cards, and it made me bitter.

"I'm burning your baby?" said Zak. I was not in the mood to play *Hedda Gabler*, either. Hedda was a bitch.

"I didn't want it anyway!" I said, and crawled into my hut, like the wretchedly immature creature I was.

A COUPLE WEEKS LATER, MY FRIEND THE ACTRESS CAME TO TOWN. She was an onstage goddess, one of the most stunningly talented people I'd ever met. She lived, to her frustration, in L.A., where she was making a reasonable if unsatisfying living doing film, television, and the occasional worthwhile theater assignment. She came to New York intermittently, because L.A. was not the town for a woman like her—wild, dreadlocked, and unapologetically exuberant.

I owed the Actress. Just prior to the beginning of my Yes Year, she'd saved me from Martyrman. I'd met both of them at Sundance, and the fact that I'd immediately felt compelled to start lying to her about whether or not I was sleeping with him ought to have told me something. I'd still been a teenager, though, just out of high school, and he'd been tenacious. For over a year, we'd had a long-distance thing, him calling me every week or so and periodically coming from L.A. to visit me, while I dated all of NYU and bemoaned him to my roommates, too ball-less to break it off. One day, the Actress had called me up.

"Diiiiiiiiiiiiiiiiiiiivaaaaaaaaaaa! Diva! I know you don't care if I sleep with Martyrman, right? I'm sick of looking for anything else in this stupid size-two town."

"Please," I'd said. "Take him! Absolutely! Need his number?"

"Does that mean he's bad in bed?" The Actress sounded suspicious.

"Not all that bad. Not all that good." I had to be honest. She was a friend.

"Oh well, screw it, I'm desperate."

She'd called me a couple of days later, and said, "Here's the good news: It reminded me that I'm tired of men. I'm trying girls again."

He, on the other hand, had said nothing about it. I'd therefore felt at least tangentially justified later that month when I'd broken up with him at a bed-and-breakfast in Bucks County, Pennsylvania, the useless folk-art capital of the universe. I'd happened upon him in the bathroom, putting talcum powder on his thighs, and that had been the end of whatever attraction I'd had left. Lubricated by an entire bottle of the bed-and-breakfast's homemade apricot brandy, I'd swiftly ended things, using his liaison with the Actress as an excuse. Yes, this was beyond shallow, and yes, I felt guilty about it. I'd behaved rottenly, but then, so had he. He'd informed me, over and over, that I reminded him of his ex-wife, an Oscar-winning actress who'd left him for a grip. She, though brilliant, was fifty, and I was vain. After we'd broken up, he'd refused to take me back to New York, saying that (a) he just wanted to spend the rest of our romantic weekend together, and (b) he'd already paid for the B&B.

I'd been too broke to escape by train, and so we'd ended up spending three torturous nights together on a feather bed, trapped by out-of-season rains, the only people within a hundred miles who weren't in love. We'd hunched bitterly over the frilly breakfast table, flinging scones like hockey pucks. By the time we'd finally made it back to the city, I'd hated us both so much that I'd puked for four days. When Martyrman had gotten back to L.A., he'd called the Actress to tell her that she was the devil incarnate.

"Diva, you owe me something better," she'd said, when she'd called me to report.

She came to New York, and we went out to dinner. I gave her a running monologue of my successes and disasters, and she said, "Well, chick, someone ought to purge you of that last thing. I promise, I won't ask you to have my baby."

While I'd thought I was done with my Sapphic phase, the Actress was someone I was crazy about. It seemed like a great idea to have a date with someone I already actually enjoyed. And to sleep with someone who fell into that category? It'd be the first time in a long time.

The Actress arrived at my apartment, the night of our rendezvous, with a full face of makeup. Foundation. Lipstick. All the various pencils and creams and paints that make a woman look like a woman from fifty paces, and like a mannequin at two. It was stage makeup. But what play were we doing? I was stunned. The Actress was a beautiful woman. Not conventional, but that was why I liked her. Why was she painting herself for me? I loved her already.

I suddenly felt like every man I'd ever hated for judging my looks. Except that I wasn't judging hers. She just thought I might, and was preempting it with eyeliner. It occurred to me that maybe I'd been wrong a few times. Maybe guys hadn't even noticed the things that I was obsessing over. Maybe they liked me because they liked me. Maybe Great Lash, or lack thereof, wasn't the deal breaker I'd thought it was.

I looked at the Actress. I was afraid to touch her face. I wondered if men had felt this way about me. I'd spent hours on my makeup on occasion. What girl didn't? We spent all our time trying to find someone who wanted to wake up next to us every morning, and every night we painted ourselves to look as much like someone else as possible.

Now that the Actress was standing in front of me, I didn't know what to do. I couldn't kiss her without kissing her lipstick. I thought she was sexy because she was raucous and crazy, because when she laughed the whole room shook, because she was hilarious and loud and irreverent, not because she was perfect.

I loved her because she was so entirely human. It sounded stupid, but this was a revelation for me. I'd tried to be perfect as much as every other girl in the world. I'd stood in other people's bathrooms, peering into mirrors, poking at my face, poofing out my lips, sucking in my stomach, pushing up my breasts, razoring my legs until they were plastic-smooth. Wielding tweezers like surgical instruments.

When I was a kid, my mom had regularly announced that we were "not far descended from the apes." My first memory of her involved a waxed upper lip, and a shriek of pain as she pulled the wax off. I'd wondered what the hell she was suffering for. Monkeys were cool. Not so, as I got older. I wanted to be not a monkey, but a mole rat. Pink and hairless. I knew people like this. People who had no body hair at all, or silken blonde legs and arms. I, on the other hand, was apprehended by my mother while shaving my entire body at the age of twelve. I'd lathered my upper lip, and taken her leg razor to it, thinking I had the perfect solution to the fact that, in my seventh-grade PE class, a boy had told me I had a mustache. And really, I didn't. Neither did my mom. Paranoia was part of our personality.

Despite the fact that my postfeminist brain had been raised on Simone de Beauvoir, Camille Paglia, and Erica Jong, I'd still done a hell of a lot to make myself into whatever I thought a male ideal was. It had taken a lot of work. And the work really never ended. Sometimes I felt like one of those toys where you turned a crank and long spaghetti strands of clay grew furiously from colanderlike heads. Part of the appeal was that those strands could be plucked, squished, and put back in the jar to use again. Not so, hair. The stubble advanced like a lame militia crossing hard terrain: slowly, but surely. I didn't want to imagine my insides as one big ball of hair, like a two-story sphere of string. I didn't want to be a roadside attraction. I wanted, albeit secretly, to be a Barbie doll.

Yet, here we were. We were so not Mattel plastic. The Actress and I stood in Vic's bedroom, totally imperfect. And that was the point. That was what was great about it. Here we stood together, and love was possible anyway, despite everything that was wrong with us. It was a minor miracle. Maybe it was a major one.

We were human. We were a mess. And we were kissing. It's always weird to kiss a friend for the first time, and this was no exception. It was weirder still because she was a woman. But we got through it. And even though it didn't seem that I was really attracted to girls, I could accept that love was larger than that. I could, at least, sleep with someone I cared about, even if she did happen to be female. I could care about her more, because of it.

We got our clothes off, and we left the bright lights on. Here we were, together against all those guys we'd fucked in the dark, against all those times we'd hidden our flaws and failures, because we thought we wouldn't be loved if we let them show. We left the lights on, and we looked at each other, and we made love.

A COUPLE OF HOURS LATER I PUT ON A PAIR OF OVERALLS without a top and meandered into the kitchen. Zak was there, standing under the glare of the fluorescents, staring vacantly into the fridge.

"Hey," he said, without turning around.

"Hey," I said.

"Hey," said the Actress, in her big, booming voice, emerging from the bedroom, wrapped in a towel.

"Oh God, who are *you*?" Zak flipped around. He'd been expecting only me. Instead, I was wearing lesbianic overalls and hanging out with a half-naked woman.

"You must be the famous Zak," the Actress said. "I've heard all about you. I'm going to go and get fried rice. Want some?"

"Sure," said Zak, looking from me to her and back again.

When the Actress got back, the three of us stayed up half the night, laughing hard together at the kitchen table. Even though I knew the Actress and I weren't going to conduct some wild love affair, it was nice to know that we still enjoyed the hell out of each other, and that after our clothes went back on, we were still friends. It wasn't very often that that happened.

"So. You don't do things halfway," Zak said when she was gone.

"I'm not gay," I said, sadly. "There are all these wonderful women out there, and I can't have any of them."

"Oh well. More girls for me," Zak told me, and patted my back. "I didn't need you as my competition. Life is hard enough."

We spoke for a while at maximum volume about Sartre and existential loneliness, and then I crawled into my hut and Zak followed me. Eventually we passed out, tangled up. We did this on a somewhat regular basis, post–deep conversation. We always woke, hours later, our limbs pins and needles, our arms trapped beneath each other, sleepily murderous. Whichever of us was in the wrong bed would stagger across the kitchen and into their hut or bedroom, respectively. This night was the same. Chaste as usual. Damn it. Or not damn it. Who could tell? Zak and I getting together could have been nightmarish.

"I love you, you know," I called, across the kitchen.

"You, too," Zak said, but I couldn't tell if he was just talking in his sleep.

'SCUSE ME, WHILE
I KISS THIS GUY

IN WHICH
OUR HEROINE
MEETS JIMI
HENDRIX . . .

MY MOM CALLED ONE MORNING IN SEPTEMBER TO INFORM ME THAT SHE HAD A NEW PLAN. "I'm sending your father to sea," she said. "If I can get him on a boat, things'll improve."

My parents hadn't lived together for years, but they were still married, and my mother hadn't had any new relationships since their split. My dad was brilliant and lunatic, and hard as hell to get over. There was no way she'd ever get him on a boat, not if he didn't want to float away, but it was a nice idea.

He'd apparently gotten worse in the months since I'd last seen him, planting a forest's worth of pennies in his backyard, so that he'd "have something to look forward to," and stringing his trees with bubblegum so that in the winter they looked like they were blooming with bright blue cocoons. The house I'd grown up in—according to my mom, who'd visited—was bedecked with shrines, and there was a tree growing into the living room.

The last time my dad and I had talked, he'd called me because he'd heard that I was dating Donatello. He wanted to inform me that he knew more about the world than I did, and though he was "not racist," he wanted me to know that black people were "not like you and me."

"Thank God," I'd responded, uncharitably. I was out of compassion. My classmates bonded over the irrationality of their stewards, telling me their parents were crazy, by which they meant that their parents wouldn't buy them a car. I kept my mouth shut. My dad was crazy in a very uncool way. He wouldn't acknowledge his mental illness, and his years of denial had tapped my reserves of empathy. We'd never gotten along very well to begin with, and even though part of me wanted him to be the rational person he'd never been, the rest was resigned to living with our stilted, gnarled relationship, one that caused him to yell unjustifiable parental maxims periodically, and me to inform him that I was now an adult and could do whatever I damn well pleased. Mostly, though, we just didn't speak.

On the same call, he'd tried to institute a long-distance curfew, something I'd never had, even when I'd lived at home. My dad, from what had become his survivalist encampment in Idaho, thought he had a mystical power over New York.

"You're three thousand miles away," I'd informed him. "You won't know if I come home at night or not. I could stay out forever, if I wanted to. And maybe I will."

He'd been to New York once, in the early sixties, when he'd been in the Navy. He'd ridden up and down on the subway all night, from the Bronx to the Battery, and never left the train. "I got the experience plenty," he'd said. "I got the deal. It's full of lazy homeless people and psychos. You don't need to go to New York. You're a small-town girl."

I'd gone, of course. Now, a year and a half in, I wasn't just living in New York, I *was* New York. Even more so, since I'd started my Yes Year. Everyone I saw, on every street corner, on every subway, had become someone I could love. I'd fallen hard for eight million people.

Like all the other citizens who'd come from nowhere to this, the great somewhere, I felt like I'd finally found home. I could relax into the hum of the trains under the asphalt, the steam rising from the manholes, the goth clubs downtown and the *clip-clop* of the horse-drawn carriages in Central Park. Every day, I wadded up and lay aside more of what I'd really come from: a crazy father who raised sled dogs in the desert, a lot of sorrow I wanted to forget.

In my experience, the mentally ill were like black holes, into which you could pour everything you had, only to find that they'd been off apprehending aliens in the desert of their dreams and hadn't been listening to a word you'd said. I was paralyzed with guilt over my dad, and helpless to help him. I had a nightmare that someday he'd hop a train (he'd been known to do things like that, though now he hardly left his house) and appear on my doorstep, demanding care, demanding housing and feeding and attention. In my brain, he was like a character out of Beckett, popping his head occasionally from under a garbage can lid, calling for something muddled and humiliating. I loved him, but I couldn't save him. I knew that much. I tried not to think about it. Every time I saw a homeless person, I thought of my dad, then cast the thought from my mind, ground it into the sidewalk like a cigarette, and walked quickly away, resisting the temptation to look back. Whatever was following me would just have to stay in Hades. I drank from Lethe every other day, and it never had the desired effect.

AFTER I GOT OFF THE PHONE WITH MY MOM, I RAN THROUGH ASTOR PLACE, late for class as usual, and tripped over a guy sitting on the sidewalk. My first instinct was fury. Didn't he know you weren't supposed to sit on the sidewalk? Then I felt guilty. I'd kicked him. Worse than that, I'd fallen on top of him, and all his belongings. How would I feel if I was camped out and someone bitchy fell from the sky on top of me? I set about my fastest apology, not making eye contact.

Maybe I could eradicate my guilt and still make it to the screening of *Five Easy Pieces* I was supposed to be at in three minutes. The class was focusing on 1970s cinema, and I was over it. We'd watched *Shampoo* the week before. The week before that, it had been *The Stuntman*. There was nothing wrong with these movies. They were good movies. There was nothing wrong with the class, either, other than that it was taught by a man who'd come of age in the seventies, wishing himself wilder than he was. Everything we watched was about the journeys of lost men, who tore the clothes off the paper dolls they screwed and didn't even care enough to dress them again before going out to stare across a forbidding landscape, waiting for a truck or a train to take them away. I was tired of lost men.

I had just opened my mouth to say my impersonal "sorry," when the guy I'd tripped over spoke to me.

"Shit. You're beautiful," he said.

"Thanks," I said, smiled politely, and pushed myself up from the sidewalk.

"No shit," he said. "I like your eyes. I like your hips. I like the whole thing. I could marry someone like you." He looked up at me, wide-eyed. I didn't look away in time to save myself from caring. He had black curls. He had a dirty face. He had fatigues. And then, eye contact. I'd been feeling fragile after talking to my mom, and so I'd been pretending that he wasn't really a person. Now I was screwed.

I didn't have much money. Not enough to make a difference. He wasn't like a child in Ethiopia, not someone I could adopt as my own, sending my four dollars a month and buying myself a peaceful existence at the same time. He was in front of me, living in New York like me, and I didn't have anything more than five bucks and my afternoon. Well. So much for *Five Easy Pieces*, Jack Nicholson, movie vagrants, the entirety of the 1970s.

"Wanna come get something to eat?" I knelt down, and put my hand on his shoulder. I watched myself do it. I knew I shouldn't, knew that I'd end up miserable, because that's the way these things always went, and I did it anyway.

"I'm good." He put his head down.

"Well, *I'm* hungry," I said. He wasn't much older than me. Gutter punk. That's what Vic would've said. And maybe so. Maybe he was just holding out for something to be given to him, like a kid waiting for Santa Claus. But I was a shitty Santa Claus, and I didn't know many people better than me. It wasn't a good living, begging. He wasn't even begging. He was just living on the street, and being tripped over.

"Come on. I owe you. If I hadn't fallen on you, I would've fallen on my face," I said, knowing, even as I said it, that the same was true of lots of things about my life. People had helped me, maybe not in the ways I would have liked them to, but still. I wouldn't have been where I was without support from plenty of places.

He looked up again. His skin was dark. He was handsome. He was my age.

"Correct," he said, smiling to reveal a missing tooth. "You don't wanna look like me."

The remaining teeth were white and suspiciously straight. Braces. He was someone's son, and I was someone's daughter, and I thought that if I could save him a little bit, the saving would transfer to my life, too.

THE FIRST BOY I EVER REALLY FELL IN LOVE WITH WAS A HITCH-HIKER. I was fifteen or sixteen. He was nineteen. He had a knapsack that contained three pairs of socks, a toothbrush, and Henry Miller's *Tropic of Cancer*. The Hitchhiker was skinny, sexily ragged, and a perfect rendition of the beatnik boy from out of town we'd all been waiting for. We didn't want to bone him. We wanted to *be* him.

We were girls, but we wanted to be train-hopping hobo drunkards. Not that I'd ever hopped a train. Or carried my belongings in a bandanna tied to a stick. Or done anything more than clean up the Boone's Farm Strawberry Hill vomit of my high school compatriots. I'd only gotten halfway through *On the Road* before I'd become bored. I'd dog-eared it for status, underlined a few random passages, and carried it in my book bag, pretending I'd read it all. This was not that hard to do, considering it seemed to be the same damned story from beginning to end. The Hitchhiker was much more interesting than Kerouac. He had wild brown Botticellian curls and no ability to protect himself from the elements. He had a tender, slender build. He looked as though he needed feeding. My girlfriends and I met him at the only all-ages club in Boise and immediately became overwhelmed with lust. We liked to pretend we were older and sexier than we were. At sixteen, some of us did, in fact, look like adults. Some of us, me specifically, had just gotten possession of breasts and hadn't learned how to use them yet.

The Hitchhiker needed a place to stay. He did not seem to be trying to sleep with any of us. I may have been wrong about that, considering that I had been, for years, the token titless tagalong. Given that the breasts had only recently materialized, I was still being left out of the adult dealings of my then-best friend, a girl who'd had, from sixth grade on, an unfair C cup. This was the friend that the Hitchhiker was most interested in. She looked twenty-five. I looked nine, or at least I did next to her. I sat at the edge of the room, nibbling potato chips and wishing that someday a Hitchhiker would be interested in me.

My girlfriends and I took him to my house out in the middle of nowhere, because it was a given that my parents were the only ones who weren't paying attention. My dad, however, suddenly had a notion of parental responsibility, for the first time in years, and decreed that the Hitchhiker could sleep over only if he slept outside on the trampoline in the rain. Despite the fact that my dad was, even then, riding a unicycle over a canyon of crazy, he disliked people he thought were lost. We got around the decree by staying up all night in the living room watching *Bill and Ted's Excellent Adventure* and reading books of Allen Ginsberg's poetry out loud. My dad crouched at the top of the stairs until dawn, armed to the teeth, a vigilante in his own house.

Later, the Hitchhiker stuck out his thumb and went home to Seattle, and he and I started exchanging letters, his typed on an ancient Underwood. They were my first adult letters, and the feeling of opening his crumpled envelopes to find his equally crumpled lines was so brilliantly romantic that I fell head over heels. I tossed aside the fact that he'd given his copy of *Tropic of Cancer* not to me, but to my best friend. I knew that I didn't have anything to compete with but my brain, and so I labored over my responses, drafting and re-drafting, obsessing over ink and paper color.

For the next six months, I devoured his articulate, poetry-strewn missives, until one day I got one from a different address. He told me he was in a mental hospital, having become severely depressed and agoraphobic after being mugged at knifepoint. I wrote back to him, and got another letter, saying that he was too afraid to leave his bedroom. This guy—who'd represented total freedom to me—was now housebound. Though I continued to think of him every moment, I never wrote to him again. I didn't know what to send. A get-well-soon note? There was, to my mind, no getting well. He sent me one last letter, wondering when he'd feel better, wondering what was wrong with him, and then I heard that he'd attempted suicide. I never heard from him again. I went into silent, guilty mourning for the things I'd imagined him to be.

Now, whenever I saw a young guy sitting on the street, I thought of the Hitchhiker, and usually, I turned my face away. I didn't give them money; nothing I had could help them. On this day, though, this guy looking up at me, his eyes so clear and rational, the rest of him so lost, something changed inside me. Maybe it had to do with love. I'd been looking and finding it everywhere, though it was never quite the romantic ideal. That didn't mean I couldn't give some out. I was privileged, really, even though I was broke and working my way through school. Even though I bounced checks on a regular basis. Even though I never slept. Two hours a night was better than the nothing he was probably getting. I was still loved by people all over the place, and I was lucky.

I held out my hand to the homeless man. I invited him to come and have a falafel with me. Yes, I was asking him out, but he'd spoken to me first, and I decided that counted.

"What's your name?" I asked him.

"James."

"Maria. Nice to meet you."

"I'm only going with you because I've got nothing to do for an hour."

"That's fine."

"I'm a busy person."

"We'll get a sandwich, and then you can go do whatever you want."

"I'm gonna let you in on a secret," he said. "I have to play a gig, but we're trying to keep the press from jumping on it."

That was the end of my fantasy that he was just sitting on the street because of bad luck in employment or, at worst, laziness. Vic had a particular dislike of young people with Starbucks grande begging cups and expensive tattoos. There was, apparently, a large population of hipster homeless in New Orleans, where she spent most of her summers, and they pissed her off. She had a menial job, she said, why couldn't they? They were able-bodied. They were young. Come on, she said. Begging was easier than working, and maybe that was true, in warm weather, in a city where margaritas could be gotten to-go.

That wasn't really true in New York City. Giuliani had cracked down on the homeless shortly before I'd moved there, and the indigent had mostly been routed to the outer boroughs as part of a "personal responsibility" campaign. The prevailing attitude toward the homeless during my time there was contempt. Legitimate living in New York was so hard that people became furious when someone seemed to be getting by without doing their part. The city had become pretty unkind in that way, though certainly there were plenty who opposed Giuliani's attitude.

Before I'd moved to New York, it hadn't really occurred to me to be contemptuous of homeless people. I hadn't seen all that many, for one thing, and the ones I'd seen had so clearly had something wrong with them, that I felt much more like I wanted to give them sandwiches than like I wanted to kick them. For all the glories of New York City, for all the things it had done to open my heart, to make me stronger and more willing, living there had also made me harder than I had been when I'd arrived. My first week in New York, a woman with a baby had asked me for money and I'd given her everything I had. Maybe I'd been a sucker. Certainly, lots of people had told me so, and I'd been embarrassed and changed my ways. Now I had much more of a tendency to suspect homeless people of being scam artists. I'd become someone who practiced selective deafness. I wouldn't have talked to this guy, for all my openness, for all my professed love for the city, if I hadn't tripped over him.

"Where's your gig?"

"Let's just say you've heard of me."

But he wouldn't tell me who he thought he was. He wanted me to guess and was definitely offended that I didn't recognize him, although he eventually proclaimed it to be a relief.

"Give you a hint," he said, and then he sang the first few bars of something unmistakable. *'Scuse me, while I kiss the sky. . .*

"Really?" I said. Hendrix, huh? I don't know what I'd hoped for. Hard luck, maybe. Just hard luck. But hard luck had side effects.

"Well, fuck, I try to keep a low profile," he said, "but when a bird like you walks by, you know, you gotta say something."

"Thanks," I said.

"I mean, how do you ignore it, when someone might be exactly what you were always waiting for?"

That pretty much said it all. I was once again ashamed of myself. My default was to think I knew everything about everything. The bottom line was that the world was still entirely surprising. That, of course, was what was wonderful about it. You could have a conversation with a homeless man sitting on a street corner in New York City, and it could change your life. For the better, I should clarify. The thought that a street corner prophet could teach me something vital was, despite my own unprivileged upbringing, somewhat foreign. It was funny. All my life had been spent reading about revelations, and a revelation was what I'd set out to have. I'd been going for a more acceptable revelation, that of falling in love. The revelations I was experiencing as a result of my Yes Year were not necessarily romantic ones, but they were preparing me nonetheless to live a better life. Every person that was wrong for me gave me a little more of the story of what a human being could be.

The Rockstar put on a pair of sunglasses, minus one lens. He stuck out his arm. I took it. We walked down the street together, and the man who thought he was Jimi Hendrix let me sing backup. Rather, he let me sing the guitar part. Which I didn't know. I just made a miscellany of high-pitched noises, and he thumped me on the back and grinned, and told me I'd learn.

MAMOUN'S FALAFEL SHOP WAS IN THE WEST VILLAGE. I'd practically lived there my first year at NYU. It was a tiny little hole in the wall, with drippy falafels and friendly employees. We cut through Washington Square Park to get there.

It was still hot out, and the park was full of everything the park was always full of: kids with backpacks, breakdancers with boomboxes and impervious skulls, waddling pigeons and the old men and women who fed them entire loaves of bread. Also the slew of dudes crouched down on the sides of the paths, whispering, "Smoke, smoke, weed, weed . . ." just in case you wanted to buy. According to my friends who'd fallen for it, the product was pretty much entirely oregano. Today, walking with the Rockstar, who was humming a disparate and hyper tune as we walked, I could see the usual coterie of weed guys looking at me with new eyes.

One of them popped his head up as we passed, and said, "What the fuck, girl?"

"I know," I said, trying to preempt him. "I know."

Every time I'd walked through the park, since I'd moved to New York, this guy had given me the same offer as I passed him, shaking my head no to the dime bags, "Smoke, smoke, weed, weed, ME?"

The only reason I hadn't ended up going out with him since my yessing had begun was that I'd carefully avoided the park. Otherwise, I'd have had to say yes. I did feel that exceptions might be made for those who'd potentially get me arrested. Washington Square Park also boasted a revolving circuit of New York's Finest, who let the park drug dealers alone, unless they caught them selling to NYU students. Hence the oregano. They figured most of us didn't know the difference, and they were right.

"You get down with him, but not me?" asked the drug dealer.

The Rockstar stared at him for a moment. "You're a loser," he said. "You think a girl like this would go out with you?"

The drug dealer stood up, aggravated. "You seen *you* lately, motherfucker?"

I had to forcibly persuade the Rockstar to come with me.

"Man," he said, definitely reluctant to leave the confrontation. "I just want some peace and quiet. The press, man, they're out of control. Leave a guy alone. Fuckers. I just want to walk with a girl somewhere, and they're all up on me."

He flipped the dealer off as we walked away. Brilliant move. The drug dealer, though, didn't want to attract the cops, and so he pursued us a few steps, bellowing, and then sat back down, the embodiment of affront.

"They're gone now," I said. But his eyes were flickering around, paranoid. "They're gone. Come on. We have to feed you so that you can sing, right?"

"I don't know." He looked at me like I was the one that was irrational.

"That's what you said."

"Well, if I said it."

It took most of my strength to keep him beside me. And I wasn't even sure why I wanted to. What experience did I think I had? How did I think that I could just give him my love, and that that would be enough to fix anything? I didn't even love him, not for himself, anyway.

Any love I had for this stranger had been allocated from my dad, from my Hitchhiker, from the variety of messed-up people in my history that I hadn't managed to save. Although, it was occurring to me, this was probably the pattern for plenty of relationships. Pick up a stranger, apply your issues, and call it love. Maybe your issues would match up enough that, for a while, no one would notice that you'd never managed to get to know each other.

Here was the reality: I'd tripped over the Rockstar while in a state of stress over my crazy father. The Rockstar was crazy. Voilà! I'd applied my savior complex to him, as swiftly as possible. My father, on the other hand, was left in Idaho, unsaved. Even then, I knew it wouldn't end well. I'd known it wouldn't end well since I was a small child, and my dad had walked me to the end of the driveway and said, with a rather glorious gesture encompassing everything around us, "One day, I'm going to set this all on fire."

"All what?" I'd asked, uneasy.

"The trees, the house, the sagebrush, the dogs, and me. If you're here, don't come looking for me. Go down the road to the neighbors' and get them to call the fire department."

Not exactly what a seven-year-old wants to hear her father say. The nearest neighbors were half a mile away. I imagined myself walking away from an inferno containing my dad. I imagined other things. My cats burning to death. My dad had already had a couple of incidents involving fire, once setting his workshop aflame, and once the entire sagebrush-covered area in front of the house. It had only been by miracle that he'd managed to put it out. We were seven miles out of town, and a fire truck would have done no good at all.

"I don't want you to burn yourself," I'd said, trying to maintain calm.

"Now, don't cry. I'll shoot myself, once I've set everything on fire. The heat won't hurt me. Don't worry, sweetie. Why are you so slow? I don't know why you're always so slow when it's you that wanted to go for a walk."

I had planted my feet. He was going to set himself on fire? Fine. I was going to cry a flood of snot.

"Want gorp?" Gorp was his patented traveler's energy mix. It had both jerky and M&M's in it. I'd never liked the fact that meat and candy cohabitated in the gorp Baggies, and so I typically busied myself with picking the M&M's out, one by one, and hiding them in my pocket. This particular gorp Baggie was mostly jerky and cashews. Disgusting.

"No," I'd sniffled.

"Suit yourself."

I'd promptly, purposefully tripped, twisted my ankle, and prevailed upon my father to carry me home on his back. If he was going to refuse to be a dad, that was just too bad. I'd force him. In subsequent years, after my parents had split up, my mom's mantra in regard to my dad was: At least, no matter what, he really loves you.

This was true. It was just that he loved me in his own peculiar, self-destructive way. If love was the most important thing, and if this was love, then I didn't want it. Love did not mean that you could stop the fire. Love meant that you'd be the sucker with the vacuum, cleaning up the ashes. Maybe this was half of my problem with men. I didn't really want to love them. And if they loved me, I got worried. I didn't like the responsibility.

Why was everything always about father issues? I'd been reading *Electra* in my Classic Drama class. *Electra,* and then *Oedipus.* Now everything seemed trite. I felt as though I had several complexes based on Greek tragedies, and it was all I could do not to burst into melodramatic verse. No, I didn't want to date my dad. In fact, most of my idea of the kind of man I wanted was based on what my dad wasn't. Certainly, I'd met girls who'd told me that their fathers were the perfect man. Bizarre, I thought, imagining my parents' relationship. It hadn't been until junior high, when I'd gone over to a classmate's house, that I'd realized that other people's parents actually had conversations. I'd had an idea that all marriages were like my parents', massively ill-matched. Yes, my parents had loved each other, in a kind of blind, whammo, this-is-your-life kind of way, but they hadn't liked each other very much. And then there was the crazy factor to consider. Once I'd discovered that people actually managed to be married and not destroy each other, I'd been dedicated to finding a relationship that was the exact opposite of my parents'. My mom had spent half my teenage years warning me away from men like my dad, wild-eyed, talented to no purpose, and rebellious.

What was the Rockstar? Worse than my dad, actually, considering my dad hadn't been obviously crazy when my parents had met. He hadn't become externally crazy until after she'd had three children with him. What was I doing with this guy? The guys at the falafel place wondered the same thing.

"You are okay?" asked one of them, about sixteen, aproned, and heavily accented. "You need help?"

"I'm fine," I said.

"You want to be with him?"

"Yeah," I said. "I do." And I did. That was the thing that surprised me.

I bought him his falafel. He waited for me to open mine before he even looked at his. We sat down together, at one of Mamoun's tiny tables, and ate from our drippy tin foil packets until nothing was left. We sipped lemon-tinged water through our straws. The Rockstar looked at me across the table. He smiled, like a kid waking up from a pleasant dream, in a pleasant bed, onto a pleasant day. He smiled like someone who'd never had a nightmare.

. . .

THE ROCKSTAR HAD A LOT OF BELONGINGS, mostly contained in an army-issue olive drab backpack. Some of the belongings were wadded-up newspapers. He had, for some reason, a drink-and-wet doll, which he brought out for only a moment before hiding her away again. He had a Bible. Most important, he had a record album. Jimi Hendrix's *Are You Experienced?* No record. Just the sleeve. He showed it to me proudly.

"Not bad, right?" he said.

"That's a great record."

"I know, I made it."

He vacillated between Hendrix and himself, whoever himself actually was. He'd grown up in Seattle. That much seemed to apply to both him and his rockstar alter ego. Then it diverged. He'd gone to Alaska after high school and started working in a cannery, which, according to him, had been hell on earth. Somewhere in there, "the bastards" had come and found him, and he'd gotten halfway home, then hopped a freight train in Vancouver and taken it all the way to somewhere near Toronto. He'd walked from there, and come across at Niagara Falls, still American, if a little bit lost. Hitchhiked to New York City, because he had a friend, but the friend had disappeared, and now, here he was, eating falafel with me on a sunny day in September, and things were good. Even as I tried to ask questions, he said something about Bob Dylan—not a normal something, but a "when Bob was over at my house" something. And then he started to sing.

> *Somewhere a queen is weeping*
> *Somewhere a king has no wife*
> *And the wind, it cries, Mary.*

"No, no, no, wait," he said. *"The wind, it cries, Maria."* He sang it a couple more times. "That's better," he said. "Maybe I'll change the song."

It wasn't all so poetic. He also gave me a long monologue about the size of his cock, and didn't look even mildly ashamed of himself.

"You ever been with a black man?" he asked loudly, very loudly, in the middle of MacDougal Street. "Because, you don't look like you know about that. You don't look like you know about the size. You're probably a virgin, right? Virgin white girl. Grew up with a million dollars, and never met a black guy, right? Never fucked one, right? I get what you are, right?"

A few other people checked into our conversation, apparently to see what my opinions were on the subject. I could see heads turning.

"Yes," I said. "I have. So you don't really need to tell me about it, okay?"

"Whoo! Don't tell your mama!" he said.

"I need to go," I said, trying to be gentle, but then he turned and looked me straight in the eyes.

"Hey," he said. "I don't mean to offend you. Maybe I'm a little rough."

"Maybe you are," I said, "but I've probably seen worse than you. Just cool it on the cock stuff, okay?"

"No problem, Maria, Maria, Miss Madame Maria. Want me to sing your song again?"

We sat on a bench, and looked out over the fall. Leaves still green, fountain still running. Things not too bad, though Bob Dylan wasn't coming to *my* house.

"What do you think, Jimi," I said.

"About what specifically? I think lots about lots."

"Living happily. Like, are *you* happy?" Even though he was living on the street, even though he thought he was Hendrix, and even though Hendrix was dead, I meant. Even though he was out of his mind, I hoped that maybe being out of your mind didn't feel too awful. Maybe he didn't even know he was gone.

"Happy is relative. Happy, I'll tell you exactly one thing about happy."

"Tell me."

"Happy's a choice. You can be fucked-up over the shit the bastards do to you, or you can decide to get over it."

He didn't look like he'd gotten over it, but what did I know? Maybe he would have been much worse without his happiness policy. Maybe he wouldn't have survived.

"All you can do is give out your love," said the Rockstar. "And hope that somebody can take it for what it is."

I looked at him. I smiled, but he was gone again, gone as fast as he'd put his finger on exactly what my question was.

"Why are you looking at me like that?" he asked.

"Like what?"

"Like you know shit you don't know."

"I'm sorry," I said.

"Fuck that," he said.

A cop walked up to us. He was youngish, his hairline beating a swift retreat, but his gun at the ready.

"This guy bothering you?"

"Why don't you ask if I'm bothering *him*? Because I probably am. He'd probably be having a nice day if I hadn't tripped over him, and then forced him to have lunch with me."

Okay, so this wasn't the wisest thing to say to a macho cop.

"Because *you're* the pretty girl," said the cop, with some definite sarcasm. "And *he's* the motherfucker. But hey, let me just ask. Is this girl bothering you?"

"Nah. She's cool," said the Rockstar.

"I'm watching you," said the cop, and strutted away. Not too far away. Ten feet.

Fuck the cop, I thought. Fuck me. Fuck all the judgment I had about bad luck, and inability to climb back up from it.

I LEANED IN, AND KISSED THE MAN BESIDE ME, the man who thought he was Hendrix, the man who knew he'd come from a cannery and hopped a train. And maybe it was disgusting. Maybe his lips were chapped from the Great Out There, and maybe his skin was covered with dirt from the city. Maybe his clothes were stiff with living. Maybe he was crazy. And maybe I wanted to get my heart broken, because after all, what are hearts for?

But I kissed him, and he kissed me, and that was all there was to that. Love was precious, however fleeting. I was kissing a ghost, the ghost of more than one person, the ghost of all those I'd never see again, the ghost of those who had changed me.

Maybe my dad would get on a ship and go out onto the ocean and be cured of his troubles. Maybe the water would put out the fire in his head. Maybe my Hitchhiker had stuck out his thumb and hailed a ride to heaven. Maybe nothing was as sad as it sometimes seemed. Maybe. Or maybe it just hurt to grow.

"When I died, I was in London," said the Rockstar, his smile crooked.

I decided that I'd just believe him. It wasn't that far from the truth. We all had to reincarnate ourselves, and that wasn't the worst thing in the world. My whole life was a reinvention of how I'd started out. If I hadn't thrown myself headlong at change, I'd still have been in Idaho, married to one of the boys I'd never wanted to marry. I was my own creation, in many ways, even though I'd been affected by everything I'd done, and everyone that had helped me along my way. So was the Rockstar. And here we were.

I knew too much to think that I could save him. All I could do was give my love.

The Rockstar waved at me as he walked away, his knapsack over his shoulder, his song carrying back to me.

I stood on the street corner, and I let him go.

REMEMBRANCE
OF THINGS CRASS

IN WHICH
OUR HEROINE
LOOKS AT REAL
ESTATE . . .

THE DAYS PASSED LIKE TRAINS. I'd fly uptown to whatever temporary job would have me, and then downtown to class, then home to write my fingers down to stubs. I wasn't making enough money, but I was making more than I ever had before. I wasn't finding love, but I was finding more than I'd ever found before. Little scraps of it, in every person I met. Everyone had something to give me. Maybe I had something to give them, too. I hoped so. I was collecting. It seemed like my cup was starting to spill over, and so what if it wasn't just from loving one person, but from loving all of them? Maybe I wouldn't find every-thing I was looking for in one place, but the world was wider than I could have imagined, and everyone's path seemed to lead to New York.

I met men from Ghana and Georgia, ate Ethiopian food with a good ol' boy from North Carolina, rode around in an ice-cream truck with a guy from Mexico City, handing out Popsicles and nut-covered cones to surging children. A Japanese student took me to a dance club, and then listened to his Walkman the whole time we were there. A Hare Krishna swung with me on a swing set, but said ab-solutely nothing. A city bus driver ferried me all over Brooklyn, late one night, when I, with some ridiculously blistered feet, due to a pair of evil turquoise cowboy boots, flagged him down from the stoop I'd made my crippled way to. I sat in the seat next to him, and he showed me his city. At four in the morning, he dropped me off at my door, and I watched his bright, empty bus drive away.

All of my writing started to be about people I'd barely met, who had, for some reason, given me their best bits. Sometime in high school, I'd read a quote from a famous author, about whether or not he actually knew about what he was writing. He'd said that if you were really a writer, you should be able to walk past a bar full of sailors, and stand outside for a minute, absorbing their talk, their catcalls, their songs. Then, you were qualified to go home and write an entire novel set at sea. I agreed with him, but I was doing it one better. I wasn't just walking past. I was getting to go inside all these other people's lives and look around. I was insanely lucky. The more I left my apartment and wandered into someone else's story, the more I thought that maybe I was making myself worthy of being loved.

Not right now, however. I had the flu. Not just the flu. Some-thing more pitiful. This flu had an emotional component, and so I was suffering from something that might as well have been called the blue or the rue. The flu had made every bad thing that had ever happened to me come back in full force. I was in my apartment, wearing my bleakest kimono, and sipping NyQuil. The only thing that made me feel better was that I knew that my neighbor nemesis, Pierre, was just as sick as I was.

I'd come home a couple of hours before, basically crawling up the stairs, and Pierre had opened his door a crack, and sneezed a bitter sneeze.

"You gave this to me," he'd rasped, apropos of nothing.

I hadn't even seen Pierre in days. There was no way I could have given him the flu. It wasn't like I'd done what we'd done as kids, when one of us had had a communicable disease: flung ourselves into sibling beds and wallowed poxily across the sheets. I was innocent. I'd never even seen Pierre's bed.

I hadn't known I was sick until I'd started seeing halos over the heads of the other morning commuters. My body ached all the time anyway, and I was always sleepy. It hadn't occurred to me that anything out of the ordinary was going on. But a train full of angels, while beautiful, was too implausible. I'd bought a thermometer when I'd gotten off the train. Fever of 102. It was midterms, though, and so I'd gone to school anyway, squinting through a watery aura to see the slides that comprised my Art History midterm. I was living paycheck to paycheck, and so, after school, I'd had to go to work. I was regretting that now, nine hours later. Normally, I just denied illness, until I was so sick that I couldn't get out of bed. This one wouldn't be denied.

"You probably gave it to me," I said, equally irrationally.

"I'm going to die," said Pierre, clinging to his doorframe.

"Me too," I said, lying on the stairs like a Slinky. I slithered up to my door, and hung from my doorknob to unlock it. When I opened it, Big White catapulted himself out.

"No," I said weakly. "Please."

"It's okay," said Pierre. "He can come distract Pepe from clawing me."

Big White, obviously self-destructive, had already thrown himself into Annie and Pierre's apartment.

Pierre's roommate, Annie, and I, like the kind of idiot parents who arrange playdates between the class geek and the class bully, had for a long time firmly believed that if our cats only got to know each other, they would be comrades. Alas, Annie's cat, Pepe, was batshit. Whenever Annie opened their apartment door, a black-and-white blur would fly up the stairs, claws extended like switchblades, and leap hissing at our door, leaving scratch marks up to the ceiling. Woe betide the person who responded to his knocks. There would be Pepe, crouched like a tiny, warlike cow, his icy blue eye glittering and his red eye radiating malice. You had to dodge before he went for your throat.

Big White, despite being three times Pepe's size, hid quivering beneath Vic's futon whenever Pepe came over. This annoyed me. They were the same species, damn it, and there was no reason why they could not be friends. Besides, they were neighbors. Annie and I thought that neighbors should like each other.

Unless, of course, the neighbors happened to be me and Pierre.

It was beyond me why Big White Cat should suddenly want to throw himself at Pepe. It had never worked before. Whatever. I made for the medicine cabinet.

After a couple of hours, I heard Pierre sneezing his way across his apartment, and knew that Big White Cat's playdate was ending. Dragging myself out of bed, NyQuil in hand, I prepared myself for the usual: a bloodied nose or ear, a cowardly Big White with tail between legs. I looked down and saw Pierre standing outside his door, pink with fever, holding onto Big White as though onto a life preserver. Big White was purring. Weird.

"Hey," Pierre rasped.

"Hi," I croaked. "Want NyQuil?" Another minute of swaying at the top of the stairs, and I'd fling myself down them, just to get the inevitable over with.

"But it's daytime," he moaned. "NyQuil is for night." Pierre was swaying, too.

"It's dark somewhere," I told him, and raised the dosage cup like a shot glass. "C'mon. Have some. You'll feel better . . ."

"Okay," said Pierre. "You want me to climb the stairs?"

"Yes," I said.

There was a sudden warp in the time-space continuum, and for reasons that I still cannot explain, the next thing we knew, Pierre and I were making out against the ladder of the fire escape. We pulled away only when we both succumbed to coughing fits.

"Oh my God," panted Pierre.

"What's wrong with us?" I gasped, and then Pierre ran a finger across my clavicle, and I grabbed his clammy bicep, and talking became futile.

Half an hour later, we got another couple of sentences out.

"Dude, I don't even like you," he said.

"I don't like you, either. Get inside before someone sees us." I grabbed him by the shirt and dragged him into the apartment.

Vic was out for the evening. Not completely, though. She was halfway single, and therefore scheduled to come home at some point. Zak, however, was in the Bay Area for the week, in rehearsal for a play. I figured that if we just went into his room and shut the door, Vic would think I was getting some obscure revenge on him by blowing my nose on his sheets. It would never occur to her that I was sleeping with the enemy.

We couldn't even converse. We were too busy kissing. And even as we kissed, I could imagine Pierre's anal-retentive nightly vacuuming, his psychedelic chef's pants, his sabotage of me with the Handyman. I could lay brain on all the reasons he made me crazy, but there was no way to resist. It seemed he felt the same way.

Finally, we paused. Both of us were so stuffed-up that kissing was almost enough to make us pass out.

"This is sick," Pierre said, blowing his nose.

"Seriously, seriously sick," I replied, daubing cold sweat off my face. "Could you feel my forehead?"

"Feels okay to me," he said. "Feel mine."

"I can't tell if you have a fever. I have a fever, too, remember? You feel cool to me."

"Question. Am I missing something here, or are we totally incompatible?"

"Not totally," I said. "We're just *mostly* incompatible."

"Then why am I hot for you?" Pierre grabbed my left breast, looking bewildered.

"Why am I hot for *you*?" I grabbed Pierre's chest, bewildered, too.

"Ow," said Pierre. "Nipple ring."

"Sorry." What was the matter with me? Nipple rings grossed me out.

We heard the front door open. I put a pillow over Pierre's face and covered him in blankets.

"Maria?" Vic knocked on Zak's door and opened it slightly.

"Hi," I croaked. "Don't come in. I'm really sick. I don't want you to catch it."

I also didn't want her to catch me with Pierre. I hoped his feet weren't sticking out of the blanket. At least he was skinny enough that he was almost invisible. I knew Vic would be pissed, despite the fact that she had, for almost a year, denied having any sort of crush on Pierre. They'd gotten their nipples pierced together, though, and that was apparently an aphrodisiac. I'd come home one day and Vic had thrown open the upstairs door, yelling, "LOOK!"

She'd been threatening to do this for a long time, but it was still a shock when she flashed me in the doorway. The piercings looked good on Vic, because the rings were big and silver. They made her look somewhat dangerous, which was probably what she was going for. On Pierre, however, it just looked weird. He'd chosen to get a delicate little ring with colored beads hanging from it. And, for some reason, he'd only done one of them. I now knew this for sure, because even as I spoke to Vic, I had my hand on Pierre's chest. It was so appalling. What was I doing?

"Can I get you anything? NyQuil? Tea?" Vic asked, looking concerned. I tried to bring myself back to Earth. No doubt, I had an odd expression on my face.

"I'm just going to sleep until I feel better."

"I thought I heard you talking to someone."

"It's amazing the kind of conversations you can have with yourself."

Vic raised an eyebrow at me.

"Have you taken your temperature?"

"Yeah, it's a hundred and two. I'm eating ice. Don't inhale. You don't want this." I also didn't want her to smell Pierre's cologne. Even though I had no sense of smell, I suspected he was wearing it. He always was.

"Lemme know if you need anything." She closed the door. I felt bad. She was so nice, and I was so deceitful. Pierre scrabbled from beneath the pillow. I lifted it off his face.

"Sorry," I whispered.

He coughed, having been deprived of air for too long.

"That sounds bad," said Vic from the kitchen. "Sure you don't need cough syrup?"

"I have some. It's just a deep cough," I said. "Like, from the guts."

"Annie says Pierre has it, too," said Vic.

"Huh," I said. It was our own little sex farce. Molière, minus the verse and plus some phlegm.

PIERRE WAS FINALLY ABLE TO ESCAPE SEVERAL HOURS LATER, as Vic talked on the phone in her bedroom. Her conversations with her sister were always raucous, and usually lasted for hours. Pierre tiptoed to the door, carrying his shiny shoes, and I followed him into the stairwell. We kissed one more time and then he fled. I heard Annie ask him where he'd been.

"Sitting on the roof," he answered. Something none of us ever did. It was black tar paper, and it was precarious. We'd been banned that summer, when Gamma had seen my friend Moon taking in the New York City skyline. She'd thought Moon looked suicidal, despite the fact that the roof was only two stories high. Moon hadn't been on an urban roof before. All you ever saw in Idaho were cows getting it on. New York City windows offered much more interesting couplings, even if they were often no more attractive.

"Let me take your temperature," said Annie. "You must be burning up."

She was right, obviously. Both of us were burning up, and what had been left postblaze was something very strange. Out of the ashes of our dislike had risen an irresistible attraction. Now it was flying through the air, crowing in triumph, and Pierre and I were left dumbfounded. And horribly, sinfully, turned on.

"We can't do this," I whispered the next day, when we were hiding out again in Zak's room.

"How come?"

"Vic has a crush on you."

"She never said anything," he said.

"Of course she didn't," I said. "That's not her style."

"She said you were utterly unattracted to me," Pierre said.

"She said the same thing about you," I said.

We soon established that Vic had been telling each of us how much the other wasn't worthy of dating. Somehow, the reverse had become the actuality. We'd been dosed with a love potion made of Vic's attempts to keep us apart. Her suspicion made us all the more perversely inclined to pursue our twisted relationship. I was still laboring under unhappiness from months before, when I'd seen Vic's diary open on her bed. Being the confrontation avoiders Vic and I both were, we'd never discussed it. I still had hurt feelings and, apparently, I was still a little bit angry at her, too. This wasn't even really about revenge, though. It was about absurd chemistry. Pierre and I suddenly could not keep our hands off each other.

We felt compelled to play footsie under the dining room table the next week, when Pierre and Annie had Vic and I over for dinner. Vic watched us suspiciously, her eyes flickering from face to face. Pierre and I pretended to be innocent, but all the while, we were holding hands beneath Pierre's lovely cloth napkins. Pierre's fingers were stroking my thigh.

Vic, not being an idiot, quickly discerned what was going on, and decided that she would never leave us alone again. She tried to drag me out to a bar, but I said that I didn't feel well enough to leave the apartment. Pierre told her that she should just go if she wanted to go. Finally, several hours later, Vic left, furious, and Pierre told

Annie he was walking me upstairs, whereupon we fell into bed. It wasn't like we were really doing anything wrong. We weren't actually having sex. We were just *almost* having sex. As long as that was the case, we could both deny what was really going on.

VIC HAD TO GO OUT OF TOWN FOR A WEDDING, and so Pierre moved upstairs for the next two weeks.

When I got home from work and school, he'd be cooking dinner. It was a strange kind of domesticity, given that we didn't actually have much to say to each other. Nothing that involved words, anyway. We both felt cheap, but not cheap enough to stop. I was beginning to wonder how long it would actually take me to grow up. I was having a strange kind of fun with Pierre and our secret liaison. Not necessarily a healthy kind of fun. Pierre was like an addictive drug that you know better than to take, but are gobbling down anyway. You know it's killing your brain cells, and still, there you are, washing down handfuls of it with champagne, and dancing the kind of dances you'd never want to see captured on videotape.

"Wait. Wait. What? Is he living here?" Zak had arrived home from Berkeley. He had graciously waited to question me, until he saw Pierre go, whistling, into the shower.

I shrugged.

"He has hair products in the bathroom. His towel is hanging from our hook. And let me just show you something." Zak led me to the closet, and flung it open.

Pierre's vacuum was neatly stowed inside.

"I found it this morning. Focus!"

I feigned ignorance. "It's just for a couple of days until Annie's friend leaves. I was by myself, and their apartment was really crowded."

Zak looked at me with extreme suspicion. I wasn't really lying. Pierre was still paying rent downstairs, but he was frustrated with his living situation.

"Welcome to the club," I'd told him, when he'd complained

that his apartment wasn't big enough for three people. Annie and Pierre already had an odd relationship, given that they had become roommates while Annie was engaged to Pierre's younger brother. The idea had been that Pierre would move out when his brother moved in. The brother had subsequently dropped Annie for a fraternity, and was now rarely heard from. Pierre and Annie had never been interested in dating each other, but had ended up stuck platonically together, due to a rent deficit. As a result of this, a friend of Annie's had moved into Annie and Pierre's living room. Now, the friend, whom Annie had met during a brief period at an organic farming collective, never left the house. She was supposedly looking for a job, but she was scared of the subway, and so she just sat around in sweatpants, meditating. According to Pierre, she was also doing a colon cleanse. Pierre had already disliked her, but her constant descriptions of wheatgrass enemas put him over the edge.

So, Pierre LaValle, most never on my List of Nevers, slept in my apartment. Late at night, I'd crawl into Vic's bed, where he was sleeping, and snuggle into his waiting arms. I'd stay there until I felt too squished to remain (this alone ought to have told me something), and then I'd crawl back to my hut. In the morning, we'd drink our coffee, kiss a clandestine good-bye in the stairwell, and go off separately to our days.

I had a feeling, though, that Pierre was looking for a more conventional life than he let on, one in which his tattoos would be hidden under a button-down shirt, his wife would wear an apron, and he would be greeted with a peck on the cheek after work. A *Leave It to Beaver* life. Maybe that was why we weren't sleeping together. Maybe Pierre didn't believe in premarital intercourse. Or maybe we had to be officially dating in order to have sex. I knew that Pierre was not the most casual person in the world, but I hadn't expected him to keep his pants on. We were playing house, and it was strangely like it had been when I was a kid. More kissing and groping, but still. We hadn't even played I'll Show You Mine, If You Show Me

Yours. If anyone had been witnessing our weird affair, they'd have thought Pierre was gay. He wasn't. He was just Pierre.

Though I hadn't told him about my yes policy, I was sure that Vic had, and I knew enough about Pierre to know that he would not have been impressed by it. He was the kind of guy that wanted to look wilder than he was. I, on the other hand, was considerably wilder than I looked. It wasn't like I was doing the things I did in order to prove a point. I just wanted to have a life, to grow, and to hopefully learn about love in the most interesting way possible. This was how it had turned out.

Other than our nights together, Pierre and I still didn't have anything in common. He still vacuumed at 5:00 in the morning, though now he was doing it in my apartment instead of his own. His shoes were neatly polished and lined up next to the door. Somehow, though, we'd gained a certain tenderness in our dealings. He came up to my apartment with freshly inked tattoos, holding a tube of ointment, and I slathered his back with it. I found myself kissing him on the forehead. He called me "sweetheart," in a tentative tone, and then smiled. When I came home one day and found a letter from the Playwright, who'd become an actual friend, Pierre was sitting at my kitchen table, next to the letter, beating something with his whisk and looking jealous. Jealous! Maybe Pierre was becoming my boyfriend. We walked down India Street together one day, holding hands.

Unfortunately, this was the day that Vic came home, and she happened to get out of a cab just as we passed. She said nothing, just gave us both a death glare, and dragged her bag into the house, denying offers of assistance.

Later that night, after Pierre had quietly moved his towel and shoes back to his own apartment, Vic chewed me out, but since she was unwilling to admit her real reason for being angry, the chewing was muzzled.

"I can't believe you and Pierre, *grrrrrrr . . .*"

"I'm sorry. What else can I say?"

"Be sorry for *yourself*! He's not good enough for you!"

"Why are you so mad?"

"Because you're debasing yourself!"

"I've debased myself before, and you weren't this mad."

"Not with Pierre!"

"What's wrong with Pierre?"

"He's Pierre!"

"Can you be more specific?"

"You don't even want him!"

"We're adults, Vic," I said.

"You're children! You're totally irresponsible! I can't be responsible for you!"

"Who are we being irresponsible toward?"

Vic glared. "He's Pierre!"

"I *know* he's Pierre. It's established. We were attracted to each other."

"You never have been before."

"Haven't you ever suddenly been attracted to someone? Someone you thought you didn't even like?"

I knew she had, given that I'd watched her through two years of various boyfriends, and that even now, her current boyfriend was someone she'd initially dismissed as being too short and too preppy.

"Not when that someone was Pierre!"

"Do *you* want to date Pierre?"

"Of course not! I've lost respect for both of you!"

"I'm really sorry, Vic, what can I tell you?"

"*Grrrrrrrrrrrrrrrrrrrrrrr,*" said Vic, and slammed her bedroom door, as loudly as paperboard could slam.

"What's wrong with Vic?" asked Zak, who had arrived about the time that Vic, by the sound of it, had begun throwing her furniture. At least Zak didn't have a crush on Pierre.

"I kind of had a small affair with Pierre. For the last couple of weeks."

I squeezed my eyes shut, hoping he wouldn't bang a cast-iron skillet on my head.

"You *what*?" said Zak.

"Pierre," I said.

"Pierre LaValle," repeated Zak, looking appalled.

"Yes."

"But you can't stand Pierre." Zak was wearing the most dumbfounded face I'd ever seen. I decided that I wouldn't mention that Pierre and I had made out in Zak's bed. Zak would probably not react favorably to this news. Even though I had washed his sheets.

"Something came over us."

"So, like, are you going to sleep with every man in the entire city? Because, you know, I think you kind of have our neighborhood covered."

"I'm not sleeping with every man in the city. I didn't sleep with Pierre. We just kissed a lot."

"Pierre is low, even for you, the most willing woman in the world." Zak's dislike of Pierre ran deep.

"What do you mean, even for me?"

"Do you want me to make a list of your personal lows?"

"I don't have any regrets."

"You will about Pierre."

"You just don't like him."

"Neither do you! Doesn't he kiss with his jaw clenched? Never mind, I don't want to know."

Nope, I definitely wouldn't mention that Pierre had stayed in Zak's room for a week. At least Zak was still speaking to me. He was planning to move out, though, and had been since the beginning of our living together. He was going back to the Bay Area. This was something I was very carefully not thinking about, because every time I did, I cried.

For the next week Vic radiated nonstop fury, and had loud and long phone conversations behind her closed bedroom door. They were in Chinese. My name was the only thing that was in English, and so it was fairly obvious what she was saying about me. The conversation was punctuated with lots of tongue clicking and the infuriated phrase, also in English, "oh no, she didnnnnn't."

But I had. I knew I had. Alas. Soon, I'd be alone with Vic and her fury, and that was not a happy thought. She'd probably strangle me in my sleep, and I fully deserved it. I started looking at the classified apartment listings.

OF COURSE, I MET A GUY WHILE I WAS READING THE CLASSIFIEDS. The apartment listings were like my pornography, especially since my roommate situation was getting worse by the minute. I'd read every ad, dreaming of natural light, eat-in kitchens, and ample closet space. Complete wishful thinking. The only thing that I could actually afford was the closet itself. I might have been able to hang a hammock from some of the closets listed, but even so, I didn't think I could afford the hardwood floor those closets were bound to come with. It wasn't like I even wanted to move to Manhattan, as that seemed beyond the realm of possibility. I just wanted to move to someplace like Park Slope. Ha. In Park Slope, I could afford my hut, if I pitched it on the Promenade.

I wanted to start over in a new apartment, with new roommates. Begin again. Minus the misery of unrequited adulation. Erase the fact that I'd made out with my roommate's crush. Take Big White Cat and run to new digs. Maybe with just one roommate: myself. I was clearly hard enough to live with, without adding other personalities into the mix. I'd been poring over the classifieds, but there was nothing appealing anywhere. Rather, there was plenty that was appealing, and nothing that I could afford.

"Are you looking for a place?" said someone, and I looked up. The guy who was talking to me was a tall, skinny redhead with freckles and pale blue eyes. He was about thirty, and as normal looking as it was possible to be. Button-down shirt. Nice trousers. Carrying a portfolio. He looked like an ad for Banana Republic.

"Maybe," I said. "But I'm having a hard time finding anything good."

"I have exposed brick," he said. "Really exposed. And wood floors."

Anyone who had never lived in New York City would not understand the profound desirability of the exposed brick wall. It was not something that could easily be explained. We were willing to pay hundreds of dollars more per month for something that bred dust, mold, and little hidey holes. At the sublet I'd lived in, prior to my apartment in Greenpoint, mice had surged forth from the walls all night long, driving Big White Cat, who had an elephantlike fear of rodents, insane. One terrible night, Vic and I had baked an apple pie. After we'd taken the pie out of the oven, we'd discovered that what we'd thought had been whole-grain flour had actually been white flour laced with mouse droppings. We fed the pie to someone who shall remain nameless, because even now, I have not confessed to this extreme misdeed. Let it be said that this someone was being incredibly annoying at the time. Still, no one really deserves mouse shit pie, and I am officially sorry.

Anyway, after two years of living mouse-free, I was back to thinking about the romance of exposed brick. The guy on the train shot up wildly in my estimation. Normally, I wouldn't have even noticed him. He was neither beautiful nor bizarre. He was a normal white boy. Not typically on my radar at all.

"How'd you get it?" I asked, with some reverence. Most apartments in Greenpoint, including my own, were drywall disasters full of cockroaches and leaks. The nice ones were never moved out of. Yeah, there were great loft spaces still to be had in the neighborhood, but they were not for rent. People had bought them years before, and were waiting for the neighborhood to become desirable. The neighborhood south of us, Williamsburg, had just been voted the hippest place in the entire universe, and we were beginning to reap the benefits of refracted cool. Rents were rising, and those cool buildings were beginning to go for ridiculous sums.

"I have a friend," he said. "Would you like to see it? I mean, I'm not trying to be weird or anything. I just thought maybe you'd like to have a tour of what's out there."

"Sure," I said.

"Great!" The guy burst into a smile. He handed me a business card. "Call me."

The card was for a design firm, and the guy was a graphic designer. He was friendly. He had no visible perversities. He lived in my neighborhood. I wasn't too attracted to him, not at first glance, but he seemed so nonthreatening and easy to deal with that I dialed his number happily. After the Pierre problems, ease in handling seemed like exactly what I needed.

We made plans to meet at his apartment the next day, and I rejoiced. I was not only going outside the building, I was going outside the block! I was going to the outskirts of Greenpoint, to an apartment that abutted the East River, and the guy was going to cook me dinner! It was very promising.

"DO YOU WANT TO TRY OUT THE BRICK?" It was the next day, and the Designer was motioning that I should sit against the wall. He didn't have any furniture. Apparently the brick had gotten him overbudget. The apartment was beautiful, yes, but it was naked. All he had was a computer and a computer chair.

"Lean against it," he said, watching me. "Feel the texture of the bricks. Doesn't that exposed brick feel great against your spine?"

I leaned. I felt. I wondered if I'd misjudged the Designer.

"A sofa is on the way," he said, and then sat down on the floor in lotus position and offered me a glass of wine. Glass? Not actually. A Dixie Cup. Well, I could deal with that. I didn't have wineglasses, either. I looked around the corner. Yes, a jug. All very familiar to me. The computer was enormous and intimidating, however, and it was playing a selection of blues CDs.

"When does it arrive?" We'd already been through the typical conversation topics and discovered that we had almost nothing in common. The Designer was very nice, but he had a tendency to look intensely at me and nod, like a bobble-head doll. He had no conversation starters up his sleeve, either. He'd have been perfectly pleased to stay silent, nodding forever, as far as I could tell, with the exception of the occasional outburst about exposed brick.

"In about five minutes," said the Designer, looking at his watch. I tried to start two conversations, then gave up and started singing along with the CD, which had become Ray Charles. The Designer nodded, in seeming contentment. We sat for five minutes, and finally, there was a knock at the door. "There it is."

The Designer opened the door to two equally normal-looking, if sweat-drenched, guys. They did not look like delivery guys. They looked like software designers. Which, in fact, was what they were. The Designer was borrowing their couch for the night. They both flashed him the thumbs-up when they left. They thought I didn't see, but I did. Kind of sweet, I thought.

I got up and went to look at the Designer's books, which were still in boxes. "How long have you lived here?"

"One, two, oh, I guess it's three years now," he said, as though there was nothing odd about living in an apartment for three years without furnishing it at all.

The Designer seemed to have a collection of books of love poems. I asked what he liked about them, and he came over, looking very excited. He pulled out a book of Neruda.

"I love Neruda!" I said, relieved that we'd now have a topic.

"I haven't read the book." He opened it to the frontispiece, and showed me an inscription. "I like the handwritten stuff," he said. "You know, love stories that got donated to the Salvation Army."

Apparently, the Designer would thumb through these books of secondhand poems, looking for inscriptions dedicating sonnets to people who were no longer adored. He liked that they'd been tossed out among the fondue makers, blenders, and leftovers of marriages. He liked to think of love relegated to curbside pickup, put into cardboard boxes with old lingerie and cat scratching posts. It made him feel as though his own life was maybe not so dismal, as though other people gave their love away, as well, as though other people had not understood its value. Love poems. Inscriptions vowing forever. Just paper in the end. The Designer was replete with other people's failures.

"Do you have any of your own?" I asked, thinking maybe that was what had started him on this strange collection.

"Any what?"

"Any books given to you by old girlfriends?"

"Oh, I don't have any old girlfriends." He sounded cheerful enough about this, despite its inherent sadness.

"How is that possible?" He had to be thirty.

"I used to be bigger. Much, much bigger. My whole life, I was, I guess you'd say, 'morbidly obese.' That's not a very nice phrase, though. Three hundred and sixty-one pounds was my top weight. Or thereabouts. I stopped weighing myself. Want to see a picture?"

He rummaged in a book box, until he found a 1970s-era photo of a poor little kid in a cowboy hat, standing in a sprinkler. The kid was wide. Very, very wide. He was clutching the kind of inner tube that is supposed to go around your waist, but it was clear this one wasn't going to.

Did this mean that the Designer was a virgin? Yes, it probably did. That was a terrifying prospect. I'd never understood the appeal of sleeping with virgins. I knew some men who'd isolated this category as their number one object of pursuit. First footprints on the moon, or something. Planting the flag at the North Pole.

No woman would do such a thing. We wanted to arrive sometime after about four or five explorers had already been there, and built a fire. We were willing to attempt to train men who were bad lovers, but we were not really willing to start from scratch. Not even when we were ourselves inexperienced. We didn't want a lost man. Men were lost enough. Besides, if something turned out to be askew, we wanted to have someone to blame. If you were the first, you could only blame yourself.

"I just decided, enough was enough," said the Designer. "One day, I stopped eating anything that made me happy." He nodded at me a few more times.

Now that I knew his history, it seemed that his bobbling was largely an attempt to get a better view up my skirt. I crossed my legs.

"And how about now?"

"Basically, mostly celery. Crudités are a wonderful weight management tool. I hope you like zucchini," he said.

"I love zucchini," I said. Not necessarily by the ton, but I did like it. He brought a platter out of the kitchen. Uh-oh. Crudités.

"It's a raw dinner!" he announced, smiling joyfully. "Raw foods are really good for you." He placed the platter in front of me. Ten pounds of raw vegetables. He sat back and watched me. I took a carrot. He bobbled.

"Aren't you having any?"

"No, I'll just watch you," he said. "I like to watch other people eat. It makes me happy."

The blues howled loud and long over the computer speakers, and I tried to crunch my carrot in the quietest way possible. I looked down at the plate. It was going to be a long night. I figured I'd just eat the crudités, and then excuse myself. I couldn't ruin what was very possibly his first date ever.

Then he brought out the cake. It looked like birdseed mixed with treacle. He smiled.

"I got the recipe from a veterinarian," he said.

"You mean a vegetarian?" I asked.

"No, a veterinarian," he replied. "Raw food is also good for animals. I mean, we're animals, too. Human animals. That's why we crave things. Like cake. It's really good! Try it."

I picked up my fork. I took a bite. Birdseed. That was what it was. Birdseed.

I pecked at my sesame seeds and suet, thinking that nice apartments were not really what mattered to me. I'd gone out with a guy on the basis of an apartment brag once before, and it hadn't gone well.

That guy, who'd owned a swanky building in Williamsburg, had made me a Bloody Mary with half a bottle of Tabasco in it, and then tried to seduce me through the bathroom door as I choked on fire.

"I just wanted to heat things up," he'd said, in a voice that was trying to be sexy.

"You did," I'd replied. "And now I'm going to die." What kind of guy used chilies to heat up a date? It was as though he'd skimmed *Like Water for Chocolate* for seduction techniques, not understanding that it had not been the chilies that had done the heavy lifting in that book, but the unrequited love.

"I'll give you a deal on an apartment," Tabasco Bastard had said.

"I don't think so," I'd said. It had not really mattered to me whether or not his building had hardwood floors. I'd developed a hatred for him, and that was all I'd cared about. Spicy foods were not something I liked. Half a bottle of Tabasco? Not only that, he'd been boring. Men who were obsessed with things like hardwood floors and mill work tended, as a rule, to be deeply dull. At least he'd eaten, though. He'd eaten all of my dinner, as well as his own, prior to the Bloody Mary interchange. What kind of person drank a Bloody Mary as an after-dinner drink? Only someone without a clue. Not that people without a clue weren't sometimes nice.

The Designer was definitely nice. He was so nice that he ate a whole radish, so that I wouldn't feel alone. I couldn't leave him mid-date. He was too lost.

He swooped toward me, a little while later, just as I stood to tell him that I'd had fun, but was really tired. He seemed to be possibly dancing to the Ray Charles. He grabbed me, and gave me a kiss that could only be compared to how it might have felt if I'd picked up a mussel shell on a beach and stuck my tongue inside it. It was, hands down, the worst kiss I'd ever had. Could I blame him? It was probably his first. He bobbled his way to the bathroom, and I pounced on his phone and called Vic, hoping I could get her to save me.

"Vic?"

"Why are you whispering?"

"I'm trapped in a gorgeous apartment with a virgin."

"Why are you calling me? Don't you want to destroy his innocence?" Sarcasm. Well, what had I expected?

"You might like to see the apartment." Vic was as fixated on exposed brick as anyone. Sometimes we'd bonded over other people's apartments. I hoped that she'd take the bait. If she came over, we could gracefully exit without crushing the Designer's self-esteem.

"Is it nice?"

"Gorgeous. And empty."

"I take it you need to be saved. Fine. You owe me."

I gave her the address.

"I'm still mad at you, you know," she said. "I'll be right there."

This was one of the reasons I loved Vic. Even if she was deathly pissed off at me, she'd still save me from a bad date. I would have done the same for her, and I had on occasion. I told the Designer that I'd checked my messages and that my roommate happened to be in the area. He was delighted.

When Vic arrived, she admired the Designer's exposed brick and water view. He fluttered around, looking thrilled to have not just one, but two girls in his apartment. He'd had his first kiss, and now he was confident.

"Cake?" he said to Vic. I shook my head surreptitiously at her.

"No thanks," she said. "Nice couch!"

"Thank you," said the Designer. "I designed it myself." He looked at me somewhat guiltily, but I didn't give him away. Vic sat down on the couch. I sat on one side of her. The Designer sat on the other.

"So," Vic said.

"So," I said.

"So," the Designer said, and then launched forward and tried to kiss me over Vic.

"What are you doing?" said Vic.

"Nothing," said the Designer.

"So, we're late," said Vic.

"We are," I said apologetically.

The poor guy didn't really deserve to be dumped this way, especially after he'd given me so much birdseed, but dumping him now seemed like a kinder thing than dumping him later. You couldn't date someone just because you felt sorry for them. I should have learned that before, but somehow it was only just becoming clear.

"Thanks for the crudités and the cake," I said.

"Thanks for the exposed brick," Vic said.

"Do you want my apartment?" the Designer asked. It was too sad.

"No, we're okay together," said Vic. "Our place is fine." She looked at me. She nodded. I wasn't forgiven, but I was on my way.

WHEN WE GOT HOME, I WENT TO THE CLOSET AND GOT PIERRE'S VACUUM OUT. I went downstairs and knocked on his door.

"I hadn't even noticed I'd left that at your place," Pierre said, looking at the vacuum. It was true. I hadn't heard his morning vacuuming in days. Maybe Pierre was changing, too.

We had an awkward hug. The insane attraction was gone, and all that was left between us was the kind of feeling that survivors share. We didn't have love, but we had a series of nights spent holding onto each other. That counted for more than I would have thought it would.

"Want to taste this?" asked Pierre, holding out his whisk. I decided that at least I might have learned how to trust him. I nodded. He put his finger into his bowl and then into my mouth.

Sweet. Not spicy at all. "Thanks," I said.

"You're welcome," he said, and grinned at me. "Now I know what you like."

I kissed Pierre for the last time, and then ran back up the stairs and home.

JOURNEY TO A
TEN-CENT UNIVERSE

IN WHICH
OUR HEROINE
TRAVELS TO
FOREIGN
LANDS . . .

I WAS WAITING FOR THE TRAIN AT FIFTY-NINTH STREET, WHEN SOMEONE TAPPED ME ON THE SHOULDER. I turned, and saw my worst nightmare made flesh. Black-and-white stripes. Expression of agonizingly good cheer. Whiteface. A tilted beret. A red flower, in the buttonhole of a black bolero jacket. I shook my head violently. No good. In front of me stood a man in the Marceau mold.

The Mime was offering me a crepe paper rose. I tried to take it, but he snatched it away, wiggling an admonishing finger at me.

My initial impulse was toward violence. Throw the Mime from the platform and onto the third rail. It was rare that I felt like a superhero, but every time I saw a mime, my guts told me that I ought to eliminate the villain. I resisted. I smiled. I was not violent. Oh no. I gritted my teeth. I was nice. I was not judgmental. So what if this person thought it was a kick in the pants to dress up in tights and plague pedestrians with false joie de vivre? What did I care? I was enchanted. I was rapturous. O Mime! I've waited for you my entire life!

The Mime seemed surprised by my welcoming smile, but then started building a wall, from which protection he played peekaboo. I started to walk to another part of the platform, but the Mime scampered in front of me and started to mime falling in love. His hands fluttered in front of his heart. His mouth formed an O of adulation. I stood there, colossally uncomfortable. People were watching. They thought I, a sworn enemy to mimes everywhere, wanted this mime. Why was the train so slow?

The Mime reached into his pocket, shyly fingering something. He gave me an invisible blush, signified by bashful patting of his cheeks. He knelt. He opened an invisible ring box, bit an invisible diamond to show me it was real, and then offered me an invisible ring.

What was I going to do? It was the Year of Yes. This was an offer. No, I didn't have to marry him, but in mime language, this was what passed for a date. I took the ring. The Mime fitted it onto my finger, admiring the results, and then came in for a kiss.

It was a peck, luckily. Mimes don't do tongue. They aren't supposed to have them.

The Mime linked arms with me, attempting to walk me down an invisible aisle. He started silently conversing with an invisible officiator, took an invisible wedding ring from his invisible best man, and stuck it onto my finger. Then, apparently regardless of the fact that I'd said nothing about taking this mime for better or for worse, he lifted my invisible veil and came in for another kiss. Another?

I was starting to wonder how far the miming was going to go. Were we going to mime a honeymoon? Apparently, yes. The Mime got ready to lift me over the threshold of what I imagined was probably one of those honeymoon resorts with a champagne glass–shaped hot tub and a heart-shaped bed. He bent down. He prepared his lower back to lift. And then he went for it. But wait.

I didn't budge, possibly because the Mime was making no physical contact. The Mime tried again, still not touching me. He strained. He heaved. Nothing. His face fell. He made the universal sign for tears of woe.

And then the Mime did the unforgivable. He brought out an invisible measuring tape and measured the diameter of my hips. His jaw dropped. He flung a hand across his forehead. He checked the measure. Again the hand was flung. My ass, it seemed, was simply too large to be lifted.

The Mime, his heart clearly breaking, took off his invisible wedding ring. He kissed it, and then put it back into his pocket. He looked at me expectantly. He motioned toward my hand. Apparently, I was meant to surrender my invisible diamond.

Well, too fucking bad. He'd called me fat. I shook my head.

The Mime turned his pockets inside out, piteously showing me the lint in them. He'd pawned his grandmother's ashes to buy this ring. And his last crust of bread. And a whole bunch of helium balloons. It was all he had left. More tears.

What the Mime did not know: I'd spent all of high school thinking that I was going to be an actress. As such, I'd spent hours in mime workshops, walking through bogs of invisible molasses, and climbing invisible staircases. My high school drama teacher had been famous for a morbid mime series, which included *Death by Dental Floss*, *Death by M&M*, and *Death by Slurpee*. Despite my inherent dislike of mime, I'd learned from the best.

I took off my invisible wedding ring, put it in my mouth, and swallowed it. I rubbed my hand over my belly. I smiled.

The Mime went into shock. He tried to enlist the support of the other people on the platform, but they mostly pretended he wasn't talking to them. Miming was only another form of madness, and New Yorkers were veterans at avoiding the insane. The Mime decided to try another tactic. He took off his beret. He took an imaginary penny from an imaginary pocket, and placed it in the hat to seed it for donations. And then he held out his hat to me, and motioned that I damn well better pay up.

I wasn't about to pay him for marrying me. I turned my pockets inside out and showed him that I'd even sold my lint. I, too, had pawned my grandmother's ashes. I, too, had sold my helium balloons. In fact, I, too, was malnourished. Could the Mime blame me for swallowing the ring? I needed the nutrients. I was probably getting rickets. The latter involved a complex mime starvation sequence; sucking in my stomach and plucking at my suddenly too-large clothes, hobbling briefly with suddenly crippled legs, swooning. And then a devil-may-care shrug, just to rub it in. The Mime motioned angrily at my midsection. I shrugged again.

The Mime drew an invisible sword from an invisible scabbard on his back. He made the universal symbol for hari-kari. He handed me the sword, jeweled hilt first.

I appreciated its hair-splittingly sharp blade, and then chopped off the Mime's hand.

The opportunity for a melodramatic mime death was too great for him to resist. He began to spurt arterial blood, looking in vain for a paramedic amongst the passengers. No volunteers, although a few more people had started watching.

Finally, the light of the oncoming train appeared. I began to walk down the platform to get a spot far from the dying mime. As the train pulled up, I looked back.

The Mime was holding his hand in front of his forehead in an L for loser. As I watched, the L converted to a straight-up bird-flipping. The Mime then mimed shitting and throwing said shit at me. Applause. Laughter. The Mime had found his New York audience. As the door closed, I could see people surrounding him, their faces joyful. He'd brought sunshine to their day.

"GOT MARRIED TODAY," I TOLD VIC, WHEN I GOT HOME.
"Funny," she said.

MARIA DAHVANA HEADLEY

"You would have liked this one," I said. "He was mute."

"The best kind of man," she said.

Vic and I had recently watched Woody Allen's *Bullets Over Broadway*. When Dianne Wiest put her hands over John Cusack's face, admonishing him, "Don't speak. Don't speak!" Vic and I, along with most of womankind, had sighed in recognition. Sometimes, everything was perfect, until the guy opened his mouth and ruined things. Mimes for everyone! If only they didn't wear those stripy tights. I'd started out the day with a mime prejudice, though, I had to admit, my mime marriage had broken me of it. Annoying as the Mime had been, he was inarguably funny. What would be next? Sweater vests? Would I have to give up all of my prejudices? Yes, in fact. Yes.

"WE'RE GOIN' TO CONEY ISLAND, BABY," said the Conductor, and grinned at me. "Goin' to see the freak show. That shit's the shit to see. Swedish Fish?"

"No thanks."

The Conductor shrugged. He'd eaten most of a bag of Swedish Fish by himself already. It was a candy, he'd told me, that he could relate to. The fish swimming upstream their whole lives, he'd said, were like conductors stuck on the G train, never making it anywhere close to Manhattan, always hoping that the train would miraculously take flight and transit across the East River. Failing that, the Conductor wanted (at least, goddamn it) some shiny new cars.

I'd met the Conductor a few mornings before, on the G. Or rather, I'd met his voice. As usual, I'd waited half an hour for the train, along with a surging pack of irritable, caffeinated New Yorkers. When the train finally pulled in, we squeezed on against our better instincts, pressed against friends and foes, elbowing and kicking to get a spot. It was a rush-hour ritual. At least one person on each car was usually speared by an umbrella. On this particular morning, a light rain had become, in about ten minutes, a torrential downpour. An hour later, our train pulled into Queens Plaza, normally five minutes away. The doors didn't open. We started to hyperventilate. Over the normally incomprehensible in-train intercom, a jolly voice boomed forth:

"Good morning, Great People of Brooklyn! As you can tell, we got some trouble. So take a deep breath and love your neighbor for just a few more minutes till we can get you all off to your day."

New York City subway conductors were known for two things: their mumbling and their irritability. Typical rush-hour messages normally sounded more like:

"Attention, Asshole-in-Red-Shirt at the last car. Step OUT OF THE DOORWAY. NOW. Don't think you're getting on my train. There is NO ROOM FOR YOU. We're just going to sit here and WAIT for you, Asshole-in-Red-Shirt."

The persons stuck on the last car with Asshole-in-Red-Shirt would direct threatening looks and/or gestures and/or streams of obscenity at him, until he got out of the doorway and back onto the platform.

Even more typically, the message went something like this:

"Wyhow? Mmmhhiummmumblemumble! Proceed to mumble-mumble! MMMMPH! Now! Hmmghrrh."

This morning, it seemed that the rain had flooded every station in the city. The entire passenger contents of the subways were to be disgorged to buses. When the doors finally opened, I took a walk past the conductor's car to see who the hell this cheerful guy was.

I got there just as he left the train. He was walking in front of me, and walking fast. Five foot three was never the best of heights, and particularly not when trying to keep up with someone tall. From behind, I could see wiry, graying hair, a navy suit jacket, and a dark neck. I started running. The sunshiniest subway conductor in New York City stopped in his tracks, causing me to run past him. He started opening his jacket. Something began to emerge from his (*horrors*) sweater vest. I recoiled. Aliens! Sigourney Weaver! High school geometry teacher! My brain, as usual, was out of control with associations. I could do nothing about this problem. I hoped it wouldn't one day end me up in an asylum, babbling about Byron and Barry White. When I forced the brain to pause, it became clear that what was climbing out of the dreaded sweater vest was an iguana. The Conductor pulled a small white bag out of his pocket, fished something out of it, and fed it to the iguana. By then I was close enough to identify the treat as a Swedish Fish. The iguana retreated into its argyle lair.

"Excuse me," I said.

The conductor looked up. He was about fifty, skinny, and startled. Then he smiled a smile like a newly whitewashed fence. I felt the rain retreating and rainbows scaling the sky. Maybe this was irrational. New Yorkers, though, weren't known for their smiles, particularly not at strangers. I felt like I'd found a kindred spirit.

"Hey, girl," he said, as though he'd known me for five hundred years.

"Hi!" I said. "How'd you get so happy?"

"What's not to be happy about?" he said. Even though he had an iguana, even though he wore a sweater vest, I liked him immediately.

"Who are you?" he asked.

"Maria."

"Pleased to meet you. I'm Joseph."

I'd watched a lot of *Mister Rogers* as a child. The train to the Neighborhood of Make-Believe had been one of the primary objects of my fantasy. I envisioned myself stepping aboard, donning a conductor's cap, and shortly thereafter arriving in a glorious place where there was not one, but *two* talking cats. There was a definite soft spot in my heart for trains. So, when the Conductor asked me if I wanted to take a little trip with him that Saturday, I was very excited. I had visions of a little trip to heaven. Or, at least, to some make-believe sector of New York City, one with sparklingly clean sidewalks and maybe a few nice elves. I thought maybe it was a secret place that only conductors knew, especially because the Conductor refused to tell me where we were going, and would only say that I needed to bring a bathing suit. It was October. Wherever we were going, it was somewhere warm. Somewhere tropical. Somewhere deep in Brooklyn that I'd never heard of before. We were taking the F train.

As we took it, though, it became clear that we were not going to the Neighborhood of Make-Believe. We were going to Coney Island.

Coney Island was about the last place on earth I wanted to go. It was cold, cold enough that hot dogs would be frozen on the spit, cotton candy would crack into spun sugar shards, and neon lights would split into splinters of color if they lit. It would be Siberia, but painted with toxically bright lead paint. It would be like one of those nightmares of juxtapositions that couldn't exist, similar to the one that had plagued me as a child: the evil Stay-Puft Marshmallow Man from *Ghostbusters* stomping down my driveway, his teeth bared to consume me. I would have deserved it, too, as I'd regularly killed his kin in campfire s'mores. Worse, I'd enjoyed it. I might as well have been a Nazi, as far as the Stay-Puft Marshmallow Man was concerned. In the dream I cowered, watching his white head bobbing above the treeline, marking his inexorable progress toward my house. He often waved cheerily at me, a bloodied parent in each paw. Periodically, he'd nibble at their skulls, and grin at me with dripping red teeth.

"It's cold," I told the Conductor, speaking with all the authority I didn't have. "I think the freak show's closed. And the rides aren't running."

"Avoid the crowds, that's my motto. I only go in the fall. Summer, you got crazies there, swimming in that ocean. Nobody need swim in that ocean in the summer. Nasty. This is the last day they're open, and it's perfect weather for it."

The train came above ground, and I looked out. Gray. Stormclouds, like giant rhinoceroses butting each other across the sky. And what was that? Oooh. A little spear of lightning! Yeah, perfect for a day at an outdoor amusement park.

I had a bad history with parks. I was scared of roller coasters, Ferris wheels, tippy things of all kinds, darts, and clowns. The last time I'd been to an amusement park, I'd been about eight, and a peacock had dive-bombed in from nowhere and taken an epic shit on my shoulder. Thinking that the cool trickle I'd felt was my dangling earring, I'd proceeded to rub my face across my shoulder, smearing peacock excrement from forehead to chin. Or perhaps an earlier memory: the time an off-kilter great-aunt had taken my siblings and me for a jaunt to Barnum & Bailey. Sometime during the acrobats, when one of us was vomiting cotton candy, she'd decided that she was done with us and had driven away. Or: the county fair when I was a teenager, at which my preternaturally developed friend won a Pink Floyd T-shirt and the ongoing stalker admiration of the vendor by flashing her tits for him and all of his twenty-something vagrant employees. I'd never been to Disneyland as a kid, because my family had never had enough money. As a result, I'd developed a deep scorn for all things Disney. Kids would come back after summer vacation, show-and-telling, proudly wearing their Mickey Mouse ears, and I would jealously inform them that mice carried the black plague and that they'd soon be breaking out in swellings beneath their armpits. The only animated Disney movie I'd really liked was *Fantasia,* specifically the "Night on Bald Mountain" sequence, and that was only because I took pride in being the only kid in the room who could watch it without wetting her pants.

"What video do you want, Maria?" the poor, deluded mommies would ask.

"Fantasia," I'd reply, handing over my own illegally dubbed copy. I'd hotly await the moment when the red devil guy would appear onscreen, and then I'd tell the story of the time I saw him come *through* the screen at a slumber party. I was not an A-list guest at slumber parties, because I had developed an early reputation for either puking or leading the other girls in somersaults through the house. I didn't care to sleep. This problem had, obviously, rippled into my present life, except that now my red devil guys were much more corporeal, and they had nothing as cultured as "Night on Bald Mountain" to accompany them. "Night with Bald Head" was where I'd ended up most of the time. God help me. At least it hadn't been "Night on Bald Mountie." Yet. I could just see it, though. Falling fool-

ishly into bed with a Canadian. Being carried off on the back of a very slow horse. The little red jacket. The hat covering the shiny head. In bed, my Mountie would cry, "Eh? Eh?"

Apparently, some portion of my traumatic thought trajectory was visible.

"Why the long face?" asked the Conductor. "It's going to be fun. You have no idea until you try it. Coney Island, baby, at the end of the season, is the best place in the world."

All my knowledge of Coney Island was courtesy of *A Coney Island of the Mind*, a book of not terribly fascinating Beat-era poems written by Lawrence Ferlinghetti, the publisher of *Howl*. I'd read it, along with a bunch of Richard Brautigan, during that high school hobo period. The real Coney Island had little to do with the book. Brighton Beach was a myth to me. I had never ventured this far on the train.

Stan the Iguana poked his prehistoric head out of the Conductor's jacket. There were strands of green yarn impaled on his spines, part of the shredded scarf that the Conductor had informed me was Stan's winter garb. Being cold-blooded, Stan required careful dressing for outdoor appearances. The Conductor gave him a Swedish Fish. Stan took it and disappeared again into the jacket, smacking his little lizard lips.

"Won't that hurt him?"

"He loves 'em. What can I say?"

What did I know about animal desire?

"That's nothing. You know what I give him in breeding season?"

"No." I wasn't sure I wanted to know, either. But this was what I'd signed on for. A date with a herpetophile. Which was not what it sounded like, but was instead a person who loved lizards. "Tell me."

It seemed that Stan's green scarf was part-time his muffler, and part-time his mistress. No wonder the muffler was so dilapidated. Stan had big teeth and claws. It couldn't have been fun to fuck him. The Conductor told me that he had to watch out if he wore anything green, because Stan would immediately decide that green meant girl.

"Stan is easily fooled by placebo pussy," the Conductor told me.

I'd been treated like an inanimate object occasionally, even in the mammal world. Sometimes I felt like the blue velvet chair that Taylor had once told me had been his first love. Sometimes I suspected I was just being used as something to rub against.

"From time to time," the Conductor told me, "I put him in a little hat. He has a collection. Sombrero. Stetson. Shit, Stan even has a yarmulke."

Every iguana owner I'd ever known had been weird. The Conductor, at least, was a joyful kind of weird. He was the happiest person I'd ever met. We sat on that train, sharing Swedish Fish with Stan, and it rocked us up high above the city, careening all the way to the Ferris wheel and the Atlantic Ocean, to the hot dog and knish stands getting boarded up for the winter. Coney Island from above was a sad-looking thing, all its bright colors stark against the sky, everything strangely tiny compared to the modern-day amusement parks in my mind's eye. Coney Island had its Wonder Wheel towering over everything, 150 feet tall, and in position since 1920. The park's old rides still stood, skeletal, the newer rides nestled like toadstools in their shadows. Or so the Conductor, a Coney Island buff, told me.

"The Cyclone," he said, reverently, pointing at the most decrepit roller coaster I'd ever seen. It was made of wood, and there'd been no attempt to hide its age. It was weathered. It was battered. It was ancient. It was still fucking running. It was so New York: a city of the most stubborn people on earth. This part of the city was especially stubborn, given that it was full of Russian immigrants, and was the home base of the Polar Bear Club, a group of elderly men who went swimming in the Atlantic year round, most notably on New Year's Day. They'd been doing this since 1903. They were skinny-chested guys in Speedos and sunglasses, for the most part. And they didn't just dash in and out. They immersed. From the beach, their long-suffering wives applauded them, and then they scampered inside for black Russian bread and soup. I assumed. I knew nothing of the Polar Bear Club, really, only what I'd seen referenced. I thought they were crazy. Who would swim in the water at Coney

Island? Particularly in the winter. Only freaks. By which I didn't mean the sideshow kind. I didn't think even sideshow performers would be loopy enough to jump into ice water. Who'd do such a crazy thing?

CONEY ISLAND ON THE LAST DAY OF THE SUMMER SEASON was not the most populated place. Some renegade parents and children, some college kids, some women in saris pushing strollers. We got off the elevated train, walked down some rickety steps, and made for the freak show, housed in a windbeaten building with old-fashioned posters of attractions. THE TATTOOED MAN, ZENOBIA: THE BEARDED LADY, THE GREAT FREDINI, KOKO THE KILLER CLOWN. Nobody outside. Too rainy. There was a small stand-up bar inside the doors, where you could get a beer and wait for the freaks to come out. Apparently, they'd stand on a plywood platform and do their crowd-catching maneuvers outside for a couple of minutes, between shifts. Sadly, by the time we got there the show was closing and everyone was going home. The Conductor and I sat on barstools and watched the Tattooed Man, dressed in jeans and a sweatshirt, pass us. Then the Bearded Lady, swathed in a raincoat. Finally, a couple of serpentine skin-and-bones performers that the Conductor identified as contortionists.

"Weren't we here to *see* the freak show?" I asked. "Not just watch them leave?"

"Girl, I see the freak show all day long. Hell no. I like to see them turn back into normal people and go home," said the Conductor. "Makes me happy to see them get on a train. I love New York," he suddenly whooped. "How can anyone not love this city?"

The tattooed guy gave the Conductor a look as he passed. A stunning, curvaceous Latina woman carrying a boa constrictor eyed the Conductor, too. Stan was scaling the Conductor's neck, and looking curiously around.

"That's my favorite part," said the Conductor. "They never ride my train. I want the F. If I had the F, I'd be more entertained. The G, the incredible folks on the G are more discreet about it. I had an opera singer on my train the other day. She started singing in the tunnel, and everybody on my train could hear it, but I never saw her face. Nobody's normal, baby, whether it's on the outside or on the inside. That's the thing."

That statement could be looked at two ways. Either it was a great thing, and I felt right at home, or it was evidence that I was destined to date weirdos until the end of time, because there was nothing else out there. The Conductor was definitely part of the weirdo category. In a good way, though. He was like a little kid, grinning and nodding at people, eating his cotton candy and spouting bits of Coney Island history between bites. The Spook-A-Rama, for example, the park's "dark ride" (a long tunnel full of thrills and chills, transited via open train cars), had been there since 1955. Charles Lindbergh had ridden the Cyclone, and had been quoted as saying that this two-minute roller-coaster journey was much more exciting than his famous flight across the Atlantic.

We watched the sideshow freaks leaving Coney Island. They melded into the people outside—the shifting mass of parents and their children, the Coney Island devotees, the Hasidic Jews and the Puerto Ricans, the Russians and the junkies—and made their way to the trains, scarcely noticed among the ice-cream clamors and the umbrellas. A stray dog skittered over the sidewalk. A guy sat cowboy-booted on the boardwalk and sang "Don't Cry for Me, Argentina," accompanied by his accordion.

We walked out into the sand. I was surprised to see that it really was sand. I'd been expecting some sort of false beach. I'd seen too many movies. The city felt like a soundstage. I'd thought the sand would be plastic pebbles.

It started to rain. It started to pour. The Conductor unfurled a candy-striped golf umbrella and a garbage bag. He pitched the umbrella in the sand and spread the garbage sack like a blanket. We sat down, and looked out over the rain and sea.

"Picnic?" he said.

"Sure," I said. As far as I was concerned, the Conductor was the coolest person I'd ever met. He made me feel like we were in some sort of alternate New York, one that was both gritty and romantic. Never mind that the grit was partially due to the sand that coated the Nathan's Famous hot dog the Conductor bought me. I ate the bun with everything on it. I gave the hot dog itself to the Conductor, who gave it to Stan to lick.

"A treat," he said. I was skeptical, but Stan relished only the relish.

"Does that count as a vegetable?"

"He thinks so."

I used the toe of my shoe to scratch a message in the sand. MARIA WAS HERE. I felt strangely compelled to make sand angels, despite the rain. I took off my shoes and wriggled my toes in the cold sand. They looked exactly like earthworms, which led me to ideas of earthworm decapitations, and made me want to put my shoes back on.

"What now? Do we go home?"

"Hell no," the Conductor said, and motioned toward the ocean in front of us.

"What does that mean?"

"Girl, we're going swimming. It's a beach, right? Got your suit?"

It was a beach only in the most generous sense of the word. I was wearing a bathing suit, yes. Under my sweater. And wool pants. And coat. And scarf. The Conductor was stripping down to psychedelic floral swim trunks. He folded his clothing neatly on the garbage sack. I could see goose bumps.

"Come on. You're joking. It's too cold to go swimming."

"Nah. I do this every year on the last day of the season. It's like New Year's Eve, you know? You make a wish, so that the next year will be good. You have to eat the last hot dog sold, swim the last swim, and watch the last tattoo go by."

He seemed to be combining several traditions into one.

Nevertheless, I started unbuttoning my coat. Something about the Conductor made me trust him. He was quirky, but, just as he'd said, nobody was normal. Not me. And he happened to be standing next to me, grinning, and hopping up and down in the wind. I couldn't let him do that all alone. I could see Stan eyeing me from the pile of clothes. My bikini was green. I shoved him surreptitiously with my foot and made sure that he couldn't climb anything to get to me. I had no intention of being molested by an iguana.

Pretty speedily, the Conductor and I were both standing there, like psychos, on the beach of Coney Island in the wind and the rain, getting ready to run into the ocean. I could see some people watching us from the relative shelter of the hot dog stands and teacup ride. Way down the beach, an old lady in a black dress lifted a pair of binoculars.

"Okay, girl," yelled the Conductor. "Here we go!" He grabbed my hand, and we ran into the water.

ICE, ICE, ICE. ONCE YOU THROW YOUR WHOLE BODY INTO ICE WATER, you feel pretty cool. Both in the metaphoric sense, and in the actual sense. I felt ballsy. But I also felt those balls shrinking. I concluded that this was, hands down, the stupidest thing I'd ever done. In a life of stupid things, that was saying something. Visions of pneumonia crossed with stomach cramps raced through my head. But somehow, I didn't care.

I'd always been secretly scared of so many things, and the months of yes had changed me. Maybe I'd been scared of falling in love, just as I'd been scared of roller coasters and sweater vests, of leaping before I looked. From the outside, I knew that I looked devil-may-care, but on the inside, I cared like crazy. Part of me was always preserving myself, making sure that I didn't get hurt, making sure that I didn't get lost. Not today. I let go of the last things I'd been clinging to. I was ready for love to come for me.

We ducked underwater and came up, gasping. The Conductor laughed his ass off.

"Dream on, Stan," he called.

I looked back onto the beach, and saw Stan crawling away from our pile of clothes.

"Don't worry," said the Conductor. "He won't go far. I have his woman."

I wasn't sure if he meant me or the muffler, but it didn't really matter. I was willing to be an iguana's woman at that point. I was fucking freezing. Reptile though he was, at least Stan had a wooly scarf he was willing to share with me. I'd done worse.

"Why'd you bring me here?" I asked the Conductor as we were leaving the water. "You don't even know me."

"I took one look at you, and I knew this was your kind of thing," he said.

"How could you tell?"

"Nobody chases a conductor down the platform to ask him why he's happy," the Conductor said. "People chase a conductor to chew his ass. So, girl, you surprised me. I owed you something special. Simple."

If I delivered something special to everyone I probably owed it to, I'd be busy for a long time. Maybe, though, I could try to deliver a little more from here on out.

"HOW COME YOU'RE SINGLE?" I ASKED THE CONDUCTOR AS WE GOT DRESSED.

"Women are like trains," he said. "They go a million miles an hour, and when they get there, they turn right around, and, you're goddamned lucky? You're there waiting. Like you, girl. You're moving fast, right? I'm not going fast enough to keep up with something like you. I just have to wait on the platform and watch you go by. But fuck, baby, that's cool. Can't drive that train. You can love things you can't have, right? Watch 'em go. Me and Stan, we're happy together. I've been working the MTA for thirty years, and I like my life. Don't need a new one. But maybe I changed your life a little, huh?"

"You did," I said. And I hugged him. He seemed surprised, but then he hugged back. Who would have thought that my guru would turn out to be a New York City subway conductor? A whole life of everything from Herman Hesse to Robert Heinlein, from Kierkegaard to Nietzsche, a childhood stocked with my mom's "spiritual" bookshelf and all of its Castaneda, *Zen & the Art of Motorcycle Maintenance, Jonathan Livingston Seagull,* and everything else of that ilk. All those things had left me cold. What really mattered? Kindness. The Conductor smiled at me, and we walked to the train.

ON THE PLATFORM, THE CONDUCTOR HANDED ME A PINK FROSTED CUPCAKE. He rummaged in his jacket and brought out a lone, somewhat crumpled birthday candle. He dug in another pocket, and found matches.

"We got one more thing to do," he said. "Don't breathe."

He lit the candle. The flame trembled, trembled, almost died. I looked questioningly at the Conductor. Finally, the tracks started to rattle, and the lights of the train glowed in the distance.

"Okay girl, now, you got to make a wish."

And so I did. Then, together, we blew the candle out.

A few days later, my wish came true.

LONG DAY'S
JOURNEY INTO TRITE

IN WHICH OUR
HEROINE GETS HER
HEART SPLATTERED
INTO FIVE GAJILLION
PIECES . . .

WHEN I WOKE UP WITH A NOSEBLEED, I should've cut my losses and run. I'd been dreaming that New York City had flooded, and that the Actor and I were on a small boat, made of silken sheets and downy pillows, floating peacefully away. Freudian. Pitiful. I knew what my subconscious was trying to say about my situation, and I didn't like it. Half through the dream, the water had turned to blood, and Ira, my high school lover-nemesis, had swum toward us, no longer in dachshund form, and instead wearing a shark fin. I'd been trying to save the Actor from Ira's gnashing, braces-bedecked teeth, when the melodrama jolted me into consciousness.

I'd bled copiously over the Actor's pillow. This was incredibly unfair. I was displaying all of the downside of a cocaine addiction, with none of the satisfaction, considering I still didn't do drugs. The nosebleed was my body's trite physical response to emotional stressors. In alternate versions, I'd be lifting my skirt in the presence of someone I shouldn't be sleeping with, and my period would gush forth, weeks ahead of schedule, with the tragic velocity of Niagara Falls. My body was bent on keeping me occupied with sopping up messes, and whether this was out of a subsumed desire to be solitary, or simply a rotten twist of fate, I inevitably ended up paying for someone else's laundry.

I felt paranoid that I was bleeding directly from the brain. The way my brain was feeling, this was definitely possible. I was hungover, but not hungover enough to be blind to the unflattering morning light, last night's makeup jigging wildly across my eyelids, the pallid ugliness of the morning after.

My bladder was about to burst, and I was paranoid about that, too. When I was a small child, my grandmother, in a misguided attempt to force me to pee prior to a short car journey, had drawn me a series of cartoon diagrams of exploding kidneys. The last panel in her diagram had featured the word "POW!" Since then, any time I'd been forced to hold it, I'd entertained panicked visions of my kidneys swelling like turgid water balloons and ultimately, horribly, blowing to smithereens. Never mind that this made no anatomical sense whatsoever. I'd been firmly branded with a belief that anything could happen.

Unfortunately, I had no idea where the bathroom might be, nor, in fact, where my clothing had ended up. The room was small and lined with bulging bookshelves. I squinted to read titles. The Actor had a collection of everything I'd ever read or wanted to read. In nice editions. This pleased me. Most of my books had been bought used and decrepit from the Strand. Hell, the bookshelves themselves impressed me. At my apartment, books were stacked in endless piles, supporting the couch, supporting the television, an obstacle course for intelligentsia. My *Complete Works of William Shakespeare* also served as a telephone stand. If you walked through the living room in the dark, you were in danger of being bludgeoned by an avalanche of textbooks leftover from a class I'd errantly taken, the Anthropology of Witchcraft, topped off with a few contusions from Zak's Ginsberg and Kerouac section.

Outside the door, I could hear the pattering feet of roommates unknown. The hissing and burbling of an espresso machine. The sound cued a vague memory left over from the night before; the Actor undressing me in the kitchen, my black lace demibra being draped over, dear God, a piece of shiny Italian machinery: brass, dials, demitasse rack. Damn their cappuccinos. I thought for a moment, and recollected perching on the kitchen counter (Who was I to perch? I didn't perch!), my legs wrapped around his waist. I concluded, woefully, that my panties were nestled somewhere in the vicinity of the refrigerator, just waiting to be discovered by the roommates I didn't ever want to meet.

These were not good panties upon which to base a first impression. I had, the night before, put on a dread pair of granny underwear. It was laundry day, and I hadn't been expecting to take them off in the presence of anyone other than Big White Cat. I owned only two pairs of sexy panties, and the rest were scraggly refugees from high school, things bought for me by my mom. I'd gone through a rebellious tie-dye phase before leaving Idaho (my mom, having lived through the sixties, moaning that tie-dye flattered no one; me muttering that if she didn't watch out I'd begin batiking my bras), so not only were the panties inherently ugly, they were a color the dye company called "atomic nectarine." Anyone discovering both pieces could only conclude that I was schizophrenic, a sex-bomb from the waist up, and an aging hippie from the waist down. Or, possibly, they'd extrapolate from my underwear that the Actor had found one girl at a strip club, and another at a drum circle in Washington Square Park, and had managed to take us both home.

I pulled the sheet tighter around my breasts. For a moment, I felt tearful, but then I looked over at the Actor and was floored by my insane good fortune.

He was still sleeping, his face creaseless, his skin perfect. I lifted the sheet and looked at his spine. I counted his ribs. I memorized the tattoo diagramming his bicep, stripes and slashes, dots and dashes, things encoded, the geometry of yearning. He was beautiful. I, on the other hand, could tell that I looked like a lunatic, my face covered in streaming blood, my hair standing at acute angles, an escapee from some East Village asylum.

I gazed at him: his dark nimbus of curls, his bitten bottom lip, and the pillow he held clenched to his chest.

Love swelled within me, like an enormous, malarial mosquito bite.

THE NIGHT BEFORE, THINGS HAD BEEN FINE. Taylor was scheduled to turn thirty at a bar on the Upper West Side, and I was dressing to defy the barometer. It was sleety, but neurosis about looking frumpy commandeered my hips into a miniskirt. Victoria took one look at me, sighed, and spun on her heel.

Defiant, I tugged on some black tights and zipped my stiletto boots. I was determined to look ravishing. This was a group of people who had, all too often, seen me looking like something warmed over at a truckstop. Taylor had directed a play of mine my first year in New York, and I had lingering regrets over my deep naïveté during that experience. There had been a few incidents of me not understanding how to use the subway, not to mention the humiliating sobbing I'd done when the production was finished, not to mention the fact that I'd been reluctantly dating Martyrman at the time and he'd accompanied me to the final show, wearing a sport jacket and a striped polo shirt, and then insisted on partying afterward with the cast. I was always looking for an opportunity to show off my evolution into a sexy, confident New Yorker, and the birthday party would be an excellent chance. I put on a not-warm-enough jacket.

Zak looked at me and raised a quizzical eyebrow.

"What?" I said.

"Someone you're trying to seduce?"

"Why do you say that?"

"It'll probably work," he said, and gave me a pat.

"You think?" I was attempting liquid eyeliner.

"Don't bend over, though," he advised, checking out the rear view.

The skirt was getting shorter by the minute, but I was not wise enough to change.

An hour later, as I walked up Broadway, the skirt inched its way up, and the tights inched their way down. Soon, the crotch of my hosiery would be visible beneath the hemline of the miniskirt. Moreover, my thighs were getting bound together by the waistband elastic of the tights, and it was becoming difficult to walk without hobbling. I ducked into a doorway, looked both ways, and attempted to remedy my situation. It was raining, after all, raining, and cold, and midnight. Who would be out?

Just as I hoisted the skirt up around my waist and began yanking on the waistband of the tights, a roughly-sixteen-year-old pizza boy meandered around the corner. I could see him silhouetted in a streetlamp and, too late, I realized that I was standing in front of a pink neon manicure sign. The pizza boy stopped and stared. I stared back. My old self would have been embarrassed, but I discovered that I was now past the point of caring.

"I'm really sorry about this," I told him, and continued to fight with the tights.

"Hey," he said. "I'm Joey."

"I'm Maria," I said. "This'll only take a minute." The tights squeezed my thighs, like a demon boa constrictor attempting to wrestle me to the ground and gobble me up. It was a losing battle. I wasn't strong enough to kill them.

"Take your time," he said. "I'm just going into that building. But I can wait."

I put my thumb through the tights, creating a massive run. I was late. I surrendered and shed them. Victorious, I threw the slain tights into a garbage can, pulled my skirt down, and rezipped my footwear.

"Later," I said to Joey.

"Thank you," he said, and saluted me. I couldn't be sure, but it seemed possible that he was blushing. It was the first New York male blush I'd ever witnessed, and it was akin to seeing a unicorn. I walked away, feeling better, even though my knees were chattering.

THE BAR WAS NOT MY KIND OF PLACE. Drinks cost more than I had in my bank account, and everyone there knew each other better than they wanted to know me. I wandered from small conversation to smaller conversation, patrolling the boundaries for scraps of sentences that I might be able to lamely respond to. Taylor's birthday was synchronized with those of several of his friends, so the group was large and diverse, full of theater people.

I'd never been good at collective socializing. I tended to either be the girl who was dancing on the tables or the wallflower, and there was no happy medium. I made my way to the bar, where I was accosted by a tray of sorry calamari. "Happy Birthday" was sung and everyone cheered. The entire world seemed to be having a better time than I was. It was my usual problem. I kept a smile of joy and rapture on my face, even though I was freezing and alienated. I was perpetually trapped in corners with people I knew only slightly, discussing Bertolt Brecht and chaos, discussing the darkness at the center of the Norwegian night and how it pertained to Ibsen's plays.

I was also getting tangentially drunk on the Maker's Mark I'd been nursing for hours. I drank bourbon because I didn't know any better. A girlfriend had offered it to me at some point, claiming that it would cure cramps, and, in fact, it did, though the cure was sometimes worse than the disease. I'd never tried anything else on the hard liquor front. Zak and I were cheap. A few days before this party, he'd leaned over the kitchen table and looked into my eyes, as though about to impart some revolutionary analysis of male-female relations.

"Big breasts do not mean big brain," he'd informed me, quite seriously.

"No shit," I'd replied.

"Would I joke about a thing like this?" he'd asked, and marched morosely into the bathroom to throw up.

We'd subsequently managed to drink ourselves into the most depressing stupor either of us had ever experienced and had been forced to stay in our beds for three days, moaning intermittently for water, Victoria stepping smugly over us as she went about her nontoxic existence. This was the tenth time we'd vowed never to buy that wine again, but despite our prestigious collegiate status, we were as broke as the winos. We'd encounter them at the liquor store, smile in preemptive recognition of pain and suffering, go home and pretend that the vinegar we were drinking was something from a wine cellar, bearing hints of cherry and tobacco on the palate, instead of hints of bile and blood.

In part, we were drinking too much because our time living together was coming to an end. Every time Zak and I walked down the street together arm in arm, or hugged, or had any damned contact at all, I shuddered with preemptive sorrow. I was trying to behave myself, but it was useless. Extremes of emotion were my nature.

Zak was trying to separate, too. The night before, I'd been leaning against his knees as he sat in a kitchen chair. I'd been gesticulating as I talked, and he'd suddenly grabbed my hand and held it. I'd sat there for a moment, afraid to breathe, feeling as though maybe big things were changing, and then Zak had complained, "Don't hold my hand so tightly."

"You handed me your hand," I'd said.

"I'm getting a cramp," he'd said.

I'd considered squishing his hand to bits, but instead, I'd just let him go.

That was half of why I was at this party. New friends, I'd thought. Distractions! And, of course, in the back of my mind was the Actor. If Zak was leaving me, maybe I could engineer a super-friendship with the Actor, and save myself some sorrow. The knowledge that there would be no more Zak to commiserate with, no more Zak to pontificate with, and no more Zak to be secretly in love with was making me even more neurotic than usual. More neurosis meant more alcohol, which meant more stupidity.

Drinking was another thing I wasn't good at. I had the tolerance of a hummingbird. This may explain why, though I'd had only the one drink, I was not in full possession of my faculties by the time the Actor arrived.

HE BLEW IN THE DOOR LIKE A HURRICANE OF HANDSOME, bringing with him reflected streetlight and pounding rain. Perhaps it was only from my perspective that he seemed to be surrounded by a starry aura of perfection. I'd been hopelessly besotted with him for years. Every time I talked to him, my tongue knitted itself into warped and purled sentences. For all I knew he was gay. Indeed, I was in denial of rumors that he was. I'd never have him; therefore, I could love him from afar. I knew I wasn't his type. If the rumors about the Actor's preferences were true, there was no way he'd ever be attracted. If they weren't, he was out of my league anyway. Adoring him was like adoring a celebrity. He'd never notice me.

I could, however, be a groupie. Surely the not-even-close-to-famous would appreciate groupies, at least as much as more legitimate superstars did. I could do his bidding, bring him drinks, smile mysteriously and never, *never* oppress him. Alas, in reality, every time I encountered him I lost control. I chronically ended up behaving like a ninny, tripping over my feet, giggling inanely, and choking on spittle.

The last time I'd seen the Actor, at a crowded cocktail reception, the back zipper of my dress had spontaneously bared its teeth, growled, and opened wide, exposing me, naked from neck to rump, to an entire room full of people. The Actor had swooped in and saved me, my zipper purring like a kitten by the time he'd finished with it. He'd spent the rest of the evening with a protective arm around me, and while I suspected this was because he'd felt sorry for me—in a pitiful, asexual, little-sister kind of way—sometimes I'd dream that he harbored certain feelings. My adulation of him had increased exponentially, even as his mystical powers over fastenings indicated, again, that he was homosexual.

I hadn't seen the Actor in months, and I'd almost managed to forget about him. I'd known, of course, that he might be at the party, but I'd pretended that it was immaterial. Now that I saw him again, however, my crush was back in full, feverish force. I could feel myself trembling. I drank the rest of my Maker's Mark in one swallow. I prayed for grace.

"HEY, BABY!" HE SAID, OPENING HIS ARMS AND HUGGING ME TIGHTLY. He seemed, as always, genuinely happy to see me. I had long ago decided that this was because he was a generosity martyr. If our roles had been reversed, I'd have started evading him long ago, dodging into darkness, swiftly engaging myself in intense confabs, leaving him teetering on the corners of conversations. I couldn't fathom why he tolerated me, given that I was quite sure my crush was glaringly obvious.

The Actor was about five foot nine and wiry. He had a smile that claimed his entire face, and, that night, he looked like he might be wearing eyeliner. He was wearing a white, wife-beater tank top and a button-down shirt, of the sort that Puerto Rican granddaddies wore to play dominoes in my neighborhood. His skin was caramel-colored, slightly freckled. He had the kind of arm muscles that only came with centuries at the gym. His gym was in Chelsea, I knew, and no doubt populated by that most glorious genre of gay man, the ones that I often saw strolling down Eighth Avenue, laying possessive hands on one another's taut asses. The ones that charitably called me "fabulous."

Why did I not care? Attraction trumped intelligence. Sticks and stones trumped bones. Some things just had to be chalked up to rules of the universe.

The most wonderful thing about him was his eyes. They were pale orange, a color I'd never seen before. They turned me into a kamikaze fly, cannonballing into amber. I could have looked at him for millennia and been perfectly happy without any reciprocity at all. That's how appealing he was. That's how appalling *I* was.

"Hi," I squeaked.

"Want another drink?" His hand was warm on the back of my neck.

"Sure," I said. At least, if I was drunk, I wouldn't necessarily remember how stupid I was about to be.

"Don't go away," he said, close against my ear, and then he brought my fingertips to his lips. He smiled again, and began to wend his way through the masses.

I WAS STUNNED. WHAT EXACTLY WAS HAPPENING? Surely, I was misinterpreting something. Surely, I was misinterpreting everything. I looked around to see if anyone else had noticed that the world had suddenly developed a rosy glow. Nope. I could see Taylor across the room, drinking, in a crowd of laughter. He caught my glance, and looked questioningly at me. I shrugged, and waved reassuringly.

I was having a psychotic break.

I was just imagining that the Actor was hitting on me. He was, after all, an actor. What did actors do, except seduce the world? Maybe I'd been inadvertently caught in his seduction spotlight, while he'd been scanning the room for the real focus of his wooing. I gritted my teeth against the inevitable: I'd look over and see him draped against the bar, arm around a hot, blond actor. I got ready to pretend that I'd meant to be left alone. I went over my exit lines in my head, preparing to protest that I was *fine, happy, having a wonderful time, thanks, but I should get back to Brooklyn, because, the trains! The G! I don't have to tell you!*

The Actor reappeared, a martini in one hand and a bourbon in the other. He hadn't spilled a drop, and I was amazed. Another thing that caused me to be enamored of actors was that they had the ability to balance on anything, be it the high wire or the shoulders of clowns. They seemed so capable, so responsible, and so stable. All these things, I reminded myself, were the antithesis of actor personalities. *Actors*, I repeated silently, *are neurotic. Actors are self-absorbed. They are performers. They never stop performing.*

Unfortunately, I loved them. I was forever suspending myself from my disbelief and twisting in the wind, trusting their lines.

"To you," he said. "It's been too long." He clinked glasses with me.

"To you, too," I said, lamely, and he grinned.

"You can do a better toast than that. Aren't you supposed to be a writer?"

"May you find joy, even in the darkest places," I said, and then felt like an ass. "Not that *this* is the darkest place," I clarified. "Not that I wish you dark places. Not that I think only bad things happen in the dark. Not that I'm an advocate of bright lights. I like lampshades. I like dimmer switches."

Words, words, words. What cruel god had given me so many of them? I wanted to transform into someone who didn't analyze her every syllable. I wanted to be a person who could accept flirtation without negation, a person who could drink her bourbon and flutter her eyelashes, and not tumble into tangential tarpits.

The Actor was squinting at me. He took a sip of his martini, and casually said:

"So, would it be fair to say you can't stand a naked lightbulb, any more than you can a rude remark or a vulgar action?"

Horrors! He was quoting Tennessee Williams! He had turned

me into Blanche DuBois! It served me right. I should never have said anything about darkness. Now I was relegated to being an aging Southern belle.

"I have absolutely no problem with vulgar actions," I said, trying to save myself.

"You know what?" he said.

"What?" I replied, faintly.

"I've always depended on the kindness of strangers." He placed a hand on my hipbone. I could feel my blood going effervescent.

Suddenly, I understood. Taylor had told the Actor to take pity on me: "She's dating homeless guys, man, I think she's losing it, can you just do me this one favor?"

I could see Taylor saying this. Though he was very entertained by the Year of Yes, he thought it was nuts.

"How much will you pay me?"

No, this was too much. I revised the Actor's dialogue.

"Okay, but you owe me. This is hardship duty."

That seemed more plausible. But was the Actor really so self-sacrificing? His hand curled around my hip, his fingers drumming gently on the bare skin between my skirt and jacket. I could feel my knees going weak.

Was it possible that he actually liked me? Maybe I'd finally worn the right outfit. Maybe I was dreaming. I was terrified that my untested heart was approaching a swift and brutal malfunction, all my theories of love revealed as false, all the willing life I thought I'd been living shown to be shallow. What if I didn't know how to do this? What if it killed me? Until this moment, every man I'd met had been implausible in some key way. It hadn't ever been a perfect fit. This was. Maybe this was. My drink splashed, and I looked down to discover that my hands were shaking.

Last call had been announced some time before, and people were dispersing. The Actor went to the bathroom. Nat "King" Cole blared over the speakers, that old dirge, "After the Ball Is Over."

After the ball is over, after the break of morn,
After the dancers' leaving, after the stars are gone,
Many a heart is aching, if you could read them all—
Many the hopes that have vanished, after the ball.

Clearly, the bartenders wanted to send a bunch of depressed drunks out into the night. The fluorescents blazed up.

I wanted this too much. What had happened to me? Exactly what I'd hoped would happen. Love. Exactly what I'd wished for when I'd blown out the Conductor's candle.

Now, here I was, more vulnerable than I'd ever been in my life. Here I was, five seconds from falling. If I stayed any longer, my heart would be pushed pell-mell by emotion, and that would be the end of any ability I had to flee in any direction other than down. I'd only fallen in love once before, and it had been with the Hitchhiker, someone I'd never even kissed. I decided that I should go home. IM-MEDIATELY.

I frantically gulped the rest of my third drink, and then choked as it burned down my throat. I stumbled to the door.

"Where're you going?" asked the Actor, suddenly next to me again.

"Nowhere," I said.

"No, I mean now." He stroked my cheek with the back of his hand.

"Um. I don't know." I did know, of course, home, but Brooklyn was three trains away, and my resistance had just left without me. There it was, sprinting down the street.

"Want to share a cab?" There was no earthly reason we should share a cab. He lived in the East Village. My part of Brooklyn required the Fifty-ninth Street Bridge.

"Of course," I said.

I could feel Taylor's eyes burning holes in our backs as the Actor and I walked out the door together, but I refused to turn around. If there was bad news to be dispensed, I didn't want to hear it. I'd spent the last several months forcibly prying my heart open, and now it seemed that it was stuck that way. So be it.

We didn't say much in the cab, just sat close against each other, me nurturing a dark fantasy that the Actor would get out on Avenue A, pat my shoulder, and say, "Okay, thanks for the ride, see you." Kiss me on the cheek, maybe.

I didn't have enough money to pay for the cab ride home, so if he left me, I was going to feel ridiculous. Only once in my time in New York had I failed to pay for a cab ride, and there were extenuating circumstances. Namely, the cabdriver had informed me, as I got in to go to La Guardia, my suitcases packed for Christmas break, that his trunk was broken and that my luggage would need to ride in the backseat. Accommodating person that I was, I settled myself into the front. Apparently, there was an entire vocabulary of passenger/driver signals that I didn't know about, and sitting in the front seat of a New York City taxi meant that:

1.   The driver was entitled to reach one arm across to the passenger side and wedge his hand down your sweater, scooping up your left breast in a grip akin to that of a Wonderbra; and
2.   When questioned as to motivation, said driver was entitled to say: "Because it was there?"; and
3.   Said driver was also entitled to be enraged at your unwillingness to compensate him for the grope he'd gotten and, indeed, to complain that he also deserved a tip.

Since that experience, I'd been somewhat suspicious. Not suspicious enough to keep me from saying yes to dates with a couple of cabdrivers, but suspicious of the ears in the front seat, wary of what they would hearken to. The cabdrivers I'd gone out with had lots of stories about passengers who hadn't cared what the driver heard. From the Actor and I, this driver heard nothing, unless he could translate the racing of my heart, the ringing in my ears, the heat that crept from the Actor's side of the bench seat to mine.

The Actor took my hand. I could feel his thumb circuiting my palm. We were three drinks into intimacy, and onto affection. I willed my hand to stay open. I tried not to hold onto him too tightly. He paid the driver.

We got out of the taxi and made our way down the deserted street. I wasn't assuming anything. Maybe he thought I lived here, too. I hadn't exactly been clear. Maybe he thought I was walking him home, keeping him safe from muggers.

We passed the Russian baths, which I'd visited a few times, accompanied by Taylor. The baths were co-owned by a feuding duo, a Russian and a Turk, and they alternated nights. The rules changed every other day, and sometimes women weren't allowed. When they were, I was delighted to put on the strange shower shoes and slog about in a mist of evaporated Alphabet City alcohol. I liked the community, the tattoos, the ancients, everyone equally undressed, everyone fallible. I liked to sit in the sauna and roast myself like a woodchip, balanced on beams that had balanced the buttocks of thousands. You could get drunk just sitting on a bench next to most of the people there. I liked to leap into the ice pool and watch the hungover shudder at my bravery. It was a great way to feel superior on a Sunday morning. Part of the allure of the baths, of course, was that I happened to know that they were next door to the Actor's apartment, and had ideas about how I might look, exiting an afternoon of steaming and soaking, a vision of vigor, all of my pallid, English/Scottish heritage abolished. I'd always thought I might even run into the Actor inside, might accidentally be topless, might woo him like the Waterhouse painting of Hylas kneeling at the side of a pool full of naked chicks. Never mind that that story ended in a drowning.

We went into a bar, dark and rosy-curtained, and had a deep conversation, the details of which I hereby grant the Actor a reprieve from recounting. Not everything needs to be written down. It was long, and it was intense, and at the end of it, the Actor and I were sitting two inches apart, and he was leaning in, and he was saying, "I'd love it if you came home with me."

He was holding both my hands tightly. If this wasn't a legitimate offer, I didn't know what was.

"Me, too," I said.

"Are you sure?"

I leaned forward, drawing reserves of ballsiness from some unknown well, and kissed him on the mouth.

"Yes," I said. "Yes," meaning it more than I'd meant it in all ten months of my Year of Yes, meaning it more than I'd ever meant it before.

He wasn't moving. I drew back, fearful.

The Actor stared into my eyes, with something that looked like wonder.

"Sometimes," he said, "my life is so amazing."

That was when I fell in love with him.

"HEY, YOU," THE ACTOR WHISPERED, HIS EYES SLITTING OPEN. I rejoiced. So familiar! So tender! So possible that he'd forgotten who I was, and was even now running an actor maneuver on me!

"You remember my name, right?" I couldn't help myself.

"Maria," he said, grinning. "*I once met a girl* . . . yeah, I think I know your name . . . Jesus! Are you okay?" He suddenly sat bolt upright. I'd forgotten about the nosebleed. He was out of bed, grabbing something that I hoped was a tissue, but which turned out to be a dirty sock. He pressed it to my nose, and pinched the back of my neck between two fingers. I felt brave, like a swaggering boxer, blinded by punches, collapsing in the corner of the ring, being ministered to by my coach. The room was spinning, ever so slightly, ever so slightly.

"Why didn't you wake me up?" He was rubbing my back.

I shrugged, and smiled weakly.

"I had such a good time with you last night," he said. "Don't bleed to death, okay?"

"Okay," I said, though I wasn't sure I could promise anything. "Bathroom?"

He looked both ways outside his bedroom door. The roommates had departed, but his cat was still home. He had a cat! Better and better! A friend for Big White! The cat meowed, then climbed my sheet-draped body and nestled into my neck.

"My roommates are all allergic," he said, by way of excuse. The cat nuzzled my chin. "Clean up, and we'll go to breakfast. Want to?"

It was so stunningly normal. It was not only normal, it was romantic. That was what blew me away. Could I have a normal existence? I never had before. A normal boyfriend? It had not occurred to me that I might actually find someone I could love in any way other than in vain. It had not occurred to me that functionality might be possible, that I could, conceivably, be half of one of those Sunday morning couples eating bagels and doing the *New York Times* crossword. I could give and receive affection in a healthful manner! I didn't need to live in consistent dysfunction! Love! Love! Love!

I flung myself upon him, hugging and kissing him.

"Okay . . ." he said, raising an eyebrow at me. "It's only scrambled eggs." He was getting dressed.

But it was more than scrambled eggs! Much more! I was feeling radiant. An entirely new world had opened up in front of me, one with possibilities, one with shared enthusiasms and multiple orgasms.

I'd finally, after all these months of dating inappropriate candidates, be able to introduce someone to my family! I wanted to sing love songs, but brushed my teeth instead. Love was possible! I didn't have to be alone forever, as I'd been beginning to think.

"Shit," said the Actor, looking at his watch.

"What's wrong?" Nothing, that was what.

"I'm late for something."

I wasn't paying much attention. I still felt like dancing. I grabbed him and lurched him into a little pseudo-tango.

"So, I can't do breakfast," he said. I was dipping him.

"That's fine," I said. "Want to have dinner tomorrow?"

"Yeah, that's not going to work, either."

"I'm free on Friday," I said.

"You know, I'll check my book, but . . ."

It occurred to me that I was, as usual, leading, and leading badly. I sat down.

"When *will* you be free?" I asked.

"Um . . . I'm not really sure. I mean, I'm actually pretty busy," he said.

This conversation suddenly felt nauseatingly familiar.

"Me, too," I said. "You're not the only one! I mean, I'm busy, too, I have school, and work, and life, and writing, a whole play, I just started this play! I have things to do!"

"So, I don't know," he said. "Can we just play it by ear?"

"Sure," I whispered. I could have given him his next line. I'd said it plenty of times myself. I felt like I'd written it.

"I'll call you . . ." he said.

"Great!" I said.

"Great," he said, sounding relieved. He picked up my atomic nectarine panties, looked at them with mild amusement, and handed them to me.

My nose started bleeding again.

"Okay, then, see you!" I was practically running to the door.

"Do you need a tissue?" Drops of blood splattered onto the floor, like sealing wax closing a letter.

"Nope," I yelped, staunching the blood with my bra. I made it to the hall before the tears fully overflowed, but I wasn't fast enough. I had to endure the tremendous indignity of the Actor putting his arms around me in an attempt to comfort me.

"What's wrong?" he asked, and kissed my hair. What was wrong? I was the thing I always dreaded: the One-Night Misunderstand. I'd left a trail of tears behind me, too, and I knew it. I'd broken hearts, all the while thinking that I was being kind, that I was saving them from me. And now, here I was, standing in a strange hallway, in the arms of the man who'd done me in. I couldn't even blame him. It was my own damned fault. Despite all my vows regarding actors, I'd fallen for him. And, despite what I'd thought the night before, despite the long and profound conversation we'd had in the bar, it seemed that he was so far from falling for me that the possibility hadn't even occurred to him. For him, this was casual. This was meaningless. For me, this was my previously state-of-the-art heart hissing and smoking, sending off emergency alarums, and finally, wretchedly, breaking down entirely.

"I'm late," I said, ridiculously. "That's why I'm crying. It's not because of you, or anything."

"You're late?" he said.

"For a very important date." I sniffled. I had lost my ability to talk. All that was left was *Alice in Wonderland*. No time to say hello, good-bye, find me a fucking rabbit hole to dive down.

"Okay . . ." the Actor said. "I'll see you around, Maria, okay? Don't cry."

And I *would* see him around. That was the worst part. He was no perfect stranger. He was someone that I regularly ran into at parties and plays. Every time I saw him, I knew, I'd be reduced to this again.

I went home on the subway, crying all the way. An old woman gave me tissues. Some guy on an acoustic guitar languished through "Homeward Bound," and I gave him all the money in my wallet. He smiled at me in thanks, and so I took my bra and panties out of my purse, and dropped them into his guitar case, too.

"Peace, lady," he said.

"Likewise," I replied, and got off the train.

"OKAY, I'M KIND OF GUESSING HE DIDN'T TELL YOU THIS, and I don't want to be the bearer of bad news, but—"

"Tell me what?" I was sitting at my temp job, trying to look like I was working. I'd been writing soggy poetry all morning and putting it into spreadsheet format, in case someone walked by and glanced at my screen. Taylor had called for details, and I was too exhausted to lie to him. Now, even though he clearly thought I was an idiot for falling for the Actor, he was trying his best to make me feel better.

"He's mostly gay. So don't feel bad. It's not you."

"What is 'mostly' gay? What does that even mean?" I didn't care if the Actor was 99/100ths gay. I loved him!

"And, he's engaged."

"To a man?" This was new.

"No, to a girl," Taylor said, as though my question was insane.

"Then how can he be mostly gay?"

"He's confused?"

"He slept with me! I'm not male!"

"Clearly, he doesn't know what he wants."

"Engaged?"

"His college girlfriend. They've been together forever. You'd like her."

No. No, I would not. I liked no one, least of all myself.

I'd already called the Actor three times, and this was supremely humiliating, because I only had his message service number, which meant that I had to speak to a woman somewhere in Long Island, who gently told me that he wasn't available, as though she had him in the next room and he was simply in the shower. I could hear her typing my message as I dictated it. I feared typos, not that that would even matter, considering he'd never call. I never responded to people who did this to me, why would he? This didn't keep me from spelling my last name meticulously, obsessively, idiotically, every time I called, like he didn't know who I was. He knew. And he was cringing. I could feel it. I was cringing, too.

I'd spent three days lying flat on my face on my linoleum, weeping, Big White Cat butting me periodically and squawking for catnip. At least he could get high. Nothing could make me feel better. I couldn't believe I'd been such a daredevil, climbing without any of my gear, and inevitably falling hard. I'd known better. Tomorrow, I kept telling myself, early tomorrow morning, I'll find my ropes and hooks. I'll start back up. It was funny, though, the air at the bottom. It was as thin as at the summit. I felt light-headed.

I called the Actor's message service.

She says she is "fine." She says she is really sorry about
falling in love. It was accidental. She says she is now
planning on staying on solid ground and that you don't
need to call her back. Unless you want to. If you do,
please call. Please. Here's that number again, in case it
accidentally got thrown away with the other garbage in
your life, which she doesn't blame you for . . .

Yes. I was that pitiful.

THE WHOLE WRETCHED AFFAIR HAD BROUGHT BACK, in excruciating detail, an incident during my first year in New York. I'd unwisely rendezvoused with one Ivan, a Russian graduate student, who had the tiniest, most irregular teeth I'd ever seen. He was so needy, so unlaid, and, in fact, such a very nice person. When it became clear that he was gaga over me, I'd thought I could charitably do something kind. I'd made out with him in a stairwell, and then walked away, thinking, Okay, that's done.

It was not done. Ivan had called, many, many times. He'd left myriad messages in his thick Russian accent, always beginning like this:

"Hhhhi. This ees Ivahn. I vas just calling to say . . . hhhi. Okay, then . . . bahhye."

He'd become a running joke among my roommates. "Hhhhi," they'd say, and crack up. I'd been mortified by the depth of his desire. In a last attempt to recover my affections, he'd brought me an enormous houseplant, some sort of lily with large, phallic blooms. It had weighed approximately seventy-five pounds, so he'd carried it to my apartment, clearly hoping to be invited in. I'd given him a glass of water, and sent him away. When the plant had died of dehydration, I'd discovered a love note stuck in its soil, Ivan asking me to forgive him for whatever he had done.

What an ass I'd been, and how worldly I'd felt. Now what had gone around had come around, and for the rest of my life, I'd be itemizing my sorrows to the Actor's voice mail.

"Hhhhhi," I'd say. "It's Maria. Headley. I was just calling to say . . . hhhhhiii. Okay then . . . bahhye." I'd arrive at his apartment bearing unwanted foliage. I could see my future strung up in front of me like frozen laundry.

I BOOKED A TICKET TO IDAHO FOR CHRISTMAS, feeling adrift, and thinking that a stint at home would help. Wrong. My dad drove up on Christmas Eve. He looked relatively okay, if you ignored the fact that his pupils were spinning like slot-machine cherries. For a moment, I entertained a fantasy that I really *had* cured him with my conversation with the Rockstar. Maybe he wasn't as bad as I'd thought. Maybe he could, like a run-down motor, still be repaired. No. He went out to his truck and returned bearing an enormous grocery sack full of cantaloupes, a misbegotten attempt to declare himself the family provider. He then brought out a thick sheaf of short stories in which I was the main character.

He read them aloud for us, sitting in my mother's living room, grinning his head off. We tried not to cry. In one of the stories, I'd written a musical that bore suspicious similarity to *Cats*, and became a wild success on Broadway. My sister, who, for some reason, he'd written as crippled, danced onstage in her "hobbled little way," and my dad got to come to the podium with me when I gave my Tony speech. All of us but him ended up sobbing on the floor. He kept reading for hours, powered by the super-strength batteries of his manic phase.

When he left, it was midnight. We got drunk on eggnog and tried to pretend that he was okay. "At least he's creative," we said. "At least he's doing something productive." Really, we were all flattened by grief, and I was already so miserable over the Actor that this pushed me over the edge. I searched through my phonebook for Idaho friends, someone to take me away from the house and remind me that I wasn't a child anymore, that I lived far away and had control over myself.

Did I have control over myself? No. I dialed Ira the Reincarnated Dachshund's number, but he didn't pick up. I dialed Zak in California, and talked to him for not long enough. I dialed Vic and got one of her relatives, someone who didn't actually speak English.

I dialed my dachshund again, and this time he answered the phone.

FIFTEEN MINUTES LATER, IRA PICKED ME UP, NO QUESTIONS ASKED. His life was as messy as mine.

It was snowing hard, and he drove up in a borrowed car.

"Hey," I said. "Merry Christmas. Sorry I called so late." I was still crying, but Ira always made me feel better. I had no idea why. We'd certainly had our share of furies, but our relationship had maintained, even when we'd wanted to kill each other.

"No worries, babe," he said. He'd picked up a British accent since I'd last seen him.

"Works well on the ladies," he explained.

"But you're from Idaho," I said, sniffling.

"They don't know that. They think I'm from London."

"Come on. Drop the British thing."

"How about Australian, matey?"

"No."

"Transylvanian? I vant to fuck your ... damn. No rhyme for blood."

"Shhh," I said.

I decided that we had enough history that we didn't even really need to talk. He seat-belted me into the passenger side, and we drove, for lack of an apartment without roommates, to a Barnes & Noble parking lot.

All around us the snow was piling up, and there were no cars but ours. Everyone else was at home, waiting for reindeer hooves. It was pitch black. If you looked up, the snowflakes were like stars falling. We might as well have been early settlers, transiting the plains and the prairie, waiting for spring to come so that we could dig out and get moving. Either that or we might, sick and snow-blind, resort to cannibalism. It'd always been a mixed bag with Ira and me.

"Whose car?" I asked, and fiddled with the stereo.

"Landlady," he said. Ira had always had a weird ability to charm those in authority.

"What are we doing?"

"Sitting in a Pontiac, babe, in a parking lot, in Boise, Idaho, U.S.A., the World. The Universe. The Mind of God," he said, quoting *Our Town*. We'd both been in it in high school. His character had been called Belligerent Man.

Then he held my face in his hands and kissed me.

Consider the previous seven years some sort of warped foreplay.

"I don't want anything to get on your landlady's upholstery," I said, as we took off our clothes. "That'd be rude."

Ira considered. "Babe, I never really liked this shirt anyway," he said, and spread it, like Sir Walter Raleigh's cape, across the backseat.

Outside, the snow built up on the glass, but inside it was summer. We were in a shopping mall parking lot in Idaho. All the other cars were gone. It was the middle of the winter, it was the middle of the night. On the car radio, "O Holy Night" was playing, and at first we laughed, but then we sang.

THREE WEEKS INTO THE NEW YEAR, THE ACTOR FINALLY CALLED ME BACK. As though our history was made of rainbows and candy hearts, I said, "Hi there, stranger! What's up?"

"Hey," he said, uncomfortably. Clearly, he was calling to defuse me. I was a ticking valentine. Nine million messages later, he was probably being chewed out by the women at his voicemail service.

"How *are* you?" I asked. Lighthearted. Bright. The Happiest Girl in the World.

"I'm great."

"I was wondering something," I said, knowing better than to ask what I was asking.

"Okay," said the Actor, through the gritted teeth that came of doing the right thing.

I closed my eyes and imagined him as I wanted to remember him, sitting in the bar down the block from his apartment, before I'd gone home with him. He'd been telling me the secrets of his soul, or at least telling me things that had sounded true. I wanted to believe they had been, that the miscommunication had happened later, that he'd loved me, for those few hours before the sun rose, as much as I'd loved him.

"I had a wonderful time with you, the last time I saw you. Remember?" I said.

"I remember," he said. His voice sounded kind, but miserable.

"And so, I need you to tell me that you don't want to be with me. I want to be with you. You knew that already. So, if you could just tell me, if you definitely don't want me?"

He'd been avoiding me for weeks. I was putting my heart on a chopping block and handing him a machete.

"I don't want to date you," he said. "I'm sorry."

"What was that night to you?" I sounded angry, but I had no right to be.

"It was. I was thinking, it was a great, an *amazing* night with Maria, you know? Just a night? Do you know what I mean?" he pleaded.

And I did. I knew. I'd been him, so many times I'd lost count. He wasn't breaking my heart because he wanted to break my heart. He was breaking my heart because there was no other option.

"Okay," I whispered.

Zak happened upon me sobbing in a corner, pitifully eating a jar of artichoke hearts with my fingers. "Why are you eating that?" he asked, with obvious trepidation.

"Because it is bitter, and because it is my heart," I said to him, quoting a bit of Stephen Crane's morbid verse. I tried to smile.

"It's not your heart, darlin', it's antipasti," he corrected.

Later, he slid a benevolent note under the edge of my hut.

"Pssst, you're beautiful and everyone knows it," the note said. There had been a time when I would have killed to have such a note from Zak, but now it was only a Band-Aid on top of hari-kari. I wanted to hide in my bed forever.

But, I still had to pay my rent. Which meant I had to go to work, which meant I had to leave the house. I had to walk down India Street to get to the subway. As soon as I did, dark circles beneath my eyes, my rainboots sloshing with tears, I met Dogboy.

ONCE SMITTEN, TWICE SHY

IN WHICH OUR
HEROINE MEETS
DOGBOY . . .

FROM THE BEGINNING, ZAK DID NOT APPROVE OF THE MAN AT THE END OF INDIA STREET. "I've seen that guy," he muttered, darkly. "He thinks he's testosterone incarnate."

"Only because he is," I said. "You can't tell me he's not sexy. Well, you can. But then I'll know you're jealous."

Zak grimaced. He didn't like the thought that any other man could have more testosterone than he did. Zak wasn't alone.

All the men in Greenpoint and the surrounding areas loathed Dogboy. Living near him was the equivalent of being Don Juan's neighbor. Every time Dogboy stood on his stoop, stretching in the sun, male self-esteem dropped with the velocity of Wile E. Coyote off a cliff. Dogboy was very Roadrunner, sprinting away, chirping, utterly unbruised by the slings and arrows of outrageous fortune. Meanwhile, the men of the neighborhood were peeling themselves up from under anvils.

Pierre, when Dogboy was mentioned, wrinkled up his nose and said, "That guy's an asshole." Pierre had started dating one of the girls who lived next door to Dogboy, and so had firsthand knowledge of his Lothario ways. I didn't care. So what if the guy dated a lot? So did I. So what if the guy was devoid of feelings? So was I. Or at least, I wanted to be. That had to count for something.

WHEN I GOT MY FIRST GLIMPSE OF DOGBOY, I WAS TRUDGING DOWN THE STREET, dressed in a 1920s men's tuxedo shirt I'd had since I was fourteen, baggy black wool tux pants, and combat boots. No lipstick. The ensemble, which I reserved for moments of deepest mourning, was meant to broadcast my disinterest in men. It was an Andrea Dworkin of outfits, a Steinem of suits. It sidled from my dresser when I was depressed, wriggling its wormlike fingers, convincing me that it was a good idea to look as shitty as I felt.

He was walking in my direction. He winked. I stopped. How dare he wink at me?

"Morning," he said, grinning the kind of grin that makes panties fall to the floor.

I had no response to that. I was still in the throes of withdrawal from the Actor, trembling and quaking, night sweating, hallucinations of intimacy. I couldn't be expected to take compliments. The guy looked like Steve McQueen, and knew it. His blond head was shaven, and he had piercing blue eyes. He was wearing a ripped-up T-shirt, which was tight over his chest and biceps. It'd been a while since I'd been this close to a man so exceedingly well built, aside from the Actor, whose nakedness I was trying hard not to think about. Six-pack, instead of beer gut? A brindled pit bull danced beside him, yipping occasionally, obviously expecting breakfast.

Dogboy kept walking. I watched him unlock his door. It was rusty red metal, and industrial. There was an open grate on the front. He was whistling. He turned his head and openly checked me out. How could he be checking me out? I looked like the misbegotten daughter of Kurt Cobain and Jay Gatsby.

"Hi," I said, belatedly.

"Later," he said, disappearing into his building. The pit bull followed him.

I stood in the street for a moment, shaking my head to clear it.

The fact that not even a guy this desirable could make me forget the Actor told me that there was something seriously wrong with both my heart and my head. I was twenty-one years old, but I felt eight hundred. I needed to stop feeling like Ophelia, which meant that I had to stop falling for Hamlets. While plenty of my stories seemed to end with bodies littering the stage, I preferred the ones that concluded with a big fat Happily Ever After. I ran to the train, intent on flipping my heart onto a new purpose.

AT WORK, INSTEAD OF DOING ANYTHING THAT I WAS SUPPOSED TO BE DOING, I sat down to compose a list of the Actor's flaws, thinking that maybe I could meditate on them until I was cured.

UNDESIRABLE QUALITIES OF THE ACTOR
(AN INFLATED LIST)

1. **NOT EVEN A VERY GOOD ACTOR.** This despite the fact that I'd dragged Griffin and Zak to not one, not two, but *three* performances of a play that the Actor had written, and was starring in. That wasn't even the sad part. The sad part was that he was:

2. **NOT REALLY A GOOD WRITER, EITHER.** Not terrible, but still. For the purposes of this list, it would

have been much better if he were officially illiterate. But he wasn't. He was smart and articulate, and mildly fixated on the plays of Edward Albee. Like I wasn't.

3. **DORKIEST HEADSHOTS IN THE WORLD,** posted on his bedroom wall. Slicked-back hair. Tight black T-shirt. Half leer. Arms bent to better display biceps.

4. **SHORT.** Never mind that I, too, was short. Never mind that anyone over five foot six towered over me. I'd seen him in his apartment, attempting to reach a midheight shelf in the kitchen, and having to climb onto the counter, his bony little knees poking out of his saggy little boxer shorts to reveal his bony little ass. I clung to this image.

5. **SKINNY.** In an I-eat-only-wheatgrass-juice kind of way. He'd been climbing onto the counter, incidentally, in order to fetch a glass for his breakfast of Vitamin-C powder.

6. **UNSKILLED/UNWILLING.** Tendency to prefer nonpenetrative intercourse, i.e., me giving him a blow job, and he patting me on the head. This gave the whole thing a sort of pre–women's lib feeling, which, at the time, I was too enamored to acknowledge. No doubt, this problem had more to do with number 7 than with chauvinism, though.

7. **HOMOSEXUAL.** Or, if not gay, ignorant of the finer points of female anatomy, which was, in itself, inexcusable for a straight man pushing thirty.

8. **EMPLOYED AS BATHROOM ATTENDANT IN HIGH-END STRIP CLUB.** Yes. He was the guy who stood in the men's room, handing out towels, spritzing cologne and getting tipped with hundred-dollar bills. It was not something I liked to think about, so when I told people about him, I left it out altogether. It had a distinct aura of skeeze, even though, I reminded myself, New York was a hard city, and he was just trying to make a living.

Still. He hung out with G-strings, boob jobs, and mafia brass all night long. Surely this would eventually have a bad effect on his psyche. Surely he'd be karmically punished for not loving me. Surely he would die in abject misery.

9. WHY DIDN'T HE LOVE ME? WHY? I could have helped him run lines! I could have edited his grammar! I could have taken new headshots that showed his radiance, and then made him look tall by standing next to him while wearing flat shoes! I could have fattened him with homemade butter-slathered scones! I could have cut my hair short and dressed like a boy!

My list started to devolve into a list of my own flaws. I was seeing the world through a fun-house mirror since the Actor. Everything looked bigger and sadder than it really was.

UNDESIRABLE QUALITIES OF MARIA
(A PARTIAL LIST)

1. DESTINED TO BE A BEARDED OLD LADY. The Actor was devoid of body hair. I, on the other hand, had to shave my prehensile monkey toes. As time went on, I was pretty sure I'd be immersing myself in soak baths of Nair. It seemed I was actually some sort of Wooly Mammoth Woman, suited only for existence in Siberia. Which would make sense, given number 2.

2. SHAPED LIKE MINIATURE MANATEE. Perfect for cold climates. I could store fat like a walrus and wallow across ice floes, congratulating myself on my solitude. If I started to starve, I could just eat myself. Basically, that's what I was doing anyway. Along with disgusting quantities of chocolate-covered raisins, which I didn't even like. Since my depression over the Actor, I had become disoriented. Did I hate chocolate-covered raisins? Maybe not. Why not buy a bag the size of Cuba and find out?

3. **SEVERE SOCIAL INEPTITUDE.** Self-explanatory. I wasn't meant to be around people. I needed to find myself a nice little cave, and meet someone named Nimue, who could enable me to go back in time and fix the problems that had begun with getting born. Maybe I could just start over. Everything that was wrong with me had been wrong with me for a long damned time.

4. **BLABBERMOUTH.** Unable to stop talking. Neurotic need to fill silences with random sentences and stories, desperate desire to be the most popular person in the room, even if the room was full of people exponentially more attractive and interesting than I was. Which was the case, almost all the time.

5. **ARROGANT.** Even in the situation of number 4, I still felt superior to almost everyone I met. Hence my unwillingness to settle for the kind of man I clearly deserved, something more along the lines of a Rosencrantz or a Guildenstern. Instead, I perpetually felt that I should date the leading men of the world, even though they kept sending me to nunneries, and dumping me fully dressed into rivers of discontent. I wanted the man with the most lines. Even if his lines were all monologue.

6. **INSATIABLE.** Someone had once asked me, not nicely, how much love I needed from him. "All of it," I'd answered. This, of course, had pissed off the person— who'd already thought I was greedy—even further. If I fell, I fell all the way. If I didn't, I threw the whole thing out like bad lettuce. No wonder the Actor/Bathroom Attendant didn't love me. I wasn't worthy. Not. Worthy. Destined to be alone forever and ever and ever. Unless I could somehow subjugate myself into becoming the woman of the Actor's dreams. Okay, so yes, the process

of conversion would be akin to that of turning a goose into foie gras. Not pretty. Not ending happily for the goose. Fuck it. I was in love. I couldn't help myself. Grasp on reality? What grasp? Masochism! Degradation! I *wanted* to be miserable.

I OPENED MY ADDRESS BOOK TO THE ACTOR'S TEAR-SMEARED VOICEMAIL NUMBER. I put my hand on the phone. Elise, who I'd hired to take some shifts at my personal assistant job, looked over my shoulder and grabbed my dialing finger.

"What do you think you're doing?"

"Nothing."

"Let go of the phone. He's dead to us."

"I want him to love me," I whimpered.

"There are millions of men, right outside," Elise informed me. "And what's this? I don't think so."

She picked up the list of my flaws and fed it to the shredder.

"Now. Available male brainstorm. How about the PR Guy?"

"Already tried him," I said.

"And?"

"He told me a story that culminated with the words 'hot, dripping treat.'"

He also spelled "scary" with two Rs. Not good for the long term. We'd never even gone out. He'd just sent me pornographic e-mails.

"Vile," said Elise. "*Scarry* and vile. Who else?"

"I might have met one this morning," I said. "We didn't speak. I ran."

"Would he have asked you out, if you'd actually spoken to him?"

"He's probably not even single. And he has a pit bull."

"Pit bulls are irrelevant. All you need is someone to get the taste of the Actor out of your mouth."

"Bitter taste," I said, and reached for my list.

"Bitter, bitter, bitter," said Elise. "How do you get the guy you met this morning?"

"He's my neighbor."

"Not Pierre. Not Pierre again. Don't tell me it's Pierre again."

"Another neighbor. Almost a whole block away."

"Stick a note in his door." She handed me a sheet of stationery from our boss's drawer. I slowly used my best penmanship to write,

> I'm the girl in the bad tuxedo. You made my morning better. Call me. I bet you can improve my night.—Maria.

Then I added my number.

"If nothing else, that's very straightforward," said Elise.

"Too much?"

"If he's a guy, it'll totally work," she said.

I stuck it in his door on my way home, and then ran.

I was breaking rules right and left. Giving him my number. Asking *him* out, even though he'd spoken to me, even though he'd given me that grin, was clearly against the Year of Yes credo. My taste was back in the equation, and though the past many months had yielded neither the perfect man, nor any sort of perfect happiness, in theory I still wasn't supposed to be going out and pursuing according to my own flawed judgment. I arrived in my kitchen, panting, appalled, and considering ways to fish the note out of the door. There did not seem to be a discreet way to do it. No doubt, the guy would catch me. Oh God. What had I done?

Zak and Griffin were sitting at the table, a jug of wine between them. I confessed.

"What?" said Griffin. "No. You didn't really do that. You don't even know this person." Griffin had faith that I was a more cautious person than I actually was. He was one of my most treasured friends, in part because he always believed me to be better than my behavior.

"She does things like that all the time," Zak told him. "Welcome to my world."

"Wait. You gave him your phone number? I thought that was against the rules."

"I asked him out," I said. I was stunned at my idiocy. Still, maybe I'd done something proactive against my sea of heartbreak.

"Well, I wish some girl would stick a note in *my* door," lamented Griffin.

"I know what you mean," said Zak. "Life isn't really fair. *Ergo bibamus.*"

Zak had taken beginning Latin. His favorite phrases were the ones that involved alcohol. *Ergo bibamus*: therefore, let us drink.

"*In vino veritas*," said Griffin, clearly in agreement with Zak.

BUT DOGBOY DIDN'T CALL ME. I started surveilling his apartment. The building exuded illicit sex. In the mornings, you could fairly hear the cinderblocks moaning. Fascinating sounds echoed from the interior: loud music, power tool growls and, most important, screaming, both orgasmic and defamatory.

One afternoon, I saw a tall, honey-blonde woman standing outside of Dogboy's place, lifting a kayak into the bed of a truck. She was wearing a white bikini top, and her muscles bulged like goldfish beneath her skin. It was November. Was she planning to kayak the East River?

"Babe!" the kayaker yelled. "Come on! I'm gonna leave you!" No response from anything human, though the dog growled. The girl noticed me staring. She laughed.

"Men," she said. "He can't even get dressed by himself."

"That's a problem," I agreed, pretending I'd been adjusting my shoe and not blatantly spying. I'd never had a man long enough to determine whether or not he would be unable to button his shirt if we were too long separated. All the men I'd known seemed perfectly self-sufficient, clothing-wise. If they failed to zip their pants, it was a choice.

"Come and get me!" someone yelled from inside.

"Shit. Must've left him tied to the bed," she said, laughing, and then carried the kayak into the house. I stood there for a moment, amazed at the kind of personal information New Yorkers were willing to share with complete strangers. I glanced back when I hit the end of the block, and saw the naked top half of the girl lean out an upstairs window and close the blinds.

OVER THE NEXT FEW DAYS, I CONDUCTED AN INFORMAL SURVEY OF THE NEIGHBORHOOD'S WOMEN. Next door to Dogboy's house was a building full of punky bands. The stoop was almost always occupied by a fantastic-looking, mascara-streaked chick. Sometimes the women were drinking from flasks as they sat. Sometimes crying and eating donuts.

They *all* knew Dogboy. Intimately.

Verdicts were mixed on whether he was good or evil, but every girl said the man was skilled. Dogboy, it seemed, was the neighborhood witch doctor. He was the cure for whatever crippling love affair you'd just crawled out of. Either that, or he was a very appetizing poison.

"Just listen, for a minute," offered a girl named Kitty, cocking her head and blowing out a smoke ring. "What do you hear?"

"Cars. Music. Jangling metal." Kitty had no less than twenty piercings, and that was just on the parts of her body that were visible.

"Huh-uh. Like, really listen."

A moment, and then a female moan. Faint, but rapturous.

"That basically never stops," said Kitty.

"It has to stop sometime," I said.

"Nope. Twenty-four/seven, fuck, fuck, fuck."

"Maybe it's a porno on endless repeat."

"That moan a minute ago? Was Sabrina. She plays bass. Blue hair?"

"Oh."

"She's my roommate. Supposedly. Her boyfriend Ryan? Is inside our apartment right now, writing angry songs and trying to paper train their Yorkie. The Yorkie is his. Ryan's been trying to convince Sabrina that lapdogs are ironic and masculine. But there's nothing he can do. Dogboy has a pit bull. Ryan knows better than to try and stop her. She'll get tired eventually, and then she'll come home. They all do. I did."

"You went out with him, too?"

"Yeah," said Kitty, and looked dreamily out into space. "He's a bastard, but he's totally worth it. His dog's name is Felonious Monk. And she's a girl. I mean, how could I resist that?"

Kitty blew another smoke ring. We watched it rise and then dissolve, as Sabrina's screams echoed blissfully down India Street.

BEEP. "HEY, MARIA? THIS IS THE GUY WHOSE DOOR YOU STUCK A NOTE IN THE OTHER DAY. Presuming you didn't stick notes in more than one guy's door, you probably know who I am. Come out dog walking with me tomorrow night. I'll be outside my apartment at seven." Beep.

I skipped to my dresser and started looking for dog-walking attire. Something that I didn't really possess. I was thinking maybe a Katharine Hepburn-esque safari suit. The dogs I'd grown up with hadn't been walked. They'd been hitched to sleds, and then pulled us down the snow-covered highway. I therefore felt that city dogs were wusses. Either a safari suit, or a 1930s silk slip? Perfect for walking a wuss dog. I held it up.

"Ugh," said Vic. She'd heard the message, too.

"What?" I said.

"I guess that's the kind of guy you want. Whatever. Get your heart broken again."

Vic and I had not really regained our solidarity. We went about our daily business, brushing past each other in the apartment and trying not to make eye contact. She'd made a brief exception during day three of my sobbing festival, and brought me ointment to put on my chapped nose. She was definitely still pissed at me, though. I again protested that I hadn't known she was so interested in Pierre.

"I wasn't," she said.

"Then why are you mad?"

"I'm not."

"Then why are you not speaking to me?"

"I am speaking to you. See? Speaking. Let the record show that you are going out with a dog walker. Just like I said you would."

"His dog's name is Felonious Monk," I said.

"That's supposed to make me think he's cool?"

She was right. He was a dog walker. I hadn't thought of it that way. This dog walker, though, was the most famous man in my neighborhood. It was too bad that Vic was mad. If she'd been happy, we could have spied together on Dogboy's house. I'd just have to wait for her to get over it. In my experience, it might take several months.

Vic forgave me sooner than I'd thought she would, though, because that night we heard thwacking sounds coming from Zak's room. Vic came out of her bedroom and stood in the living room, her ear cocked for a minute. *Thwack. Thwack.* Vic gave up her grudge and ran across the living room to my hut.

"Hear that?"

"How could I not?" I said.

"Is it what I think it is?"

"Spanking."

"Gross. So, so, so gross," giggled Vic, and crawled into my bed.

"It's not gross," I said. "It's just kind of loud."

Zak's new girlfriend, Malibu Barbie, was in his room with him. Malibu Barbie was not a stupid person. In fact, Malibu Barbie was a pleasant and intelligent person. But I was jealous, humiliatingly jealous, and when I learned that her Los Angeles plastic surgeon father had given her a teenage nose job, that was the end of any good feeling I'd had about her. She had yards of blonde curls, and Zak was wrapped around her manicured finger. Princeling One had been her boyfriend at some point, and they were a perfect match, gorgeous and commercially viable. They were poster children for NYU. Zak and I were the opposite half. We were prime examples of what happened if you went to an expensive school without anywhere near enough money. You ended up living in a hovel, working too many jobs, and not focusing on school at all. We were rotgut; Malibu Barbie and Princeling One were gin and tonic. Apparently, Malibu Barbie had been a very bad girl. The floor of our apartment shook. The walls of my hut vibrated. Vic giggled. The spanking went on for a long, long time.

THE NEXT MORNING, ZAK WAS IN A STELLAR MOOD, though he had sacks beneath his eyes. Vic and I sat down at the kitchen table, and smiled at him.

"What?" he said. "Good morning!"

"Good morning," we said.

"Right, good morning. Why are you staring at me?"

"Are we staring?" Vic asked.

"I don't think so," I said. "I think Zak's paranoid."

"You guys are acting freakish."

"It's a freakish house," I said, "Don't you think, Vic?"

"I do."

"At least you're smiling again," Zak said, "but that smile is kind of scary. Wait." He looked worriedly at the bathroom door. "Did the toilet explode again?"

"Nothing like that."

"No, nothing, no explosions," said Vic, and then had to leave the table because she was laughing too hard to stay in her chair.

"Is she high?" asked Zak. "I don't think I've ever seen her that cheerful before. Wait. Is she getting laid?"

"Is that why *you're* in a good mood?" I asked, innocently.

"Maybe," said Zak. Clearly, he was totally unaware he'd been overheard. Ah well. I'd leave it, for the time being. For the right time. Maybe for when he was mocking me in front of Griffin.

"Going on a date with Dogboy tonight," I told Zak. He groaned.

"He hits on everything that breathes, and some things that don't," said Zak. "His ego can be seen from outer space. I'm telling you."

"What's your point?" I asked.

"He's what you always like," he said. "He's also what you always hate."

"He's sexy," I said.

"He's a jerk," Zak said.

"Sexy jerk," I said, shrugging. "*Sua cuique voluptas.*"

"You're not allowed to use my Latin against me," Zak said. I'd been flipping through his phrasebook. "Everyone has his own pleasures" seemed like a useful thing to know how to say. Even in a dead language.

THAT NIGHT I WENT OUTSIDE IN THE BLACK NIGHTGOWN, high heels, and a parka. The wrong attire for almost any public appearance, particularly in December, but I was determined to impress Dogboy. He was walking Felonious Monk down India Street. Windows were opening, and skinny, cuckolded hipster boys were peering forlornly out. Their tattooed and pierced hipster girlfriends were emerging from doorways up and down the block, drawn like mutts to filet mignon.

"About time. Hold the dog for a sec," Dogboy told me, handing me Felonious's leash and disappearing into the bodega. Felonious stomped her dainty pit bull feet. Her friendly was the friendly of an ex-girlfriend who's well aware that your man will never get over her.

Señor Chupa and a couple members of his old man posse strolled by on the other side of the street. Señor Chupa's shirt tonight was pink and ruffled, his hat at a rakish angle. He tipped it in my direction and did a little shuffle dance. The posse imitated. I could hear their finger-snapping song carrying across traffic, and so I mimed a little applause for them. What else was there to do? They were my personal Greek chorus.

Dogboy returned with a carton of chocolate ice cream. He squinted at Señor Chupa, who was dancing into the distance.

"Know him?"

"Yeah," I said. "Louie."

"He stole my girlfriend's underwear from a dryer once. He hangs out at that Laundromat, stealing G-strings. Disgusting."

"Always been nice to me," I said. I preferred to keep the mystery of my association with Señor Chupa to myself. Dogboy was clearly intrigued.

We walked to the end of the India Street pier and looked out toward Manhattan. Even though the water was polluted beyond repair, it was still a fantastic view. And though I'd expected Dogboy to be dumb, a Neanderthal with preternatural bedroom talents, he turned out to be both intelligent and funny. We walked back to his apartment, and he used an enormous ring of keys to let us in. At last! I rejoiced. And shivered. Nightgowns in snowy weather were a bad idea.

The building was cavernous, and seemed to have no interior walls. There was a large metal staircase flanking one side. It was a testament to Dogboy's personal charisma that he'd ever managed to get a woman into this, the ultimate bachelor lair. Not a pillow to be seen. All iron filings and half-full soda bottles. And then there was the thing I could see at the top of the staircase. A freestanding toilet.

"What exactly do you do?" I asked.

"Sculptor." Relief! Clearly, the toilet was an art piece. Some sort of Duchampian tribute. Still, a toilet at the top of the stairs. *Gaaaaah.*

"Wanna see my coal bin?"

Somehow, I didn't think it was weird to climb down a ladder into a coal bin, forty-five minutes into a first date. I liked him, I guess. I knew that Vic would have been screaming at me for my stupidity. Pretty much every horror movie we'd ever seen began this way. Brainless Girl says, "Sure, Mr. Creepy, I would *love* to see your coal bin." Aforementioned Mr. Creepy proceeds to whack her on the head with a shovel, and bury her in coal. Dogboy, however, was just proud of his coal. Real coal. Real bin. Real welded-iron tulip, seven or eight feet tall, balancing against the wall. He told me he was planning to install it secretly at the edge of the East River, so that it was sometimes visible, sometimes not. Obviously, I was into this. A *subversive* sculptor. I ascended the ladder, and the stairs, ignored the toilet and bathtub next to it, and sat down on a couch that was also in the middle of the room. Next to the bed.

"Not even gonna ask about the toilet, huh?" Dogboy gave me his best grin.

"I assume you put it there on purpose. *Fountain Number Two*, right? Ironic commentary on the nature of modern art?"

I was showing off. I happened to be midway through a colossal survey of modern art, taught by a professor improbably named Pepe Carmel. The good thing about the class was that Pepe Carmel loved female nudes, and would happily have devoted the entirety of the semester to various representations of them. The bad thing was that the class was on modern art and, therefore, the female nudes we were looking at, with the exception of Gustave Courbet's *L'Origine du Monde*, a pre-porno close-up of an amply fleeced female crotch, were abstract. I'd discovered sometime in week two of the class that I found most of modern art to be a pretentious load of bullshit. Signed urinals. In five hundred years we'd gone from Sistine Chapel to pissoir. If this was cultural evolution, it was depressing.

"It's a test. I happen to like women with brass balls. Want to play Scrabble?"

I assumed he meant the board game, and not some sort of wall-climbing erotic escapade. I didn't see a climbing wall. That didn't mean there wasn't one. The place was huge, and not exactly well-decorated. He rattled a box. Scrabble. This was just weird. However, it was a better weird than some things. I sat down at the coffee table.

"Bring it on," I said, falsely confident. I was awful at Scrabble. The moment the little tiles appeared in front of me, I lost language completely. Dogboy was a Scrabble fiend. He had the *Scrabble Dictionary*, and used it. He kept score on little tablets. This was not what I'd expected. At all. After an hour, Dogboy gave up on me. I'd forfeited many turns, and his score was in the stratosphere. I'd also marched to his freestanding toilet and peed, largely a distraction tactic.

"I'm impressed," he said. "You passed the test."

"Why?"

"No one ever does that on the first date. They all make me close my eyes."

"I thought it was part of the deal of dating you?"

"Nah. Girls are all modest."

"Not when their bladders might explode." Let it never be said that I was unable to learn from my mistakes. Half of my accidental love for the Actor had probably been caused by the fact that he'd shown me where his bathroom was. I wasn't going to let a full bladder make me get my heart broken again. Irrational? Maybe. So what?

"Point taken. Still, you're better than I expected you'd be," he said.

"What'd you expect?"

"Emotional wasteland."

"Why would you expect that?"

"I've seen you crying every time you walk past my house, for weeks. Ice cream?"

He fed me a spoonful of chocolate ice cream before I could answer.

"You've been watching me?"

"You're kind of hard to miss. Every day you're wearing a cocktail dress and high heels. Every day you're carrying a backpack the size of your body. Every day you fall up the subway stairs. Plus, in case you didn't know this, you've got like five or six old men trailing behind you like a pack of stray dogs. Wait. Excuse me. *Singing and dancing* old men. Tell me how I wouldn't notice that?"

However illogical this was, I'd thought my weird life was visible only to me.

"Hang on," said Dogboy, putting out his finger and wiping ice cream from my chin. "And, you've been spying on *me* for the last week or so, which, for an egomaniac like me, is totally intriguing."

This was disarming. I'd thought I'd been so discreet.

"Believe everything Kitty says, by the way," he said. "She's right about me."

"I met your girlfriend, too," I said.

"The Alaskan? She's great, right? She could break me like a toothpick."

"But you cheat on her."

"I'm not cheating. We're just eating ice cream and playing Scrabble," Dogboy said, giving me another spoonful. Felonious Monk barked a bark of yearning.

"She's jealous," said Dogboy, and then he picked me up and carried me to the bed.

"Who's jealous?" The pit bull or the Alaskan? I was scared of both.

"Now, *this* might be cheating," he said, as he slid his hand up my thigh.

"Who's jealous?" I asked again, but Dogboy didn't answer me. He'd torn the strap off my slip, and he was happily sinking his teeth into my left breast.

"Actually, I want to keep that," I told him, grabbing him by the ears.

"Come on," he said, and grinned. "Self-destruct a little. Isn't that why you're here?"

I considered his logic. I pictured myself asymmetrical. Picasso. *Guernica*. No.

"I don't know you well enough to give you body parts," I said, prying his jaw open.

"Some girls would," he said. "Most girls."

"Yeah, well, I'm not most girls."

"Clearly." He went back to eating ice cream. He dripped it onto my collarbone and nonchalantly licked it off. Felonious Monk whimpered and threatened to board the bed. Dogboy waved his hand and she desisted, though not happily. He went back to applying his mouth to my skin, this time my neck.

"Why do you think I'm self-destructive?"

"You're letting me leave tooth marks. For one thing." A growl floated up, rattling in the air for a moment like the chains of Jacob Marley. Dogboy dropped a spoonful of ice cream. The growl shriveled. Sounds of lapping.

"That doesn't mean there's anything wrong with me," I protested.

"Don't get me wrong. A broken heart will always make for great sex."

He sunk his teeth into my thigh. I let him. He bit my neck. He bit my arms. He bit my stomach and my calves. He bit everything, and I rejoiced. Witch doctor, sex therapist, asshole, or angel, I was getting cured. No more leaving messages, no more wailing on my floor, no more wandering around the East Village hoping to run into the Actor. Nope. I was over him. So. Over. Him.

THE NEXT MORNING, I DID THE WALK OF SHAME DOWN INDIA STREET, clutching my torn slip to my chest, and feeling pleased with myself.

I ran into the Handyman, who said, "Damn, mamita, I bet you need me to rewire that buzzer, 'cause the way you're lookin', some dude's gonna be ringing at your door."

"Nothing's broken," I said. Not my heart, anyway. Maybe some capillaries. I hadn't seen a mirror, but I figured I might have a hickey or two.

Pierre was standing in his window when I got to my building. He opened the door and beckoned me into his apartment.

"What exactly happened to your neck?"

"Nothing."

"If you say so." Pierre went to his refrigerator and casually got out an egg.

"I do," I said. "I do say so."

"*This* is your heart," Pierre said, holding the egg up to the light.

"My heart is not an egg," I said.

"This is your heart on Dogboy." Pierre cracked the egg into a frying pan. It sizzled.

"Are you about to segue into the Just Say No campaign? Because that didn't work very well," I said.

"I'm about to scramble your heart with a little butter," Pierre said. "And then I'm going to eat it. Want some?"

"Can't. I'm late for class."

Pierre shuffled the scrambled egg onto a plate and took a bite. "Not a bad heart," he said. "I wouldn't give it to that guy, if I were you. He won't appreciate it."

"Thanks for your cooking lesson," I said.

"What are neighbors for?" Pierre smiled at me.

BY THE TIME I GOT OUT OF THE SHOWER, I'd forgotten about what Pierre had said about my neck. I was late for my sign language class.

I was in sign language because I'd thought it could pass for a foreign language requirement. Foreign languages were something I was awful at. It turned out that ASL was not considered a language, but a dance form. I'd already been halfway through the semester when I'd found that out, though, so I was screwed.

I went into class and took off my sweater. The teacher started laughing in his high-pitched way. He pointed at me. He put his hand beneath his chin, wiggling his fingers, and then made a sign I recognized. Two Ps, banging together.

"Dirty fucking," the teacher wrote on the board, and then signed it again, slowly, for the remedial students. I looked down at my arm, and saw a trail of bite marks beginning at my wrist. My sign language partner informed me that my neck was covered, as well. Several others in the room attempted to ask why they didn't get laid as well as I clearly had. Why lie, I thought. Sign language was a blunt thing and everyone was obscene, all the time. It was the only part of the language most of us really understood. Plus, extra points were given for successful dirty joke tellings.

"Yes," I signed. "He bite."

"Fun!" signed the teacher.

"Fun!" agreed several students.

"Love is big hurt," I signed, in a paroxysm of honesty. "One month before today, me heart break from a boy actor. Boy actor maybe gay, but sex with me anyway." Here I got exactly the right facial expression, and the teacher applauded.

"Men bad," I signed, and the teacher agreed. He was himself

gay, and his regular complaint was that the gay deaf community was tiny, ugly, and not well hung.

"But poor me love bad men," I continued. "Now, I meet another bad. He bite!"

The class applauded. It was the longest sentence I'd ever managed to get through without breaking into an inappropriate smile.

"Introduce me?" signed the teacher.

"Straight," I signed.

"Shit," signed the teacher.

"Shit," signed several other people in the room.

LATER THAT NIGHT, ZAK, GRIFFIN, AND I WENT TO A HORRIBLE MARGARITA BAR deep in NYU's backpack jungle. The bar's claim to fame was that its sign was an enormous yellow taxi cab careening out over the street. You could get a pitcher full of soapy, lethal margaritas there for about seven dollars. The bathroom of the bar was difficult, involving a teetering descent down the steepest staircase in New York. When I'd first moved to the city, I'd once fallen all the way down the stairs and been picked up from the floor by a tiny Mexican busboy, who'd balanced me like I was just another tub of dirty dishes.

Zak, Griffin, and I ended up waiting in line for the bathroom together and Zak could not restrain his impulse to question me.

"How exactly did you get tooth marks on your arms?" It wasn't just my arms. I looked down and saw tooth marks on my upper chest. I slowly raised the hem of my skirt to my thighs.

"Attacked by a vagina dentata?" I said.

"Latin will not save you. Attacked by a pit bull–owning neighbor," Zak said. "What is he? A vacuum cleaner? A suction cup? No, wait, I know. A giant leech. That's what that looks like. Leeches." He put his hand over his eyes and groaned. He peeked out and groaned again. "That's horrible. Go back to Pierre. At least he was repressed."

"Want to know the worst part?" I asked.

"Probably not," said Zak.

I danced down the cramped hallway.

"It was SO MUCH FUN!" I sang.

"Oh God," said Zak. "You're a freak."

"Why do you always have stories about biting?" questioned Griffin. "What's the deal here? What is this pattern?"

"I can't believe you let some strange guy bite you," said Zak.

"You've never done anything kinky, huh?" I said.

"I don't want to hear this," said Griffin. "Yuck. No, I am not hearing this."

"Not like that," said Zak, self-righteously.

"*La, la, la, la,*" said Griffin, who had put his fingers in his ears.

"So the other night," I said to Griffin, who looked at me in horror, probably thinking I was about to give a blow-by-blow of Zak and me finally sleeping together, "there was a thwacking sound coming from Zak's bedroom."

"A thwacking?" said Griffin, weakly.

"What thwacking? There was no thwacking!" said Zak.

"A spanking sound," I said, and Zak's face showed revelation.

"You heard that," he said. "Oh my God."

"Thin walls," I said. "It went on for a long time. Vic and I both heard it."

"*So,* the margaritas are really good here," said Griffin.

"They are," said Zak. "Fantastic margaritas." He was laughing, though, and laughing hard. So was I. Things were looking up. For the moment.

"I HAVE TO FIND A GIRL TO DEGRADE," DOGBOY SAID, giving me a quick once-over to check my reaction to this, and then peering out onto the street again. It was a few weeks later, and he was looking for the new neighbor, who walked around in ice storms wearing almost nothing, her nipples standing up like tiny antlers.

"I'm here," I pointed out, unbuttoning my jeans, irritated that he wanted to go out and find someone else.

"I don't think I could degrade you," he said fretfully. "You're not in love enough."

"I don't want to be in love with you," I said. "It's on purpose."

"Be my new girlfriend," Dogboy said, turning on the taps of his bathtub, so that he could hide from me underwater. "Maybe that would help."

Only a fool would agree to be Dogboy's girlfriend. From my vantage point across the street, I could easily see that Dogboy cheated on six or seven women at once. Shortly after our first night together, he'd informed me that he was madly in love with the Alaskan, and therefore couldn't see me anymore. Not a week later, I'd been walking past his house, on my way to a date with someone I already knew wouldn't be anything I wanted, when Dogboy had opened his door and said, "Remember that girl?"

"That Alaskan girl you were madly in love with? Yes. Actually, I do."

"She decided I wasn't worth it."

"Hmm," I'd said. "Are you?"

Dogboy had run a finger up my thigh.

"I have to go," I'd said, and didn't.

The Alaskan had broken up with him not because of me, who she didn't know about, but because he'd spent the night with someone else entirely. *Two* someone elses. If he was going to cheat anyway, why not with me? I, at least, had decided not to care.

I'd decided that a person like Dogboy was the best possible thing for me. The parameters were clear. We'd spend a couple of nights a week having very loud, very emphatic sex, and that would be all there was to it. I wouldn't be his girlfriend. I'd just sleep with him. We were compatible in the dark. Maybe this was as good as it was going to get.

LOVE? HA! I WAS NO LONGER IN THE MARKET FOR LOVE. Why I'd thought I'd wanted it in the first place was beyond me. I didn't know anyone who was actually in love. I knew a lot of people who were in pain. Though I could easily have loved Dogboy, I was, at least, smart enough to know that falling for him would be like hitching myself to a line of lemmings. I didn't need him to love me. I didn't need to love him. We had an understanding.

So what if I was totally unhappy about it?

So what if I still wanted the Actor?

"You don't want to be with me," Dogboy said, and submerged himself in his bathtub. The man could hold his breath a long time.

"Why not?" I asked, when he surfaced.

"I'm bad for you, that's why."

"Who said I wanted something that was good for me?"

"You *deserve* something that's good for you. I don't care if you want it or not. I'm not going to be the guy that fucks you up and convinces you love isn't possible."

Under the water again. Could it be that he had a conscience? I'd been lamenting the Actor again, having burst into tears in Dogboy's bed because he'd put a Radiohead CD on. He'd played the song that goes, *I'm a creep, I'm a weirdo . . . I don't belong here.* The Actor had been a Radiohead fan. Sob. Even worse, Ira had played that particular song for me, years prior, as part of a pity-me extravaganza that had also included Beck's "Loser," and a date to see *Schindler's List.* Now I understood how Ira had felt. *I wish I was special . . . you're so fucking special! But I'm a creep!*

Dogboy was a creep, too. Except that, really, he was just a more jaded, more confident, definitely more well-endowed version of me. A little lost, definitely a little lost. But then, so was I.

"Go screw the guy again," decreed Dogboy, from his tub. "See if there's really any love there. If there isn't, you'll be cured."

"But he doesn't want to sleep with me," I said. "Or love me, or *anything* me."

"Excuse me. Is he, or is he not, a guy?" said Dogboy. "He'll sleep with you. Particularly if you offer him no strings. Take it from one who knows the male mind. If you offer it, they will come."

I decided to ignore the fact that he was paraphrasing *Field of Dreams.*

"But he's gay," I said.

"He's not gay, or he wouldn't have slept with you to begin with. You're not the kind of girl that can be mistaken for a boy."

"But what if there is?"

"What if there is what?" said Dogboy. He'd gotten out of the tub. "Mind if I handcuff you to the bed?"

I held out my wrists.

"What if there is *love*?" I asked.

"If there is, Maria, you have to chase him until he falls down," said Dogboy, looking at me with his blue eyes, looking at me with his unsatisfied face. Dogboy hadn't had an easy life. The week before, he'd told me about his father's suicide by hanging, and how he, a fourteen-year-old, had found him.

"Hey, Dad, why are you still hanging around?" he'd said, laughed wryly, and then submerged in his bathtub before I could really tell what he'd been thinking. There was more to Dogboy than met the eye. He seemed to care enough about me to help me get over the Actor, and for that, I was grateful.

"Blindfold," said Dogboy, unfurling a black silk scarf.

"You or me?" I asked.

"Both," he said.

AND SO, POSSIBLY IN A SUICIDAL MANEUVER, I WENT TO A PLAY THE ACTOR WAS IN. There he was, two hours of him, his radiant skin, his Puckish curls. There he was. His Celtic tattoo, his amber eyes, his mind, his walk. His everything that I wanted, and nothing that he'd let me have. There were all the things that had made me love him, and, even with the history of heartbreak, made me love him still.

"Hi," I said, and he came and sat next to me. "Good work tonight."

I was lying, but it didn't really matter. The Actor's performance hadn't blown me away. *He* was the thing that blew me away, and even as I could now see that it wasn't really justified, that he was just a guy, I was still up there with the hurricane, clutching Toto, not in Kansas anymore.

"That means a lot to me," he said.

Skip the long, lame conversation in which we dealt with nothing of our past pain and misunderstanding. Skip the theater history we discussed instead. Skip the section where he asked me where I was going, and we both had déjà vu when I said, "Nowhere."

Arrive back in the East Village, the Russian baths still steaming, the weather still freezing, and my heart still wavering on the brink of dreaming and denial.

Skip the part where I unbuttoned his shirt, memorizing and then forgetting every inch of his skin, tracing and then erasing his ribs, inhaling and then exhaling his neck. Skip the part where I stayed dressed myself. Skip the part where I held him tightly to my heart, needing to give him something, even if he couldn't give anything back.

Finish it up in the shower, early the next morning, the water running cold, he kissing me, me kissing him. Finish it up with me looking into his eyes and seeing lots of things: sadness, ego, insecurity, drama. There was plenty to this man, but there was nothing there for me.

"What's this?" he asked, standing behind me at the bathroom mirror, as I twisted my hair up. He was running his finger across a bite mark left over from Dogboy. Since he hadn't looked at me the night before, he hadn't noticed it.

"This is me getting over you," I answered. "Thank you."

"You're welcome," he said, looking puzzled, his hand still on Dogboy's kiss.

"See you around," I said, and walked out the door, sad, but no longer brokenhearted.

"I'll see you, Maria," he said.

When I got to the street, I could see him standing in his window, watching me leave. I raised my hand to wave good-bye, but he'd already closed the curtains.

. . .

DESPITE SENDING ME AWAY, DOGBOY CONTINUED TO WHISTLE IN MY DIRECTION EVERY COUPLE OF WEEKS. I'd listen to his phone ring, his answering machine picking up, the suggestive messages left by women I didn't know. He'd give me their one-line biographies. The forty-five-year-old stripper, who wanted to be a concert pianist. The pretty blonde, whose angry eight-year-old daughter kicked him in the shins every time she laid eyes on him. The bulimic Hawaiian trust-funded artist, who wanted to move into his bachelor building. I'd feel superior for a moment, and then I'd wonder why I wasn't as willing as they were, and why he wasn't willing, either, why we didn't just want each other. I wondered why nothing was easy. I wondered what he said about me, when one of them was sitting on the rim of the tub. "The neurotic writer who . . . who . . ."

That's as far as I ever got, because as soon as I referred to myself as neurotic, I started to feel defensive and had to begin proving my perfect stability.

At least Dogboy and I understood each other. He was a player, and I was playing. Though there was no great love here, there was plenty of sex and Scrabble. Maybe people wondered why I was willing to date a guy who was dating half the women in New York, and maybe I wondered that, too, but then I took a look at myself. What was I doing? What was the Year of Yes? Maybe he was a little more like me than I wanted to admit. We were both throwing ourselves completely into the quest for love, at least. We were trying, in whatever way we were capable of trying. He told me a story about one of his girlfriends asking how many girlfriends he'd had before her. He'd rounded down. Way down. He hadn't wanted to upset her.

"Only twenty," he'd said. Her face had fallen. He'd cringed. He'd aimed too high.

"Two," she'd said.

"Two what?" he'd said, though he'd known.

"Two boyfriends." She'd broken up with him shortly thereafter. He'd told me he was glad he hadn't told her the real number, which was somewhere more around a hundred and twenty. And that was girlfriends, not just women he'd slept with.

"You'd better not be counting me," I said. He smiled. He was. And that was sort of okay with me. Not ideal, but what was? I was treading water until it was time to swim again.

One morning, Dogboy handed me my bra and then ruffled Felonious Monk's head. She growled a happy growl. She was the only woman in his life, the only constant, and she knew it. He was getting rid of me.

"You can have whatever you want. Now go and get it," he said and kissed me hard for good measure.

"Besides," he continued. "I need you to leave. One of my friends has a broken bathtub, and she's coming over to take a bath."

"And sleep with you," I said.

"See how much you don't want a guy like me?" he said.

I went home, kind of happy, kind of blue. It was the end of the eleventh month of my year, and here I still was, bitten and bruised, walking down India Street, toward some sort of vision that hadn't appeared.

MEETING MR. WRITE

IN WHICH OUR
HEROINE FINDS A
HAPPILY EVER
AFTER . . .

WE'D ALWAYS KNOWN THAT ZAK WAS MOVING BACK TO BERKELEY. He considered it home, and I didn't blame him. It was a great city, and most of his favorite people lived there. No surprise that I didn't want him to go. It was just that I felt like I was losing an arm. More than an arm. Half of my brain. Half of my heart. Maybe more than half. I wouldn't think about that too much.

Zak was insanely planning to take a cross-country Greyhound, and so he packed everything he owned into a duffel bag, gave me his mattress and some of his books, and got ready to leave.

"I can't wait to write you letters," he said.

"I'd rather have you here," I said.

"Yeah, but in letters, everything looks better than it really is," Zak told me. "You can tell me all about every perfect man you meet, and I'll pretend I really think they're perfect."

"You can tell me all about every perfect girl you meet, and I'll pretend I really think they're not jailbait."

"Very funny," said Zak.

Both of us suspected that there was no such thing as perfect. If we weren't perfect together, who would be? And we weren't. We loved each other, undoubtedly, and that was miraculous. It wasn't miraculous enough, though. We were, in the end, just destined to be friends. Ultimately, maybe that was better. As friends, at least, we could love each other without anyone's issues getting in the way. I'd only lived with Zak a year, but I felt like we'd been together forever. Maybe this'd be how it would feel when I finally met the right man. Except that, if I had any luck at all, that man wouldn't get on a Greyhound and leave me.

I MADE ZAK WAKE ME UP AT FIVE IN THE MORNING on the day of his departure. I handed him a mix-tape full of singer-songwriters, for listening to on the bus. We hugged until our bones cracked.

"I'm gonna miss the fuck out of you," said Zak, and we kissed hard on the mouth for exactly five seconds, which was as long as I could kiss him without sobbing. Then he dragged his bag out the door and was gone.

I watched him walk through the courtyard, gave him what I hoped was a relatively cheerful wave, and then went into the bathroom to cry my eyes out. I curled into a ball at the bottom of the shower and sobbed for half an hour, hoping that Vic was still sleeping. After a while, though, she knocked on the door.

"Maria?"

"Yeah?" I sniffled.

"Are you okay?"

"No." I came out in my towel. "Do you need the bathroom?"

"I'm sorry Zak left," Vic said, and hugged me. Sometimes I loved Vic. Sometimes she loved me. Maybe we weren't entirely compatible, but we had the weight of history behind us, and that history included a lot of commiseration. That was worthwhile, even in the face of a bunch of nonsuccesses. Love wasn't the only thing that mattered, after all. Or maybe it was. I didn't know anymore.

A FEW DAYS AFTER ZAK LEFT, I WOKE UP AND DISCOVERED OUR FRONT DOOR WIDE OPEN AND ALL THE LIGHTS ON. Since Zak's departure, I'd taken down my hut and moved into his bedroom (where I looked nightly at the thumbtack holes he'd left behind), and the door to the bedroom had been left open, too. My light was on. Nothing was missing. Big White Cat was fine. But I'd definitely locked the door and gone to sleep in darkness. I couldn't sleep with the lights on.

Someone had been in our apartment.

I went downstairs and got Pierre to come up with a big skillet in his hand, to patrol the closets and make sure no one was hiding. When I'd come home the night before, everything had seemed fine, but now I had the feeling someone had been hidden, waiting for me to go to sleep. I was scared out of my mind.

Vic had been sleeping at her boyfriend's apartment, and I had a faint hope that maybe she'd come home very early in the morning and then left again, but no such luck. When she came home, we examined our door and lock to see if maybe it had just blown open. No. Instead, we discovered that someone had gotten a screwdriver and moved the deadbolt latch, so that the deadbolt couldn't catch. Worse and worse. Who was it? Maybe Junior, the landlord's son, who would have been able to use his dad's keys to get in and mess with the lock. Junior had never shown the slightest interest in us. If it wasn't Junior, though, it was someone we didn't know, and we didn't want to think about that. We started sleeping with chairs pressed against our doorknobs. If sleeping was the right word. It wasn't. I tried to focus on other things.

For example: the fact that the Playwright had left me a message, telling me he was coming to New York and that he'd love to have dinner.

Dinner, I thought, not calling him back. I'd been having what amounted to dinner for eleven months, and dinner was no longer what I wanted to have. I didn't want to get up from the table disappointed, wiping my mouth and pushing back my chair. I wanted more than dinner. I wanted to be eaten alive. I wanted to fall so far in love, I'd never be found. I wanted bliss and kisses and adoration and joy, and I was quite sure that I would find none of these things with the Playwright, a married man.

I called Dogboy, who told me that he'd just been dumped again, this time by someone he might have loved.

> **DOGBOY:** "I'm wrapped with guilt. I have to stop thinking about it."
>
> **ME:** "Wracked."
>
> **DOGBOY:** "That's what I said."

I thought sadly about the predicament of the modern man, wrapped in a silky shroud of guilt, comfortably wallowing across guilty sheets. Were there any good ones left? If so, where the hell were they?

I tried to focus on school, on living, and not on the fact that the Year of Yes was almost over. Though I'd changed from the inside out, I hadn't found someone willing to take me for what I now was. Unfortunately, there was no going back.

On paper, it was so easy to search through your old drafts and find that darling you'd killed. You could reinstate the passage, as though you'd never even thought about murder. In life, not so. You'd change a part of yourself—a flawed part, maybe, but a flawed part you might have, secretly, been a little bit in love with. You'd know it was for the best, that you'd only manage to proceed if you revised whatever thing was messing up the overall structure of your existence. But inevitably, at some point, you'd want to go back on the changes. It would be easier to stay the same old rumpled version, the same typos and blotches, the same old severe climactic flaws.

I found myself trying to think my old judgmental things as I walked down the street. Instead I'd end up talking to everyone I saw, spending half my day sitting down next to strangers. Letting them tell me everything. Giving them love.

It wasn't like I'd made myself perfect. Far from it. I'd just gained awareness, and now I noticed even more how acutely imperfect I was. I was willing to do all kinds of things that I knew better than to do. Like, for example, fall madly in love again. With someone I knew very well was a very bad idea.

Luckily, though, this particular bad idea was out of state. I figured that if I had to fall, at least I could be graceful about it. I'd do it secretly, in the dark, and I'd never tell the Playwright anything about my ridiculous emotional state. I'd leave him no messages. I'd send him no valentines. No one would have to know.

By the time I returned the Playwright's call, I hadn't closed my eyes in days. I was back to reading *Prometheus Bound*.

The Playwright sounded extremely enthusiastic. We agreed to meet for dinner. He said that he had something important to tell me, in person. I had no idea what. He'd written me some letters, but he'd never really gone into any detailed description of his life. We were having the kind of correspondence friends have. I'd tell him about my latest bad date, he'd commiserate. I'd tell him about my latest play, he'd send me his, and we'd exchange notes.

Unfortunately, the night before my scheduled dinner with the Playwright, I walked past the new mirror I'd installed in the kitchen and saw a red laser-pointer dot appear on my forehead. The mirror was on the same wall as the windows. Which meant that someone was aiming something at me, right that moment. I ran to my bedroom and hid under the covers, shaking. I knew this was not the perfect course of action, but I had no idea what to do. Someone was watching me. I called the police, and they said that they couldn't do anything unless there was a concrete threat. This felt pretty damned concrete to me, but the cop who came to my apartment said, "I can't arrest someone for looking, can I?"

"No," I said. "I guess not."

"If I did that, half the population would be sleeping at the precinct. Get some thick curtains, that's my advice."

"But then, if something bad happened, no one would be able to see it through the windows and call the police."

"This isn't Hitchcock, lady," said the cop. "It's New York. Take away the girl a guy wants to look at, and he'll find someone else. Sleep well, now."

Was he kidding? Apparently not. Needless to say, this basically sent me over the edge. I tried to create amnesia. If someone was spying on me, if I was unsafe on a regular basis, I didn't want to think about it.

I DECIDED TO OBSESS OVER WHAT TO WEAR FOR DINNER WITH THE PLAYWRIGHT INSTEAD. Fuck red laser dots. Screw people staring from darkness through my windows, people who obviously knew that Zak had moved out and that Vic and I were two girls living alone with one nonthreatening cat. I'd never really been scared living in New York before. Now I wanted to hide from everything for so many reasons, but there was nowhere to go.

The effect of the whole event was that I became frivolous. I put on a cocktail dress with a feather boa, walked defiantly past my windows, and went defiantly to sleep. With a chair braced against my door. And a paring knife under my pillow.

"Should I wear this?" I asked Vic the next morning.

"Only if you want to have your boobs fall out."

I was trying on outfits for dinner. A black V-neck sweater. A black skirt. Conservative, except for the slit halfway up the thigh. I tugged at it, trying to expose a little less leg. No cigar. Maybe I could sew it shut.

"Can I borrow your black high heels?" Vic's feet were a size larger than mine, but all of my shoes were scuffed and made of plastic. The Playwright was classy. I didn't want to look like the poverty-stricken college student I was.

"I wouldn't wear that. What if you're platonic and you just don't know it?"

"We *are* platonic," I said.

"Not according to that outfit," Vic said.

I put my hands on a pair of striped overalls I normally used for painting. They were platonic, all right, but so platonic that I wasn't sure I could manage to wear them outside. I was too much of a girl to enjoy not looking like one. Even if the world was a creepy place.

Vic continued. "What if he wants a secretary to type his plays for him? What if he's taking pity on you because he thinks you're starving and *that's* why he's buying you dinner?"

All those things were possible. However, he'd left me a voice-mail the day before:

"I'm finally here. Staying at the Rihga Royal, thanks to my gig for Ron Howard. You have to see my bathroom. That sounds weird, but it's wonderful. Meet me at the hotel, okay? I know that's not what we talked about, but I hope that's all right. Can't wait to see you tomorrow."

I realized that the invitation was seriously up for interpretation, but still, he wanted me to come to his hotel room. To see the bathroom. I'd fall apart if this cultured, Pulitzer Prize–winning playwright, this articulate, intelligent, charming man, asked to pee on me. It would be too much disappointment for one lifetime. I was already too on the edge. I tried not to think about it. I put my rain slicker in the back of my closet and didn't give in to the impulse to bring it.

WHEN I LEFT THE HOUSE THE NEXT MORNING, I thought I looked pretty good. However, after eight hours straight of meditating on it, I was convinced that I looked like something out of *My Cousin Vinnie.*

I dashed into Banana Republic on my way to meet the Playwright. I bought a clearance-priced, high-necked sweater, which I wore out, over the slitted black skirt.

I was stepping happily onto the downtown bus, when the slit suddenly ripped, hooker high. I leapt off the bus and ducked into another clothing store. There, I found a twelve-dollar ankle-length skirt, which I put on with the sweater. Perfectly prim. Puritanical ancestry finally on display.

It wasn't until I was on the street again that I noticed the blatant panty lines. I was forced to throw myself, screaming, into yet another store.

By the time I finally made it out of the Upper East Side, I'd spent two hundred dollars I didn't have on five stores' worth of clothing that didn't look good on me, and was carrying a big bag full of the clothing I'd rejected. I was completely paralyzed with neurosis, and I was late. I was reduced to hailing a cab I couldn't afford and asking my turbaned Indian cabdriver if I looked okay.

"You look sexy, honey! Yes! You want some Indian whiskey? Indian massage? Good Indian company! Eh?" He laughed his ass off. "I am making the joke."

"No! I'm having dinner with this guy . . ."

"Ohhhh! Your boyfriend!"

"No! No, he's married. My friend. Sort of."

"You look like you go to dinner with your boyfriend."

"Why?" I frantically tried to adjust my top to reveal absolutely nothing.

"Maybe he propose, eh? In my country, you look like you are going to meet your new husband."

"I'm not! He's someone else's husband!"

"Then why your blouse so tight, honey? Eh?" He erupted into uproarious laughter.

Because everything in every store was tight. Because even if things were not tight, they looked tight on me. Because the universe was conspiring against me. Because despite my legitimate Puritan blood, I simply did not look puritanical. Ever. Maybe this night would turn out to be the worst idea I'd ever had. Very likely, in fact.

I could see the cabdriver eyeing me in the rearview mirror. He reached his hand back through the cash window and shook my hand.

"He propose, you trust me, honey," said the cabdriver.

"But—"

"No, no, no! I do not listen. Your boyfriend, he is lucky man, huh?"

No man that had to deal with me was a lucky man. I was a walking volcano. I could explode at any moment, and God only knew what kind of emotional outburst it would be.

THERE IN FRONT OF US, MUCH TOO SOON, WAS THE RIHGA ROYAL. It wasn't the most elegant hotel in New York City, but it was more glamorous than anywhere I'd ever been. I paid the driver and got out of the cab. My shoes informed me that if I attempted to walk more than three blocks, I'd be carrying my little toes in my purse, but there was nothing to be done about that now. I hobbled up to the doorman and went through the revolving doors to confront my fate.

The Rihga Royal was a hotel made of glass and brass and pomp. I glanced casually into the lobby mirrors and saw a bag lady with crooked bangs wearing a leather jacket clearly scavenged from a Dumpster. I wondered who the hell she thought she was. This was no place for her!

Then I realized that she was me.

The only thing that kept me from leaving was the elevator attendant smiling and asking which floor I wanted. I felt too guilty to ask him to let me out. He was pushing the button for me, after all, and that was generous because I couldn't have done it for myself.

THE PLAYWRIGHT'S DOOR. I HOPPED ON ONE FOOT, TRYING TO GET UP MY NERVE TO KNOCK. Just as I was turning around to go back to the elevator, coward that I was, it opened.

"Umm. Hello . . ." said the Playwright, and I stopped hopping, mortified. I raised my head, and there he was, standing in the doorway, his eyes kind and blue, his smile wide, and his arms open.

"Do you remember me?" I said, at a loss for anything remotely appropriate to say. Of course he did. He'd called me. I blushed.

"I was kind of waiting for you," he said, and laughed.

I put out my hand to shake and he ignored it and hugged me. My tear ducts decided that just then was the perfect time to cut loose. I tried to hide my tears in his collar. Red plaid. Laundry detergent. Cologne, faintly.

Why was I crying? I had no idea. Once I started, though, there was no stopping me.

"Hey," he said. "Hey, what's the matter? This is a happy occasion, isn't it? I hope?"

He led me inside, where I dropped all my possessions on the carpet and fell into a chair. I frantically tried to stop crying. He brought me tissues.

"No real reason," I said, lamer by the minute. "I'm just happy! Very, very happy!"

"Tell me about it," he said, and sat down across from me.

So I did. I couldn't help myself. He looked so nice, and seemed to actually care that my apartment was unsafe and I was broke, that I'd been roaming around New York for eleven months, throwing my heart like a water balloon and watching it explode all over people who had no use for it. That I hadn't slept in what seemed like two years and that my famous, expensive school was not all it was cracked up to be. That this might have been fine, if only I'd been able to fall in love with someone who was also able to fall in love with me.

Even though now, finally, I knew what I was looking for: kindness, compassion, intelligence, sense of humor, all other qualities negotiable. It seemed that that combo didn't exist. I was tired to the bone.

I sobbed on the hotel couch, and the Playwright took my hands and patted them, even as I blew my nose.

"It'll be okay," he said.

"*Warghghhhhhhhhmmmphhhh,*" I said.

"I didn't quite get that," he said.

"*Blerghhhhmrrrhmwahhhhhhhhhhhhh* sniffle sniffle."

"I know what you mean." He smiled at me. "How about you wash your face and we go get some food in you. I made a reservation for Japanese, because you said you didn't eat meat."

"Good memory," I said. Better than mine, considering I had no recollection of saying any such thing.

"I pay attention," he said, picking me up off the couch and hugging me again.

Pull yourself together, I thought. Stop crying. Suck it up. Have dinner with someone you actually like. Even if you can't have him.

"You look great, by the way," the Playwright said. I looked down at the avalanche that was me and smiled as much as it was possible for me to smile.

"Oh! You have to see the bathroom."

Despite myself, I wished for that rain slicker. I walked down the hall, as slowly as I could. I didn't want to look at a toilet. Looking at toilets reminded me of Dogboy. Maybe that's what this was. Maybe I'd have to pee in front of him in order to prove my bravery. Didn't seem likely, but I didn't know him all that well.

In fact, no. The toilet was heated. There was no way to gracefully discern this. I had to place my hand on the seat. There was a phone and a fax machine next to the toilet. It was that kind of hotel. The Playwright was excited in the way that a child is excited on Christmas morning. I liked this. Most people didn't get excited about anything other than their own discontent. So what if it was about a heated toilet? I was just happy he hadn't made me regret the stowing of my rain gear.

"This is a wonderful toilet," I said.

"I know!" he said. "It's the best thing about the hotel. That's what it means to work in Hollywood. Great toilets. Fitting."

SUSHI. SAKE. THE FISH ARRIVED LIKE JEWELS ON A LITTLE TRAY. The sake was warm as it went down my throat, as we toasted to meeting again, to another meal at another Japanese restaurant, to friendship.

The Playwright ordered tempura and told me a story about almost dying after suddenly becoming allergic to oysters. He'd happened to glance in his rearview mirror as he'd been driving home from lunch and seen his face swollen to three times its normal size.

We looked down at my raw fish and agreed not to die that night.

He kept alluding to some story that he wasn't ready to tell me until he'd had some more sake.

"It's not a happy story," he said.

"I already cried all over you," I said. "It can't be that bad."

"I don't want to make you cry again," he said. "You won't, will you?"

"No promises. If it's a really sad story, I might. If it's a really funny story, I might. The only story that might not make me cry at this point is a boring story that puts me to sleep."

"Fair enough. This is probably a boring story. It's not a story you've never heard before, anyway. No good way to begin."

He looked at me for a moment and then he put his left hand on the table.

"I'm still wearing this," he said, "but my marriage is over."

I'd heard variations on this theme before. I was instantly wary.

"Does your wife know that?" I asked.

"She should, considering she asked for the divorce."

"Why?" I asked, because I couldn't imagine anyone would leave this guy voluntarily.

"I don't even think she knows. But I'm done holding the marriage together by myself. It's killing me. In the middle of our fourth attempt at marriage counseling, she announced that she wanted a divorce, and I said, 'Do you really mean that?' She said, 'Yes,' and I said, 'Okay.' The next day, I called my lawyer. You know how you can stubbornly hold onto something, despite the other person stepping on your fingers, and then one day, you just let go? That's what happened. I let go. It's the strangest kind of relief."

I did know what he was talking about, though my drama with the Actor had been on a much smaller scale, and certainly, thank God, hadn't taken fourteen years to unfold, as the Playwright's had.

He told me more about the relationship and why it had dissolved. A million horrible, heartbreaking things that all ran together because I was hyperventilating, and because the Playwright looked so sad. He talked about the disappointment of finding out that your life was not going to go according to the plan you'd had forever, the one where you find someone to love, and they love you, and you have kids and stay together in peace and harmony until the end of time. The disappointment of discovering that love was not what you thought it was. This sounded familiar to me, though in this moment, I was having the opposite realization. That maybe love was sitting right in front of me, and maybe it was larger and more wonderful than I'd imagined.

I fiddled with my chopsticks, then stuck an entire roll in my mouth and felt an obscene amount of wasabi snatch at my sinuses.

The Playwright slapped my back. "Water?"

"It's okay." My mind was racing. This wasn't dinner. This was more than dinner. That was what I'd wanted. Was this what I'd wanted? Not from him. I wanted him to be happy, which meant, in my twisted logic, that I didn't think he should want me. But maybe he didn't. Maybe he just needed someone to talk to. Maybe I could have been anyone.

I wanted either to upset the table and dive headlong into one of the fish tanks lining the walls or throw my arms around him and try to save him from his pain. Neither seemed like a good idea. I looked up, and saw tears overflowing the Playwright's eyes. I couldn't help it. I put out my hand. I took his fingers. I squeezed them.

"The kids don't know yet," he said. "I can't believe I'm going to do this to them."

"It's better to do it now, when they're little," I said, repeating something I'd heard on TV, or maybe read in a magazine in a doctor's waiting room. I knew nothing about divorce, nothing, as far as I could tell, about anything. The Playwright was holding my hand like I was a lifeguard, the only thing keeping him from drowning. One problem. I didn't know how to swim, either. I felt like I should give warning. But somehow, we made it out of the restaurant and we walked back to the hotel together.

Halfway there, he put his arm around me and pulled me in to his side, and I found myself dropping my head onto his shoulder. Despite everything, despite all the potential for complication, here we were, and I could feel something happening to my heart. Joy? Was this what joy felt like? Or was it bad sushi? No. No, definitely, improbably, joy. Was this why fools fell in love? Because we couldn't help ourselves? Maybe so.

AT THE HOTEL, WE WERE BOTH AWKWARD. I sat on a chair. He sat on the couch across the room. "So," I said.

"So," he replied.

There was too much to say and neither of us was brave enough to say it.

I stared out the window, desperately seeking something, a bird, a plane, Superman, to talk about. Nothing out there but night. And not even any stars. New York City, after all. No place lonelier than a New York City hotel room.

Then, a miracle. Some light surfaced out of the black. Glowing red letters. TON, they said. I knew it was meant for me. A sign from heaven. A sign saying, yes, this is very fucking big, big enough to squash you, but you have to do it. No matter how scared you are, no matter how much you've just realized that you're unfit for anything this real, no matter that he has so much baggage you'll never be able to carry it, no matter that this man is everything you thought you didn't ever want. You were wrong. He's everything you need. Get up off your ass and get across that room.

Never mind that this message was delivered via half of the HILTON sign.

This was the kind of moment that changes your life, and even though I didn't know which way it was going to change it, I stood up. I drew on every ounce of courage and stupidity, recklessness and hope, everything that had made me do this year in the first place.

"What's that light outside the window?" I said, walked across the room, and sat down on the couch next to the Playwright. I put my head on his shoulder. He didn't look at me. I put my hand on his chest, inside his shirt, and I felt his heart beating fast. And, then, I leaned in and kissed him on the mouth. He kissed me. We kissed each other. There is no way to describe a really wonderful kiss. There's nothing to compare it to, because it is like nothing else in the world.

The Playwright kissed the marks my bra straps had made on my shoulders, kissed me all over my face, kissed me like a man who'd been starving for years. He looked at me hard.

"Please, tell me now, if you don't want to do this. Don't say yes if you mean no, okay? I know this is a big deal, because it's a big deal to me, too. That's the only question I have. Do you really want me?"

I put my arms around his neck. I took a deep breath.

"Yes," I whispered.

LATER, MUCH LATER, LYING IN THE PLAYWRIGHT'S ARMS, I thought, so this is what all those books were saying, all those songs. The Playwright had cried against my neck as we'd made love, and I had cried with him, because some things were ending and other things were beginning. My life was about to change irrevocably and so was his. Maybe it would be together. Maybe not. That, I was stunned to discover, wasn't the point.

I could hear the announcer in my brain tapping his feet and singing out over the roaring crowd, "This is it! This is the moment you've all been waiting for!"

"Why are you crying?" I'd asked him.

"Because this is possible," he'd managed, and I'd stretched my arms out and held onto him as he'd sobbed. It was worth sobbing over. It was worth laughing over.

When you find the real thing, there is nothing to do but let it take you.

The Playwright slept, and I curled against him, listening to the sounds of the city: a helicopter passing overhead, taxis honking, dogs barking, and people calling good night. I listened to the bootleg music vendors touting their boomboxed wares, to the subway far beneath us rattling our foundations, to room service rolling down the hallway. I listened to Pierre pushing his vacuum, and the Handyman pushing my buzzer. I listened to the Boxer telling the story of our failure, and the Princelings telling the story of their success. I listened to Baler peddling away, unbitten, and Jarzhe calling down the elevator shaft, unblown. I listened to the Prom Queen's crinolines rustling, and Marie Antoinette's bellowing. I listened to Louie and his old man chorus, singing "*Chupa, chupa*" as though it were a love song. I listened to Wonderwoman telling me she was going to kiss me, and the Actress laughing and ordering Chinese. I listened to the Rockstar singing his revisionist song, and the Designer crunching his radish. I listened to the flutter of the Mime's fingers flashing through the air, and the whoosh of the Conductor's breath as he blew out our candle. I listened to the Actor telling me that sometimes his life was amazing, to Ira singing "O Holy Night" in a British accent, and to Dogboy breathing out from underwater. I listened to every man I'd ever met, calling out like a chorus of ghosts, and I knew they'd be with me for the rest of my life.

Some fumbling pair of lovers were making their drunken way not to their own room, but to someone else's. A whoop of surprise, a slamming door, hysterical laughter. Running footsteps. Water coursing through pipes. Heating vents. The Playwright's heart beating directly under my cheek.

How do you describe what happens when you fall in love with someone? It's much easier to tell tales of brokenhearted nights, falling up the subway stairs into some sort of light. Easy to make lists of your loathing. Easy to itemize and appreciate your disenchantments.

Love is hard to pin down. There is no language for it. A glorious sparking inside you, an alchemy. All your hurt suddenly turned into joy. Love is inexplicable. Of Dante's *Divine Comedy*, the *Inferno* is the half that gets read. The *Paradiso* is ignored, because it repeats those same, trite descriptions of bliss. Love is too enormous to diagram, too complex to re-create on the page. Even if, as Dante did, you glimpse your beloved only a couple of times. Historically, he met Beatrice once, when he was about eight, and again, when he was a teenager, and she, married to someone else, smiled at him. That was it for Dante. He was blown away. They never even touched. She died young, and Dante ended up married to someone else. And still, his love for her was so large that, in the *Paradiso*, Beatrice leads him out through the solar system. The Earth isn't enough to contain them. It's like that with love. Nothing could have prepared me for it. All I could do was open my heart. I didn't understand everything that I was holding. I only knew that it was right.

It was 3:00 A.M. in New York City, and I was lying wide awake in a midtown hotel in the arms of the man I was going to marry. I didn't know that then. I didn't know it for a while. That wasn't the point. This night was the beginning of something I could never have imagined, even though all my time was spent imagining and you would have thought I would have been able to write my own happy ending. I couldn't have written this. It was, as love always is, a miracle.

I looked over at the Playwright. His eyes were closed and he was smiling. The noise of New York City was all around us.

I shut my eyes and let it sing me to sleep.

ACKNOWLEDGMENTS

MASSIVE, EARTHSHAKING THANKS TO . . . My brilliant and hilarious editor at Hyperion, Kelly Notaras, for understanding just what it's like to come from nowhere to the great somewhere, and to everyone else at Hyperion (Beth Dickey!) for being behind me all the way. My brainy, ballsy agents at William Morris, Suzanne Gluck and Andy McNicol, for helping me give a relatively scream-free birth to this baby. David Lubliner at William Morris, for believing that I was more than just his writer's wife. Shana Kelly at WMA UK for a great London day. Carole Tonkinson and company at Thorsons Element, for exuberance. Michael Rudell, Jason Baruch, John Power, and Steve Twersky for forcing me to wheel and deal in my high heels.

THE BREADLOAF WRITERS' CONFERENCE, WHICH ALL WRITERS SHOULD ATTEND, if not for the career advancement, for the opportunity to see a bunch of literary luminaries dancing to Nirvana's "Smells Like Teen Spirit." Trust me on this. The fabulous girls who roomed with me in Breadloaf's oh-so-inappropriately named Cherry Residence Hall: Erin Brown for ongoing screaming laughter from a fellow Ida-Ho, Julie Farkas, Emily Choate, and Bonnie Nadzam for too much gin and tonic in the afternoon. The wildly talented Michael Fairbanks, for marking up the very first pages of this book. Meredith Broussard, for telling me how to write a proposal. Murad Kalam, for giving an evening over to a massive conversation about the heart, the soul, and human nature. Matthew Dickman, for reading a heart-stoppingly gorgeous love poem involving a lizard, which climbed into the between-the-lines of this book. Douglas Kearney, for being the best dancer on the floor, and a hell of a poet, too. Matthew Power, for inspiring the fuck out of me with a motorcycle and a brain full of fascinating things I'd never seen before. Jessamyn Smith, for conversations about big bad love, Suzanne Rivecca, for glorious causticity, Daniel Wallace, Jamil Zaki, Carrie Amestoy, Aimee

Pokwatka, Amy Holman, Andrew Hallman, Hannah Tinti, Pete Duval, Esmond Harmsworth, Andrew Miller, Antonya Nelson, Lewis Robinson, and Margaret Ellen Zamos. You all rock, and I owe you all a drink or three.

MY BELOVED NYU PROFESSOR, MARTIN EPSTEIN, not only for making me write prose, but for a certain story about a walk-up apartment, a bohemian bitch, and a bite at the top of the stairs. Zay Amsbury, for years of communion, feet in the mouth, and bullshit detecting. Mark Bemesderfer, for stories about the secret parts of small dogs. Sam Brietz, for reading each chapter hot off the printer and for being my adored scissor twin. Hallie Deaktor, for countless shared kvetches and for introducing me to both T. C. Boyle and G-strings. Greg Kalleres, for much all-night laughing, major heart sharing, and an abortive viewing of *Repulsion*. Vivian Liu, for the red paint and the staples and years of tears and crack-ups. Ruth McKee, for being my first Gemini friend and sharing one of those notorious bad boys. Ben McKenzie, for a deep conversation on a shallow L.A. day when I needed a comrade. Dana Nelson, for always believing, even when the *chupas* ground us down. John Olive, for saying "obviously" when I sold this book and for being a brilliant writer in his own right. Alex Steffen, for being my new Seattle soul twin. Kimberly Scott, for noticing the toeprints on the ceiling and for about fifty million other things. Ira Amyx, for your Belligerent Man self. You know I love you. Sullivan Walsh, for obscene generosity. Heather Moon, for fifteen years of reading the pages. Michelle Shaw, for always calling me back to tell me that my neurosis was just neurosis. Jenny Mercein, for big, fat, coffee-fueled conversations about sex and longing. Trevor Williams—huge thanks here—for inadvertently commissioning much of the very first incarnation of this thing. I owe you all more than a drink. Probably a hefty slice of my heart. But you already have that.

ADRIANE HEADLEY, FOR LOVING ME NO MATTER WHAT KIND OF STORY I'm telling, and for letting me write my name backward on all the walls. Molly Headley, for her notorious Shelfie story and for her raucous cackle on a trans-Atlantic flight. Mark Headley, for that same raucous family cackle, and for a woeful comment about Judas as linked to the male sex drive. The three above for being my long-suffering familial audience, and the most unique and talented bunch of fabulousity I could ever hope to encounter. My dad, for dogsledding in the desert, may you find the calm you never found in life. I owe you. My grandma, Marguerite Moulton, for always laughing, even if the stories *are* obscene. My grandpa, Dwayne Moulton, for telling me tales of which I was the star . . . look what happened. The rest of my family, dead and alive, for all the good and bad and glorious that goes into a writer's brain and comes out as inky pages. Without you, I'd be normal, and normal was never the goal. Thank you to the entire spectacular Schenkkan clan for being the best group a girl could marry into. Sarah Schenkkan, for giggle fits over brunch. Joshua Schenkkan, for bonding over piles of books. You two are a couple of the greatest surprises I've ever had, and as soon as you're old enough, I'll owe you some drinks, too.

ROBERT SCHENKKAN, FOR BEING MY MAN, the only one on this green earth who could take me, the whole thing, and never run screaming into the night. For sleeping beside me, and waking beside me, and letting me love you like crazy. For endlessly encouraging me to write this book, despite it being all about sex, lugs, and lost control. You're the most generous, tender, brilliant man I've ever met. And . . . well, I've met a few men. You fucking blow my mind, baby, and you blow my skirt up, too.

And last, but absolutely not least (with apologies to Willie Nelson):

> *To all the guys I've loved before,*
> *who've traveled in and out my door . . .*

I trust you know the rest. Thanks, boys. And girls.